INTERNET LITERATURE IN CHINA

GLOBAL CHINESE CULTURE

GLOBAL CHINESE CULTURE

David Der-wei Wang, Editor

Internet Literature in China

MICHEL HOCKX

COLUMBIA UNIVERSITY PRESS   NEW YORK

COLUMBIA UNIVERSITY PRESS
Publishers Since 1893
New York   Chichester, West Sussex

cup.columbia.edu
Copyright © 2015 Columbia University Press

Library of Congress Cataloging-in-Publication Data

Hockx, Michel.
    Internet literature in China / Michel Hockx.
        pages cm. — (Global Chinese culture)
    Includes bibliographical references and index.
    ISBN 978-0-231-16082-7 (cloth : acid-free paper) — ISBN 978-0-231-53853-4 (ebook)
    1. Chinese literature—21st century—History and criticism. 2. Literature and the internet—
China. 3. Literature and technology—China.   I. Title.

PL2303.H5833 2015
895.109'006—dc23
                                                                        2014026762

Columbia University Press books are printed on permanent and durable acid-free paper.
This book is printed on paper with recycled content.
Printed in the United States of America

c 10 9 8 7 6 5 4 3 2 1

COVER DESIGN: ELLIOT STRUNK / FIFTH LETTER
COVER ART: © GETTY
BOOK DESIGN: VIN DANG

References to websites (URLs) were accurate at the time of writing.
Neither the author nor Columbia University Press is responsible for URLs
that may have expired or changed since the manuscript was prepared.

IN MEMORY OF MY FATHER,
Jacques Hockx
(1925–2001)

CONTENTS

ACKNOWLEDGMENTS

➡ I STARTED PAYING ATTENTION to Internet literature in China around the turn of the millennium, having noticed during a trip to China that *wangluo wenxue* was being widely debated and that printed versions of works originally published online were starting to hit the shelves of bookshops in major cities. What interested me especially was that such born-digital works, even if they looked exactly the same as conventional prose or poetry, would still end up in a special section of the bookshops and be identified as "Internet literature." The potential emergence of an entirely new genre, possibly even a new literary field, in China fascinated me, and, over the years that followed, I tried to stay informed about what was happening. Around the same time I also began to talk about Chinese Internet literature during classes and lectures. My first opportunity to give a class on the topic came in 2000 when my SOAS colleague Kevin Latham invited me to make a contribution to his Chinese Cinema and Media course. Around the same time, Jie Lu from the University of the Pacific invited me to contribute a piece on Internet literature to a special issue of the *Journal of Contemporary China*, which she was editing, and in this context she also invited me to visit her university and give a talk on the topic to her students. I am grateful to both Kevin and Jie for encouraging my early interest in this topic.

While Internet literature was booming in China and its practices, sites, and terminologies rapidly became part of serious literary discourse, the phenomenon continued to be very marginal in the United Kingdom, where I have been living since 1996, and in other Western countries. For many years, the majority of presentations I gave on the topic were descriptive introductions, simply because without ample explanation, most of my audience would have no idea what I was talking about. Often my audiences were surprised to find that such wide-ranging literary creativity existed online in China. After all, the most pervasive image about the Internet in China present in Western people's minds is that of the "Great Firewall." Although I am strongly interested in literary censorship as a field of study and often intrigued by how difficult it is to study it objectively, I soon found myself compelled to resist the trend of talking about only what could *not* appear on the Internet in China, and instead I focused on what could. After all, there has never been a period in China's long history that literature was not subjected to state censorship, yet we study and appreciate Chinese literature from ancient times to the present. The existence of censorship per se can never be a reason to dismiss any literature, nor can it ever be argued that only literary fields with weak or no censorship institutions are worth studying.

Over the years I came to realize that the book I wanted to write, this book, would first and foremost need to be a general overview, useful not only for specialists but also for general readers interested in present-day China and its culture. In addition to that general intention, however, two further aspects are explored here in more depth: the ways in which Internet literature brings about literary innovation and challenges existing paradigms of "electronic literature," and the ways in which this literature specifically challenges the established publishing system of the People's Republic of China, bringing about changes and adjustments in the regulation regime.

A small group of other scholars has shared my enthusiasm for Chinese Internet literature. I believe we all shared a keen sense of doing something new and exciting, and I greatly enjoyed our many discussions, often via e-mail, and the exchange of materials and manuscripts. I want to mention especially Jin Feng from Grinnell College and my former student Heather Inwood, now at the University of Manchester. I should also mention Mei Hong from Southwestern Jiaotong University in Chengdu, author of the first-ever Chinese textbook on Internet literature, who spent a year in London including six months at SOAS in 2011–2012. Finally, I want to mention Shao Yanjun from Peking University, a recent convert, initially quite critical of Internet literature but actively promoting its study in the past few years.

I have many reasons to thank many people for their contributions to this research. Three names stand out in my mind: Helen Hockx-Yu, whose expertise in web archiving developed over the same period that I was doing this research, has been a constant source of advice in all matters related to the study of the World Wide Web. Second, the author Chen Cun, whom some refer to as the father of Chinese Internet literature, patiently responded to many questions through e-mail and also generously granted me a very long interview in Shanghai in 2010. I am also grateful for his generous permission to reproduce online work by him that is no longer available on the live web. Third, I owe a similar debt of gratitude to Dajuin Yao, the earliest online literary experimenter in the Chinese language, for kindly allowing me to preserve his work from the 1990s, despite its having disappeared from the live web many years ago, and refer to it in presentations I have given over the years, and in this book.

What follows is a list of people who have enabled me to present or publish my work, engaged me in discussions, helped me find materials, taught me crucial new computer skills, advised and inspired me, or supported me with their friendship and collegiality. With apologies for any unintentional omissions, my sincere thanks go to the following: Cosima Bruno, John Cayley, Kang-i Sun Chang, Shih-chen (Sheila) Chao, Chen Pingyuan, Chen Taisheng, Eileen Chow, Maghiel van Crevel, Susan Daruvala, Kirk Denton, Jennifer Feeley, Bernhard Fuehrer, David Gauntlett, N. Katherine Hayles, Margaret Hillenbrand, Pamela Hunt, Ann Huss, Wilt and Eveline Idema, Sara Jones, Joan Judge, Nick Kaldis, Paize Keulemans, Uganda Sze Pui Kwan, Wendy Larson, Charles Laughlin, Li Chao, Li Nan, Andrea Lingenfelter, Liu Shuling, Chris Lupke, Ma Lan, Paul Manfredi, Bonnie McDougall, Liansu Meng, Barbara Mittler, Stephen Morgan, Meesha Nehru, George Paizis, Xenia Piëch, Carlos Rojas, Fiona Sampson, Lena Scheen, Dan Stillman, James St. André, Julia Strauss, Liying Sun, Xiaofei Tian, Jing Tsu, Wang Qiang, Gerda

Wielander, Xia Xiaohong, Michelle Yeh, Yuan Jin, and, last but most definitely not least, the inventors of Zotero.

Special thanks go to David Der-wei Wang for encouraging me to publish with Columbia University Press, to Jennifer Crewe at Columbia for her great patience, and to Mike Ashby, Jonathan Fiedler, and Roy Thomas for their editorial work.

Research for this book was supported by a research grant from the Arts and Humanities Research Council in 2010–2011, and further enabled by periods of sabbatical leave granted by SOAS, University of London, in 2005–2006 and 2010–2011.

Portions of chapters 1 and 4 have drawn upon material from within Michel Hockx, "Virtual Chinese Literature: A Comparative Case Study of Online Poetry Communities," *China Quarterly* 183 (2005): 670–691 © SOAS, University of London, published by Cambridge University Press, reproduced with permission. Other parts of chapter 1 first appeared in Michel Hockx, "Links with the Past: Mainland China's Online Literacy Communities and Their Antecedents," *Journal of Contemporary China* 13, no. 38 (2004): 105–127. (See the journal website at www.tandfonline.com.) Parts of chapter 2 previously appeared in Michel Hockx, "Master of the Web: Chen Cun and the Continuous Avant-Garde," in *Text, Performance, and Gender in Chinese Literature and Music: Essays in Honor of Wilt Idema*, ed. Maghiel van Crevel, Tian Yuan Tan, and Michel Hockx, 413–29 (Leiden: Brill, 2009). I am grateful to all three publishers for granting permission to reuse the material.

My most heartfelt thanks go to Hong for her ever-present love and support and to our son, Dylan, for bringing so much joy to our lives, and for showing us how the next generation grows up with the Internet. But as I write these words, my thoughts go out first and foremost to my father, Jacques Hockx, who bought a computer to catalogue his books, a project he was unable to finish. This book is dedicated to his memory.

▶ ALL URLS MENTIONED in the notes were accessible in early March 2014, when the manuscript for this book was submitted. In cases where the original web pages that I consulted are no longer available on the live web, the URLs in the notes refer to archived copies of the pages in question, usually those preserved by the Internet Archive Wayback Machine (IAWM, http://web.archive.org). If a page was not preserved by the IAWM or other web archives, but I saved a snapshot of it myself, the URL in the notes refers to the copy in a Zotero group library where I stored my material. To access this archive, readers must contact me with a request to become members of the Zotero group "Internet Literature in China" (https://www.zotero.org/groups/internet_literature_in_china).

The Zotero group library is organized by chapter and by note number. In addition to snapshots of material not available elsewhere on the web at this writing, it also contains snapshots of all the other web pages referred to in the notes. This means that readers of this book can view all the material I used even if it disappears from the live web in the future.

INTERNET LITERATURE IN CHINA

▶ **IN OCTOBER 2011** the seventeenth Central Committee of the Chinese Communist Party (CCP) held its sixth plenum. The theme of the four-day gathering was culture. China watchers writing for the U.S. and U.K. media had difficulty coming to terms with this fact. Although it was acknowledged that culture was related to soft power, which had been high on the CCP agenda for a number of years, the general tenor of the reports was that it was inexplicable that the Central Committee would talk about culture, rather than more significant issues such as the economy and the imminent transition of political power to a new generation of leaders. Many commentators concluded that the Chinese leaders must have had major disagreements on important topics and therefore opted for a relatively safe debate on culture, so as to be able to present a united front to the outside world.

This is not the place to complain about the quality of coverage of China in the U.S. and U.K. media, especially since the foregoing analysis is in fact quite plausible. In addition, readers of U.S. and U.K. newspapers probably do not expect governments to spend much time debating culture and tend to see culture as something quite separate and different from economics and politics. It is difficult to imagine a government that

considers itself obliged to regulate culture in all its aspects (form, contents, production, distribution, canonization). Yet it is not so long ago,
only a few decades, that the socialist system in China worked exactly that
way. Well into the 1980s, cultural development in China was subject to
state planning, just like the economy. Much has changed in China since
then, and the state-controlled planning principles that are core to any
socialist system have long been reformed or overhauled, but that does
not mean the underlying principles and mentalities that shaped Chinese
socialism have disappeared without a trace. There is a residue of socialism to be found in many aspects of society and politics in the People's Republic of China, and this residual socialism often explains behavior that
might otherwise appear unpredictable or strange. For the Chinese ruling
party to devote an important congress to questions of culture is, I would
argue, ultimately a completely normal thing to do and not considered
as an evasion of more important duties, nor indeed as separate of other
duties, but as an integral part of what that party believes it should do,
namely to set out the ideological guidelines for the governance and development of the Chinese nation in all its aspects.

When socialist institutions such as state planning, collective work
units, guaranteed job allocation, housing distribution, free health care,
and fixed pricing have all disappeared but residual socialist mentalities,
sensibilities, and hierarchies continue to impact on people's behavior, the
term "postsocialism" becomes useful. It will be referred to throughout
this book. A discussion of the history of this term and its usage across different disciplines will follow shortly, but for the moment it should suffice
to note the parallel between my understanding of postsocialism and the
commonly accepted term "postcolonialism," which refers to the lingering
of colonial mind-sets, language habits, power relations, and practices in
societies where colonial institutions no longer exist.

In the very long document publicizing the outcomes of the sixth plenum, the postsocialist condition is omnipresent. Most of the document
hinges on the assumption that cultural production should be as much
as possible privatized, deregulated, and profit making (i.e., not socialist),
but that at the same time it should be healthy in content, represent the
interests of the masses, and support China's international soft power.
Reading the document, one is struck by how very different this approach
to culture is from what was prevalent thirty or more years ago while at the

same time sensing a strong residue of a mentality that holds that cultural producers should be guided by political ideology and serve the nation. In the case of literature and the arts, where, apart from making profits and promoting the correct ideology, there is also the element of aesthetic value to consider, the situation becomes even more complex. The following passage from the document, listing what needs to be done in the area of artistic evaluation, is a good example of this complexity, which most Western media observers tend to underestimate or choose to ignore:

> Perfect the evaluation systems and encouragement mechanisms for cultural products. Maintain that following the progressive direction of socialist advanced culture and the satisfaction of the masses of the people constitute the highest standards for evaluating works, *unifying evaluation by the masses, evaluation by experts, and market testing*, so as to shape scientific standards of evaluation.[1] (emphasis added)

This is followed by a number of sentences calling for more cultural awards and prizes, better criticism, promotion of the best cultural work to wider audiences through mainstream media, setting up dedicated funds for the arts, supporting preservation of important cultural works, and protecting intellectual property rights.

Cynics would argue that statements like these are too convoluted to have any meaning at all, but it seems to me that the passage I highlighted is crucial for a good understanding of cultural production in today's China. Unlike the situation in countries like the United States and the United Kingdom, where cultural products tend to be measured on scales expressing critical success, commercial success, or both, the Chinese political elite insists on including a third dimension: "evaluation by the masses." Since the Communist Party is of course the vanguard of the masses, this essentially means that ideological control remains integrated in the overall mechanism of evaluation. This is a far cry from the ideological campaigns of the Mao period, when cultural workers were specifically instructed to conform to particular propaganda aims. It is also different from the situation in the 1980s, with its occasional backlashes against "spiritual pollution" and its continued strict control over literature in terms of printing, distribution, and pricing. Instead, ideological control is now part of a complex, postsocialist mix of factors determining what takes place in the literary sphere of the People's Republic. Adding to this complexity has been the rapid development of the Internet in China since the late 1990s, and the huge popularity of Internet literature (*wangluo wenxue*[2]) across a wide variety of genres and styles.

Internet Literature

According to annual statistics published by the China Internet Network Information Center (CNNIC), around 40 percent of all Internet users in China in 2012 made use of applications providing access to online literature.[3] The percentage is roughly equal to that of people using the Internet for online shopping. Although the growth rate of online shopping is now much higher and the CNNIC report suggests that online literature might have passed its heyday,[4] the percentage of online readers is still incredibly high. Even the sheer fact that these statistical reports perceive the need to include "online literature" as an independent category is remarkable.[5] It points to an overwhelming popularity of online reading and writing that have been a major feature of Chinese literary life, and of the Internet in China, for well over a decade. Because this phenomenon has been so significant in China (and in other East Asian societies as well) yet has no real equivalent of the same scale and scope in Western countries, my first aim in writing this book is simply to describe and showcase the phenomenon. That it is now in relative decline, with the number of users of online sites growing more slowly than the number of Internet users as a whole, is somewhat of a fortunate coincidence. Although nobody can predict how the Internet will develop in the future, it may well turn out to be the case that the period covered in this book (roughly 2000–2013) has seen the rise, climax, and gradual demise of a unique form of Chinese-language cultural creativity.

So what, then, is Internet literature in China? A detailed overview of its emergence and early development is provided in chapter 1, but its basic features are as follows: it is Chinese-language writing, either in established literary genres or in innovative literary forms, written especially for publication in an interactive online context and meant to be read on-screen. The addition of the words "in China" here and in the title of this book means that I am limiting myself to mostly work written to be uploaded to servers in China, although this scope will be widened as I go along, especially in the final chapter. The reason why I impose this limitation is exactly because I am interested not only in the formal or technical characteristics of this body of literature but also in how its practitioners interact with, and at times pose challenges to, the PRC system of state-regulated publishing and literary governance.[6] To put it briefly: the aim of this book is to tell its readers what Chinese Internet literature is, how it challenges literary conventions and hierarchies, and how it operates within the specific context of the PRC's publishing system. I will touch upon all aspects of the postsocialist mix (aesthetics, market, ideology), but literature will be the focus. This is not a general study of the Internet in China, nor is it a general sociology of online communities. This is a study of a newly emerged literary community, its practices and products, and its interactions with other, more established communities and institutions within the wider Chinese literary sphere.

Although much of the born-digital literature discussed in the following chapters is conventional in form and some of it appeared in print at a later stage, for most of the period under discussion even its printed editions were considered generically distinct from print publications that had gone through the regular system. This led to the paradoxical situation that, for instance, bookshops in China would group "novels" together on one shelf and "online novels" on another shelf, the only formal distinction between them being that the latter had originally been published on the Internet. Toward the end of the period, the increasing popularity of e-books had started to blur this distinction, but some distinctions did remain in place, even at the level of terminology. For instance, whereas established writers in the print-based system are generally referred to as *zuojia* (authors), those active on the Internet tend to be referred to and refer to themselves as *xieshou* (writers). The former term functions as an honorific and indicates elevated cultural status, whereas the latter term has connotations of low-level labor. Hiding behind these distinctions, however, lies a wide variety of different styles, genres, and motivations for writing online, which will be explored in the chapters that follow. Before giving an outline of the contents of each chapter, I shall try to capture the main debates in three areas of study that are directly relevant to my topic: electronic literature, Chinese Internet studies, and postsocialism.

Electronic Literature

Electronic literature is the collective name used for any and all literature that has a substantial electronic element, normally involving some sort of computer programming or code. It is also the name of a growing field of academic inquiry, especially in the United States and western Europe. Much electronic literature is created by artists in unique, stand-alone versions or downloadable applications that, once they are running, do not require the user to be online. It is fair to say, though, that the World Wide Web has come to play a significant role in electronic literature, as well as in the preservation of both online and stand-alone works in web-based archives such as the Electronic Literature Collection[7] and the Electronic Literature Knowledge Base (ELMCIP).[8] A significant body of scholarly and critical work has accumulated around a canon of works that are characterized by a strong desire to experiment with nonlinear processes of writing, alienating audiences from traditional line-by-line reading experiences by making ample use of hypertext links, other interactive features, machine-generated transitions, and multimedia effects. For most scholars and critics working in this field, nonlinearity is a paradigmatic feature of all electronic literature. Only electronic works requiring "nontrivial effort" to "traverse the text," that is, only works that come with an instruction manual, are within the scope of their inquiries.[9]

In her influential essay "Electronic Literature: What Is It?" N. Katherine Hayles provides an exhaustive overview of the history of electronic literature, mentioning various forms of hypertext fiction, interactive fiction and drama, computer-generated writing, three-dimensional installations, and multimedia visual work.[10] All these varieties of electronic literature are (or were once) brand-new art forms, demanding nontrivial effort not only from their readers but also from critics and scholars, while generally not at all fitting into established systems for publishing and distribution. As Howard Becker insightfully argued when first confronted with the notion of hypertext fiction, the fact that there were no existing conventions for dealing with such work and no support structures for promoting it meant that electronic literature authors were forced to carry out on their own many of the routine tasks that print authors would never need to worry about (sales, distribution, providing user instructions, and so on).[11]

At the same time, this tendency for electronic literature producers to work in isolation on their projects has ensured that the community, at least until now, has continued to support a very conventional perception of the author as a creative genius, with the creativity in this case dependent not only on conventional writing skills but also on programming and design skills. Consequently the majority of entries in, for instance, the Electronic Literature Collection are of works associated with a single named creator, thereby continuing long-standing models of assessment, canonization, and preservation that are clearly inherited from the print culture community.

Although experimental nonlinear electronic works and their consequences for our understanding of literature are discussed by scholars in China as well, Chinese scholarship of this nature tends to draw only to a minimal extent on material published in China.[12] In my own reading as well, I have come across very little work on PRC websites that is experimental in the specific sense of trying to undermine the linear experience of reading and writing.[13] However, this does not mean that Internet literature in China does not feature any form of radical innovation. I am not convinced that nonlinearity is a necessary condition for being innovative when writing online. One contribution I hope to make to the study of electronic literature is to show how linear online writing can have innovative characteristics that pose unusual challenges to scholars using conventional methods, especially when it comes to undermining the idea of a clearly recognizable, single-authored work.

As Hayles points out, there is another side to electronic literature that is the opposite of challenging convention. When the Electronic Literature Organization (ELO) decided by committee on a definition for the core subject of their new field, what they came up with was "work with an important literary aspect that takes advantage of the capabilities and contexts provided by the stand-alone or networked computer."[14] Hayles rightly notes that the definition is tautological, since it relies on a prior understanding of what are "important" literary aspects, and such prior understanding can be based only on knowledge derived from the print-based system. Hayles continues,

> Readers come to digital work with expectations formed by print, including extensive and deep tacit knowledge of letter forms, print conventions, and print literary modes. Of necessity, electronic literature must build on these expectations even as it modifies and transforms them.[15]

In its own preservation and canonization activities, the ELO builds on the conventional expectation that each work must prominently display the name of its author (as it is on the book cover in the print system). The ELO (and Hayles) also largely ignore online popular literature, such as fan fiction, presumably because it is conventionally not seen as "important literature." This is a shame because communities devoted to such work may use the capabilities of computers and the Internet in original ways. At the very least, by contrasting their activities with those at the high end of electronic literature production, one might be able to add some detail to the perception of the latter's qualitative superiority, thereby removing the need for tautology. In electronic literature studies, as in the study of print literature, popular fiction and similar genres attract more interest from social scientists than from literature scholars.

In this book I have taken a somewhat different approach, trying to keep an open mind about what is or is not important and looking at a wide variety of genres, ranging from avant-garde experimentalism to mass-produced semipornographic fiction. Despite this relatively tolerant approach, in line with my ambition to map and describe a newly emerging field of literary production in its entirety, my own decisions about what was and was not within the scope of my inquiries were still based at least to some extent on conventional expectations about literature. This is the case for two reasons: first, because I have a clear preference for work that presents itself as literature and whose authors demonstrate a certain level of reflexivity about the aesthetic aims of their writing, and second because I prioritize discussion of work that explores boundaries or can be considered transgressive, not just in the sense of challenging literary conventions but also in the sense of pushing the limits of the post-socialist publishing system. With politics and ideology forming such a clear element of the mix of factors involved in literary production in the PRC, we should not expect innovation to come only from those pursuing an autonomous aesthetic.

China and the Internet

The transgressing of boundaries is a key theme also in the fast growing field of Chinese Internet research, which, especially among scholars working in the United States and United Kingdom, revolves predominantly around the question of whether or not the Internet can bring about democratic changes in China.[16] As pointed out by David Kurt Herold in a recent rather gloomy state-of-the-field article, the scholarly overemphasis on the Chinese Internet's potential for political change can be seen as a form of "digital Orientalism," based on a probably mistaken assumption that Chinese Internet users want (or ought to want) something different from the Internet than users in other countries. Herold points out the relative lack of studies on "how people in China are using the Internet to do what they want to do" (as opposed to what "we" feel they ought to want to do) and ends with a leading question: "Is politics and the pursuit of democracy *really* the most important issue for Chinese Internet users, or is it just the most important issue for us researchers?"[17]

I sympathize with Herold's dissatisfaction, having experienced many times over the course of my research that audiences asked very political questions about Chinese literature, of the kind that they would never ask about, for instance, English literature. A good example of this somewhat skewed perspective is the case of the author Han Han, who has been revered by millions of Chinese readers for his novels but studied by Western scholars almost exclusively for his politically oriented blog posts (see chapter 2). At the same time, as pointed out earlier, political ideology and state regulation are part of the mix of factors one should take into account when studying present-day Chinese literature, online or otherwise. The issue here is one of perspective: whether to highlight the political factor as a kind of alien element that should have no place in literature, or whether to accept that it is an integral part of the literary system one wants to study.

Related to this is the large number of publications discussing Internet censorship in China, exploring both the real and the perceived boundaries that prevent Chinese netizens from accessing specific non-Chinese sites (behind the so-called Great Firewall) or from uploading certain content (so-called sensitive keywords) to sites inside China. In the popular imagination, Chinese Internet censorship is scary, invariably filtering out every online occurrence of unwanted language while preventing Chinese netizens from accessing the likes of Facebook, YouTube, and Twitter.

None of this, of course, is even remotely true, as many scholars have shown by now.[18] The Great Firewall has been so easy to get around that, at some point in 2011, even ranking services inside China were listing YouTube in the top fifty of most frequently accessed websites in China, despite the fact that it was officially blocked.[19] As early as 1997, when the Chinese Internet was in its infancy, Chinese government officials accepted the reality that they would never be able to monitor everything. In the memorable words of "Comrade X," cited in a 1997 article by Geremie Barmé and Sang Ye, in which the phrase "Great Firewall of China" was first introduced,

> Naturally, many questionable sites still go undetected. So the way we prefer to control things is through a decentralized responsibility system: the user, the ISP, and China Telecom are all held responsible for the information users gain access to.
>
> People are used to being wary, and the general sense that you are under surveillance acts as a disincentive. The key to controlling the Net in China is in managing people, and this is a process that begins the moment you purchase a modem.[20]

Nowadays, keyword filtering is carried out predominantly not by state censors but by Internet companies and website moderators themselves, to the extent that, as shown by Rebecca MacKinnon in research published in 2009, not a single "sensitive" topic could be proven to be banned consistently across a range of different blog sites. Large blog sites hosted by big companies, such as the SINA Corporation, would delete potentially risqué posts much more vigorously than smaller sites that have less to lose and are willing to take risks.[21]

These findings were recently confirmed and further refined, using a different method focused on social media posts rather than on blogs, by a research team at Harvard University led by Gary King. Their research convincingly showed that most censorship is indeed not done automatically by keyword filters but based on decisions by human readers, and that there are no specific bans on any individual words or expressions. In an interview with King for *Harvard Magazine*, his team's results are summarized as follows:

> Scholars have long debated the motivations for censorship in China, but King said that his research offers an unambiguous answer: the Chinese government is not interested in stifling opinion, but in suppressing collective action. Words alone are permitted, no matter how critical and vitriolic. But mere mentions of collective action—of any large gathering not sponsored by the state, whether peaceful or in protest—are censored immediately. [22]

The Harvard team also found that two topics were invariably censored, regardless of whether or not they were attracting any attention or threatened to inspire collective action. Those two taboo topics are criticism of the censors and pornography.

When dealing with online literature, the situation is somewhat different, as might be expected. It is rare for literary authors in any country to want to inspire collective action through their writing. However, the sheer volume of online literary publications in China, including countless full-length novels, amounts to a massive collective onslaught on the traditional state regulation of publications, which relies on state offices issuing "book numbers" to publishers in order to approve specific publications.[23] Moreover, literature tends to have greater leeway when it comes to descriptions of sexuality, which might be considered pornographic when encountered in other contexts. Questions of what does or does not constitute redeeming artistic quality in a sexually explicit literary work and whether or not such works should be made available only to those over a certain age are worth examining, as I do in chapter 3, since they shed light on changing norms of moral censorship in China, as opposed to the frequently studied political censorship. In looking at these issues, too, my choice is not to treat censorship as a polluting factor but as an integral component of literary life in China.[24]

A very good study of online practices in China, and one of the foundational books of Chinese Internet studies, is Guobin Yang's *The Power of the Internet in China*. Yang focuses on the potential of Chinese netizens to use the Internet to express contention and promote activism, drawing on material such as Internet use by civic associations, which shows that by far not all collective action generated with the help of the Internet is suppressed in China. Yang also pays prominent attention to cultural phenomena, especially what he calls "the changing style of contention,"[25] showing that online activism and contention often use a much lighter and satirical tone when compared with the heroic, self-sacrificing discourses employed by activists and dissidents of the 1980s.

The use of puns and homophones to circumvent overly aggressive keyword filtering on some sites is especially well-known in this context and has even given rise to the online publication, by Xiao Qiang, of a lexicon of words and expressions used for the purposes of humorous censorship avoidance.[26] The expression "grass mud horse," pronounced *cao ni ma* and thereby homophonous with the Chinese words for "fuck your mother" has been widely adopted as representative of Chinese netizens' playful opposition to censorship. This is clearly a case of resistance against moral, not political, control: the only reason why some websites in China might censor the phrase "fuck your mother" is because they might consider it obscene. Yet it is widely assumed that the use of an obscene term in this case represents a broader resentment against censorship in general.[27] Again, this raises complex questions of how to interpret the redeeming aspects of obscenity and how to evaluate the CCP's efforts to promote what it calls a healthy culture. Such efforts include censorship of phenomena such as pornography, which pose no overt challenge to the regime at all but which the regime feels it has the responsibility to keep away from the public. This tendency to set "parental controls" for all its web-browsing citizens is a clear remnant of the socialist system.

Postsocialism

At the beginning of this introduction, I illustrated my understanding of the term "postsocialism" by comparing it with the much more widely used term "postcolonialism." If the latter refers to the lingering impact of colonial mind-sets following the official dismantling of colonial institutions, the former must refer to residual socialist mind-sets in a society that has done away with the institutions of socialism. However, in scholarly discourse of the past two decades or so, the term has in fact been given many different, at times even contradicting, definitions. In this section I provide a short account of my own readings around the topic, outlining the different positions and tracing the genealogy of my own.

The one thing everybody agrees on is that the term "postsocialism" was invented by Arif Dirlik and first put forward in an essay written in 1988 and published in 1989.[28] This fact alone is remarkable: I know of no other scholarly term that was coined by a China scholar and subsequently widely adopted by academics working in other areas. For Dirlik, as for many others in the late 1980s, the main challenge was to come to terms with the discrepancy between socialism as an intellectual ideal on the one hand and its practical application by self-declared socialist states, commonly referred to as actually existing socialism, on the other. The widespread disappointment of left-wing intellectuals with actually existing socialism had led to what Dirlik calls a crisis in socialism, requiring the rethinking of socialism in new, more creative ways."[29] In his analysis of Deng Xiaoping's "socialism with Chinese characteristics," Dirlik comes up with the term "postsocialism" to describe a "condition of ideological contradiction and uncertainty," allowing him to take "Chinese socialism seriously without sweeping under the rug the problems created by its articulation to capitalism."[30] Toward the end of his essay, Dirlik explains that his use of the term "postsocialism" was inspired by reading Lyotard on postmodernism, especially with regard to the latter's "incredulity toward metanarratives." Dirlik goes on to say, "I would suggest by analogy that the characteristic of socialism at present is a loss of faith in it as a social and political metatheory with a coherent present and a certain future."[31]

In order to do full justice to Dirlik's ideas, it is important to note that they were formulated before the June 1989 massacre. By the time his article appeared in print, his hopes for Chinese socialism to offer a way out of the worldwide crisis in socialism will have been summarily quashed. However, his newly invented concept proved to have real staying power and was adopted by many scholars, many of them not in any way left-wing, and developed in a range of different ways, each drawing on different aspects of Dirlik's original, tentative proposal. In Chinese studies, and especially in the realm of studies of Chinese culture, the differences in interpretation have at times been extreme, as demonstrated in detail in an excellent overview article by Sheldon Lu[32] and confirmed in more recent publications. Some film scholars, following a lead from Paul Pickowicz,[33] have drawn upon Dirlik's original comments about the loss of faith in the grand narrative of socialism to designate as postsocialist all those cultural products that express disappointment with socialism at a time when socialist institutions were still in place. This perspective is developed at length by Chris Berry in his book on Chinese films from the period 1976–1981.[34] In contrast, Xudong Zhang in his study of Chinese literature and film of the 1990s develops Dirlik's points about postsocialism's ideological contradiction and uncertainty, as well as its potential to herald something new. Zhang's definition is worth quoting in full:

> The use of "postsocialism" does not suggest a more advanced, superior—or, for that matter, more backward and inferior—form of socioeconomic and political development. Rather, it is an experimental way to address a bewilder-

ing overlap of modes of production, social systems, and symbolic orders, all of which lay claim to a fledgling world of life.[35]

For Zhang, and for many others, Chinese culture of the 1990s is clearly distinct from that of the preceding reform era of the 1980s, when "high culture fever" swept the nation in a manner that, in retrospect, was shaped largely by the Deng regime and relied to a very large extent on the continued support of state institutions and state subsidies.[36]

Several China scholars have explored postsocialism in wider geographical contexts, suggesting that the condition is not, or should not be, unique to China. Film scholar Jason McGrath, for instance, conceives of postsocialism as a global condition: the state of the world after the end of the Cold War and the demise of socialism. Within this wider context, according to McGrath, Chinese intellectual and cultural life of the 1990s actually continues to be relatively attached to the grand narratives of modernism, such as the pursuit of a humanist spirit and the resistance against entertainment culture.[37]

Outside the China field, too, scholars have begun to equate postsocialism with post–Cold War. The term has been especially popular with social scientists working in central and eastern European countries, as well as countries formerly part of the Soviet Union. In these scholars' usage, postsocialism represents the transition (actual, perceived, or aspired) from socialism to capitalism, most clearly pronounced in those countries striving to meet the conditions for membership of the European Union.[38] This understanding of postsocialism as a transitional phase in a development toward the distinct goal of becoming a capitalist country may turn out to be applicable to China as well, but for the moment this seems highly unlikely.

Several scholars have taken up Dirlik's challenge to consider postsocialism in the specific context of Marxist theory and the worldwide socialist movement as a whole. A strong contribution to this debate comes from Lydia Liu, who reminds left-wing scholars critical of the effects of global capital in countries like China of the fact that their use of Marxist terminology carries an entirely different weight and meaning in the Chinese context. At the same time, she rebukes "China watchers" for their tendency to overemphasize residual socialism as the sole or dominant explicatory factor for everything happening in the country.[39]

Anthropologist Andrew Kipnis, who also cites Liu's work, launches a similar critique of the lack of reflexiveness of some left-wing scholars but goes significantly further as he postulates that what he calls Marxian theory should be rethought in its entirety. Flatly denying the artificial distinction between theoretical and actually existing socialism, and noticing the unwillingness of scholars like Arif Dirlik to give up on socialism altogether, he draws up a long list of similarities between left-wing theory and socialist state governance, focusing on tendencies toward holistic thinking, politicization, and polarization. For Kipnis, the challenge of postsocialism is to come up with new theories that do not rely on the assumption that left-wing thought is per definition superior to or more intellectual than that of other schools.[40] Kipnis emphasizes what he calls the real messiness of the world and the inability of grand holistic theories to provide an insight into it, but he lethally harms his own argument when he goes on to state that "only the empiricism of the social sciences" can give insight into this messiness, whereas the humanities will never be able to achieve such understanding—thereby descending into the same unnecessary mode of polarization and conflict creation that he critiques so convincingly in his introduction.[41]

Finally, critical theorist Nancy Fraser, in her book-length study of the postsocialist condition, stands diametrically opposed to Kipnis, as she openly deplores the "sceptical mood or structure of feeling that marks the post-1989 state of the Left"[42] and warns against modes of inquiry that prioritize "recognition" (of specific groups, identities, etc.) without considering the (in her view) greater cause of "redistribution" and social equality.[43] In the current context, the most significant chapters in Fraser's study are those discussing in great detail the notion of the "public sphere" and its problematic relation with socialist governments. How to conceive of socialist governance of public opinion, for instance on the Internet, in a society no longer dominated by socialist propaganda institutions is a question that lies at the heart of my study.

It is remarkable how wide-ranging the interpretations of postsocialism have been since the concept was first introduced in 1989. Some view it as a phenomenon unique to China, others as a global phenomenon. Some think it expresses itself through loss of faith in socialist myths, despite the existence of socialist structures; others, including myself, hold the exact opposite. Some don't think it should apply to China at all, because China, unlike eastern Europe, has not yet officially relinquished socialist governance. Others see it as a theoretical problem in the study of socialism. Yet we all appear to have one thing in common, namely that we prefer not to talk about Chinese society and culture having been overtaken by, or responding to, some sort of global "neoliberalism."[44]

With regard to the study of Chinese literature and culture, my impression is that the position taken in this book has already won the argument. Scholars from very different persuasions now seem to agree that the socialist system in China lingered on until the 1980s, and that it is the disappearance of core socialist institutions in the early 1990s that heralded the arrival of the "messiness" of postsocialism. I develop this point in more detail in the next chapter. Here I should make special mention of what is probably the most comprehensive and provocative study of Chinese culture of the 1990s, Geremie Barmé's *In the Red: On Contemporary Chinese Culture*. Barmé does not refer to postsocialism at all,[45] but he is clearly sensitive to a rupture between Chinese culture of the 1980s and that of the 1990s. His main thesis is that after the open conflicts between intellectuals and the state in the 1980s, the 1990s witnessed the advent of a culture of negotiation and accommodation, which he links with the rise of commercial culture:

> The cultural purges of the 1980s may have achieved little in narrow political terms, but they had repeatedly stunted the numerous sprouts of autonomous culture. As a result of these regular attacks, as well as the grinding administrative sanctions that the authorities placed on specific people and works, artists and intellectuals throughout the country had gradually evolved various nonthreatening alternative cultures. In the 1990s, popular or commercial culture seemed to many writers, from po-moists to traditional-style humanists, to be the most efficacious as well as safest way to promote cultural revolution in China.[46]

Barmé is especially convincing in those parts of his study where he describes the 1990s phenomenon of "packaged dissent," that is, the pursuit of commercial or reputational gain by taking ostensibly provocative political positions in works of art that never really cross the line, as in his case study of the film director Zhang Yuan. In a later passage, he sums up the idea that artists of the 1990s had acquired a disposition that was different from that of their immediate predecessors, to the benefit of the quantity but not the quality of cultural production:

Artists had gradually learned how to combine political acuity and market sense to produce works that earned them enough notoriety to advance their careers but not so much that they were banned. Other nonofficial artists were trading on the international market and were not directly involved with the local critical climate. Furthermore, far from there being a cultural downturn in the 1990s, the publishing industry had burgeoned and the number of writers had grown. There was more culture than ever before. As it has been argued throughout this book, however, the voracious appetites both of the cultural industry and consumers did not necessarily mean that artists were enjoying an unconditional freedom to create.[47]

As a conclusion to this section, it is worthwhile to contrast Barmé's views with those of Xudong Zhang referred to earlier. Zhang's monograph *Postsocialism and Cultural Politics* is as impressively documented and as knowledgeable about intellectual life in China in the 1990s as Barmé's. Both agree that the principled, socially committed stance of many intellectuals during the 1980s gave way to a greater variety of less outspoken positions in the 1990s. Both also agree that the uncompromising avant-garde high culture of the earlier decade later became something more mixed and more attuned to popular tastes. But whereas Barmé concludes that 1990s China is "an environment with a cultural deficit" (hence "in the red"),[48] Zhang remains hopeful that Chinese intellectuals, as they "stay and live in contradictions and chaos in a mixed economy and its overlapping political and cultural (dis)order,"[49] will eventually come up with a genuine "Chinese alternative" to global capitalism. In the end, it seems, their positions differ mainly as a result of their evaluation of the state of the world outside China.

Neither Barmé nor Zhang were able to take into consideration the effects of the arrival and rapid development of the Internet in China from the late 1990s onward.[50] None of the other studies referred to in this section made any meaningful references to online culture either. Yet the postsocialist condition is nowhere more recognizable than on the Internet, a mixed, messy space where the socialist publishing system has been left far behind, but residual socialism lingers through novel regulation systems and continuing censorship; where commercialism is rampant, but where there is plenty of room for independent expression and creativity; and where genuinely novel forms of communication and interaction are integrated with artistic and political ideals constantly and on a daily basis. This space was always going to be far too big to grasp in its entirety, so in the remainder of this introduction I shall explain the choices I made in my research and how I made them.

Managing the Mess

Since there were no established methods for doing research on Internet literature when I started looking at it a decade or so ago, I made up my methods as I went along. The most important lesson I learned early on was about archiving and preservation. When my first article on Chinese Internet literature was published, about two years after I had written it, virtually all the URLs referred to in my footnotes had become inaccessible, leaving me in the unenviable situation that I was unable to prove (or so I thought at the time) that any of the material I had mentioned had ever even existed. Anyone citing any URLs in any article about anything should really think twice before doing so, but for a study such as this one, the ephemerality of online material is especially problematic. Over the years I built up a personal archive of entire downloaded websites or snapshots of web pages, using software such as Offline Explorer (for PC), Sitesucker (for Mac), and, more recently, Zotero. I also learned about citation repositories, where one can deposit snapshots of cited URLs at web addresses hopefully more permanent than the original ones.

Eventually I also became familiar with the Internet Archive Wayback Machine (http://web.archive.org, hereafter IAWM) and its truly impressive collection of linked snapshots of web pages from around the globe, taken over the course of sometimes well over a decade. In the chapters that follow, all references to URLs in my personal collection that can no longer be found on the live web have been replaced by URLs pointing to the IAWM. Although IAWM snapshots typically lack some or all of the original image data, they can at least give some impression of what a site originally looked like. Unfortunately, the National Library of China has so far not attempted to keep a general archive of Chinese websites, unlike other national libraries such as, for instance, the British Library, which has legal permission to download at regular intervals the complete contents of all UK websites into the UK Web Archive (http://www.webarchive.org.uk).[51] This means that, apart from what has been captured by the IAWM and the materials preserved by Chinese netizens themselves, or by people like me, the literary publications discussed in this book will not be passed on to posterity.

Even if they were passed on to posterity, the question would be: how? A second lesson I learned during my research was that many of the texts I was interested in are not in any way stable. Unless one has a very narrow definition of what constitutes a text (i.e., unless one completely ignores all the visual and textual information appearing on-screen alongside a conventional piece of prose or poetry), the majority of the works I looked at appeared differently at every reading, and will appear differently again to you when you read them. There are different reasons why this might be the case. It might be that the site in question displays user-targeted advertising. I have lost count of the number of times I was staring at a Chinese text online with, next to it, an English-language advertisement for some product similar to something I had bought online the day before, or a recruitment ad from some British university. Another, more interesting reason why sites may look different at each visit is that their content is interactive, as is the case with the majority of Chinese Internet literature. Since the last time you read the text, readers may have uploaded comments, which may have inspired the author to make changes, publish additions, or remove certain phrases or certain images. There are also texts that simply do not end, or that go on for such a long time that one has to decide whether or not to wait for the ending before starting some sort of analysis, a question generally not considered by those analyzing printed novels. In the meantime, other versions of the text, either identical or different, may have begun to appear on other websites, sometimes even connected to other authorial pseudonyms. These are not problems faced by most literature scholars (although they will sound familiar to those dealing with manuscripts or oral traditions). When working with Internet literature, the first question one has to ask oneself again and again is: how do I define the text? Sometimes there is an obvious answer, sometimes there is not.

The instability of the text also offers opportunities in the realm of interpretation. Since most literary texts are typically open to multiple interpretations, it goes without saying that different readers read the same text differently. Even the same readers will read the same text differently at different times of their lives, but what if the text itself changes over time as well? In that case, the reading experience and the act of interpretation almost automatically take on more of a temporal quality. In some cases I have tried to make this explicit by avoiding the use of the present tense in describing texts or sites. Traditionally, literature students are trained to use present tense to describe their material ("The book *is* in two parts. The first part *describes* this, the second *continues* like that."). In contrast, some of my readings in this book are more like travel journals ("When I visited this site in 2003, the text looked like this; when I visited again in 2011, it had changed into that.") Even the simple necessity to go back frequently to a site to make sure it is still online adds to the temporal experience of reading.

Even more challenging are experimental works that rely on user interaction (e.g., clicking on hyperlinks) to determine how they take shape. Such texts are different for each reader and, as they often rely on visual aspects of language (words moving around screen, for instance), they are difficult to paraphrase and difficult to reproduce in print, other than by still images. Some examples are discussed in chapter 4 and can probably be understood properly only if the reader makes the effort to visit the URLs in question.

My selection of topics for each chapter is necessarily quite random but conforms to the three aims I stated at the outset: to describe the general phenomenon of Internet literature in China; to analyze examples of literary innovation taking place online; and to show how online publications push the boundaries of the state-regulated publishing system, especially the moral boundaries of what is ideologically considered to be healthy literature. In addition to general description and analyses of specific online literary practices, each chapter contains at least one reading of a specific work or group of works. Chapter 1 starts with a descriptive overview of the early history of Chinese Internet literature, making grateful use of canonizing efforts already under way in China. The second half of the chapter looks at the Rongshu Xia (Under the Banyan Tree) website, generally acknowledged to be China's first successful literary space, before zooming in on a work that helped make the site famous: the online diary of the cancer patient Lu Youqing. Drawing on different versions of the text I observed at different times online, as well as snapshots from earlier versions and a copy of a later printed edition, I show how both the author himself and the people supporting him carefully tried to maintain the serious literary nature of the publication, despite the media attention it created. Lu Youqing's writing was among the earliest work demonstrating the potential of the diary or chronicle form for online literary expression.

Chapter 2 looks in detail at online chronicles by three very different authors. The first is Chen Cun, whose long, meandering, never-ending online writings are clearly linked to his earlier avant-garde experiments from his pre-Internet days, when he was always striving to find ways to liberate himself from what he considered to be the stifling conventions of fiction, in favor of a more immediate manner of written expression. Chen's awareness of avant-garde gestures and ironies at some point even resulted in me being included in one of his works, putting me in the unenviable position of having to do research on a representation of myself. A very different chronicler is Wen Huajian, author of China's first microblog novel, whose work is less serious than Chen Cun's but nicely thematizes the community aspect of social media while constantly blurring the lines between the contents of the novel and Wen's actual interactions on Weibo. Finally, chapter 2 looks at the celebrity blogger Han Han. Although, as mentioned earlier, Han does not publish literary work online, his early blog posts (no longer on the live web but captured by the IAWM as well as preserved by individual netizens) are important for their frontal attacks on the established publishing system. More recently as well, Han Han has been engaged in several projects aimed at widening the space for independent literature publishing in China, both in print (through his involvement with a short-lived independent magazine) and on the Internet (through his recent promotion of a magazine-style application for mobile phones).

Chapter 3 is about online fiction. It describes the tremendous commercial success of online genre fiction, based on a business model pioneered by Qidian (Starting Point), which went on to become one of the most visited websites in the world. Much of this is romance fiction and has been studied in great detail in a recent monograph by Jin Feng, who not only scrutinized the texts but also did extensive fieldwork among members of online romance fiction communities.[52] My own analysis focuses on a variety of genres and on the regulatory context of online fiction publishing. I look at how state regulators deal with the sudden emergence of countless online publications of full-length novels appearing without the "book numbers" normally required for printed publications. I pay special attention to the proliferation of erotic fiction, highlighting the shifting interpretation of PRC laws aimed at banning the distribution of obscene publications. I show how moral censorship is a typical feature of postsocialist publishing, with the state regulator insisting on imposing "healthy" morals on all readers, regardless of age, but the interpretation of what is healthy and what is not in practice becoming increasingly tolerant. I also show how authors' responses to censorship requests for cuts and changes can in fact be quite playful and add to the level of interest of the texts in question. The chapter ends with a short case study of a very different site, Heilan (Black and Blue), home to a fiercely autonomous group of highly serious creative writers, who have been honing their technical writing skills, bringing out an independent online literary magazine, and awarding their own literary prize for well over a decade. My reading of some stories in a recent issue of *Black and Blue* focuses on the authors' aestheticized treatment of otherwise base or obscene subject matter, which contrasts meaningfully with the erotic fiction discussed earlier in the chapter.

The fourth chapter deals with online poetry, widening the scope to work published both inside and outside China, including experimental work done by non-Chinese authors of electronic literature using Chinese characters for their visual qualities. The chapter looks at some poetry forums that I visited a few times over a number of years, discussing ways in which online poetry crosses boundaries: between poet and reader, between those inside and outside China, and, once again, between what is and is not considered morally acceptable. I look in detail at the work of the female avant-garde poet Datui (Thigh), which originated in the context of the now-canonized "Lower Body" group of poets but turned out to be too explicit to be accepted by critics as having poetic value, resulting in her work being deemed obscene and subjected to moral censorship. The chapter also contains a long discussion of the highly experimental online visual poetry of Dajuin Yao (Yao Dajun), one of my personal favorites, who, for artistic reasons, also operates largely outside established systems, to the extent that he designs his own software to create some of his works. Starting out in the mid-1990s when he was a graduate student in the United States, Yao built up a fascinating body of work that disappeared from the live web a number of years ago but has been preserved in the IAWM, and on my hard drive. The combination of case studies in this chapter, highlighting the social, political, moral, and aesthetic aspects of online Chinese writing, recaptures all the themes addressed in the previous three chapters, and in this introduction.

Finally, in the conclusion, I look back at the first decade and a half of Internet literature in China against the background of what appears to be the onset of a decline, or perhaps the start of something even newer.

ONE

Internet Literature in China

HISTORY, TECHNOLOGY, AND CONVENTIONS

▸ **INTERNET LITERATURE**, like any other literature, is shaped by general technological developments and by specific social conventions. In the early twentieth century in China, the spread of mechanized printing and the demise of the literati lifestyle conspired to produce a richly varied magazine literature. This literature catered to a wide variety of tastes and was written in an equally wide variety of linguistic and cultural registers, but the many magazines of the early Republican period also had some notable shared characteristics. Most of them reveled in the opportunities the new printing technologies offered for combining textual and visual contents. Photographs, illustrations, and advertisements all played a role in distinguishing different journal styles or genres from one another. The magazine format also helped to continue and strengthen the traditional preference for linking literary production to collective activity. Many journals were affiliated with literary societies or clubs and used their publications as newsletters to stay in regular contact with their members and supporters. Finally, most of them promoted the spread of personal information about authors, encouraging biographical interpretations of literary work, as well as ad hominem criticism. This continued the Chinese tradition of considering text and author as two sides of the same coin (*wen ru qi ren*) while at the same time laying the foundation for a modern literary celebrity culture.

Following the establishment of the socialist literary system after 1949, both the technology and the social organization of literary production came under state control. Of the hundreds of literary magazines that were in circulation throughout China in 1948 and 1949, not a single one survived the introduction of the new system.[1] Instead, the cultural bureaucracy of the socialist state founded a number of nationwide and regional literary journals run by editors appointed by the various branches of the All-China Federation of Literary and Artistic Circles (Zhongguo Quanguo Wenxue Yishu Jie Lianhehui, or Wenlian for short) and its subsidiary, the Chinese Writers Association (Zhongguo Zuojia Xiehui, or Zuoxie).[2] Literary magazines became part of a network that also included official literary prizes, financial and nonfinancial benefits and incentives for writers, stipends for editors to travel around the country, distribution via the network of New China bookshops, as well as, specifically in the case of magazines, via the network of post offices. The system whereby readers could subscribe to magazines at dedicated post office counters survived well into the 1980s. All this was part and parcel of the socialist literary system, as described in great detail in Perry Link's book-length study *The Uses of Literature.*

During the Cultural Revolution, Wenlian and Zuoxie ceased to function, and literary magazines closed down. For a while, literary production was reduced to carefully selected book publications and the occasional appearance of literary texts in newspapers. The quantity of literary publications gradually increased during the last few years of the Cultural Revolution, in the early 1970s, and periodical publishing recommenced during that time, although the major literary journals of the pre-1966 period did not reestablish themselves until after 1976.[3] By the 1980s, the institutions of the socialist literary system were all back in place and literary magazines once again flourished. The 1980s also witnessed the gradual bifurcation between "official" (*guanfang*) and "nonofficial" (*fei guanfang* or *minjian*) literary circuits. As Xudong Zhang has argued, however, the preference of the nonofficial circles for apolitical, modernist writing tied in well with the policy of the Deng Xiaoping regime to promote the autonomy of cultural work in exchange for its depoliticization and noninterference with the overarching course of economic reform.[4]

The result was that the 1980s avant-garde movement (*xianfeng pai*) in fiction, widely celebrated by critics for its radical opposition to the socialist realist paradigm, was in fact very much dependent on direct support from the institutions of the socialist system. Professor Shao Yanjun from Peking University has described this paradoxical situation, in which a literary elite used a nationwide support system, designed for distributing mass-produced propaganda literature, to promote instead a kind of literature that could be appreciated only by a tiny minority:

> Writers were showing off to editors, editors were showing off to critics, critics were showing off at conferences, and behind it all was the magazine publication system supported by the Writers Association, and the university system. Inevitably, this developed toward cliquishness—and these cliques were not communities of individuals with similar tastes but interest communities of individuals sharing the same privileges.... From the postal system that allowed the free sending of manuscripts for submission, to the patronage of and generous instruction to writers by the editors of the big magazines; from the formal establishment of culture bureaus at prefecture level to the assistance with revising manuscripts, free travel and lodgings provided by the big magazines, the whole emergence and development of the avant-garde movement relied on the latent continuity of the traditional literary mechanism.[5]

In her influential 2003 monograph *The Inclined Literary Field*, Shao describes how, when literary magazines were weaned off state support from the late 1980s onward, the literary elite was ill equipped for assuming leading positions in the emerging literary marketplace because its previous cliquish behavior and its denigration of more mainstream and popular work had alienated it from the tastes of the wider reading public.[6] Without state support, the 1980s avant-garde collapsed, and the kind of "economic world reversed" described by Pierre Bourdieu as typical of European literary communities never developed in China. Instead, the literary field tilted toward the side of economic capital, with the frantic production of best sellers (*chàngxiaoshu*) balanced out only by the steady popularity of traditional realist "long sellers" (*chángxiaoshu*).[7] It was against this background of typical postsocialist uncertainty, with familiar institutions disappearing, market mechanisms kicking in, and traditional tastes lingering, that Internet literature began to emerge.

A New Literary Space

The noticeable commercialization of Chinese literature in the 1990s was the outcome of two simultaneously occurring processes. One was the withdrawal of state support for the literary system already just mentioned. The other was the relaxation of state control over publishing houses and the rise of what is generally referred to as the second channel (*er qudao*) of semiofficial, market-driven print production.[8] The second channel, studied in detail by Shuyu Kong in her book *Consuming Literature*, is "a grey area of publishing that . . . includes both unofficial publishing and private book distribution" and that "represents the most commercialized and liberated area of book publishing and distribution."[9]

The phenomenon of private distribution of books and journals emerged in the early 1980s and was initially associated with the sale of illegal printed material, including pornography. During the 1990s, partly as a result of repeated government campaigns and a nationwide reregistration of publishing houses, as well as decreasing state control over printing and distribution, a workable system was forged in which state-owned publishers collaborate with private entrepreneurs, with the former providing access to formal "book license numbers" (*shuhao*) and the latter doing most of the work in terms of production, marketing, and distribution.[10] The outcome so far has been that the number of official publishing houses in China has remained stable at around five hundred, but the number of private companies involved in producing books and journals is many times larger. At times the distinction between the state-owned and the private elements is not obvious, especially as the official publishing houses themselves have begun to adopt corporate business models. Changes in this area continue to the present and are reflected, for instance, in Xin Guangwei's authoritatively comprehensive overview of publishing in China, where he states, in one and the same section of his first chapter, that "all publishing houses in the Chinese mainland are state-owned," only to correct himself a few pages later to say that, since Liaoning Publishing Group was listed in the stock market in 2007, "gone are the days when all publishing houses in China were state-owned."[11]

Especially relevant to the present discussion is Shuyu Kong's analysis of the main differences in private-sector publishing between the 1980s and the 1990s. After pointing out that, in the 1990s, state sector and private sector became more integrated, she goes on to say that second-channel publishers of the 1990s were "better educated" and produced "better books."[12] As we shall see in later chapters, the expectation that publishers and editors in the private sector, including those operating online, are professionally trained and have certain qualifications is part of the conditions under which private publishing ventures can obtain business licenses from government regulators. These policies undoubtedly raise the level of publications, but they are also meant to discourage the second channel from getting involved in projects that move beyond state-sanctioned boundaries of "healthy" content. Nevertheless, as Kong's study convincingly demonstrates, the introduction and semilegalization of the second channel has created a vibrant publishing climate, and market incentives can at times encourage cultural entrepreneurs to push the limits, or be instrumental in shifting them.

In the conclusion of her study, Kong turns to the recent emergence of online literature and asks the question if the Internet is providing "a new literary space." She gives an excellent summary of the development of the major literary website Rongshu Xia (Under the Banyan Tree, http://www.rongshuxia.com), which will feature in my discussion later in this chapter as well. She notes the site's rapid development toward a commercial business model, which leads her to the following gloomy observation, worth quoting at length:

> On the surface, the Internet promises a democratic zone where everyone has the right to freely produce and publish, ignoring literary conventions, political censorship, and not least the prolonged and cumbersome publishing process. However, most objective observers would conclude that up until now, cyberspace has remained a huge virgin territory untouched by deep passion, originality, and talent. Anyone who browses through the gigantic database of literary works stored on Banyan Tree's site would agree with those critics who decry Internet literature as, at best, simply a form of "literary karaoke" for self-entertainment and, at worst, "literary detritus" freely and copiously discharged onto the screen. The subject and style of these works tends to be narrow, trite, and monotonous, full of conventional and clichéd expressions of predictable personal sentiments. Although traces of unique style and language can be found in certain individual works of Internet literature, in general one must search hard to find any literary innovation. Rarely are

the new technological possibilities of the medium, such as the potential for
interaction between visual images and words, and the ability to link back and
forward between pages, fully explored.[13]

As I will argue in the next chapter, I do not believe that multimedia and
hypertext are the only means of literary innovation on the Internet, and
I am less pessimistic than Kong about PRC authors' ability to create new
literary conventions online. More important, however, it is worth not-
ing a slight but significant contradiction in Kong's argument. The well-
known modernist aesthetic that she favors (depth, originality, talent) is
intimately linked to the ideals and conventions of an established professional print culture community in which authors, editors, proofreaders,
designers, illustrators, and publishers spend large amounts of time polishing and perfecting literary texts meant to be presented as works of art.
It is not feasible to expect online literature to have developed such an "art
world"[14] within the space of just a few years, nor is the Internet the kind
of environment where one would expect such an aesthetic to develop. In
some ways, Chinese Internet literature is reminiscent of the often hast-
ily produced work that featured in the countless literary supplements of
newspapers during the Republican period, which one scholar has aptly
described as "literature in its primary state" (*yuanshengtai wenxue*).[15] In
other ways, it is quite simply something new to which old value systems
might not apply.

In short: it is worth pointing out that a new literary space does not
necessarily need to be a new space for "high" literature in the traditional
sense. As we shall see in chapter 3, the rise of online genre fiction is a
tremendously important new development in PRC literature, even if it
means flooding the Web with pulp. In my view, there can be no question
that the Internet does provide a new literary space and that it has established and will continue to establish its own conventions and values,
which are not identical with the conventions and values of print culture,
even though all kinds of intriguing forms of overlap between print media
and digital media are in existence. In the following, I provide an overview of the early history of Chinese-language Internet literature. Following that, I give a brief description of the way in which Internet literature
forums operate and introduce some of their conventions and the related
terminology. This is followed by a more detailed look at the Banyan Tree

site, which stands out among PRC online literature portals of the early period. Finally, I give a brief case study featuring Lu Youqing's work "Date with Death," which propelled Banyan Tree and online writing to nationwide popularity in the year 2000.

Chinese Internet Literature: Early History

The earliest Chinese-language web literature was produced outside China. As scholars and critics are starting to write the history of this new form of Chinese literature, there seems to be an emerging consensus that the first works of Chinese web literature appeared in the online journal *Huaxia wenzhai* (*China News Digest—Chinese Magazine*, hereafter *HXWZ*), established by Chinese students in the United States in 1991, which was also the world's first Chinese electronic magazine.[16] The magazine was distributed through various electronic channels (LISTSERV, FTP, e-mail) prior to establishing a web presence in 1994. The last issue, number 939, appeared on April 18, 2009. Right from the start, issues of *HXWZ* included literary writing in various genres, both original writing by contributors and republications of printed work by well-known authors. U.S.-based Chinese students also posted their creative writings to the Chinese-language newsgroup alt.chinese.txt, founded in 1992.

The earliest Chinese-language electronic journal devoted entirely to literature was the monthly *Xin yusi* (*New Spinners of Words*), launched by Fang Zhouzi in 1994 and named after the famous independent Republican-period journal *Yusi*, which was founded by, among others, the brothers Lu Xun and Zhou Zuoren. *New Spinners of Words* was originally distributed via alt.chinese.txt, with back issues available on various FTP sites. In October 1997, it established its World Wide Web domain, http://www.xys.org, where it continues to be published every month. Other influential literary publications founded in the United States around the same time and mentioned in all histories of Chinese Internet literature are *Ganlanshu* (*Olive Tree*, http://www.wenxue.com) and *Huazhao* (*Cute Tricks*, http://www.huazhao.com), both launched in 1995. *Cute Tricks* is said to have been the first Chinese-language literary publication to obtain its own domain name and ISSN number. It is also noticeable because it focused mainly on literature for and by women. *Olive Tree*, cofounded and edited by the poet Ma Lan, has been praised

↑ Figure 1.1 Front page of Olive Tree website, captured by the IAWM on June 24, 1998. https://web.archive.org/web/19980624202450/http://www.wenxue.com/.

for its professional user-friendly design, which included in-site search functions that would not become commonplace on the web until much later.[17] Both sites are no longer active. *Olive Tree* has been archived by the IAWM, whereas an archive of *Cute Tricks* survives at the URL http://www.huazhao.org/huazhao.php.

The year 1995 also saw the appearance of Bulletin Board Systems (BBS) on servers at universities in mainland China, starting from Tsinghua University in Beijing and quickly spreading elsewhere. According to Ouyang Youquan, some original literary works were distributed via BBS, but the main trend was to copy works from Taiwan. Three years later, the first online work to become a print best seller in China also came from Taiwan. Using the pseudonym Pizi Cai (Ruffian Cai), a Taiwanese man called Cai Zhiheng serialized the novel *Di-yi ci de qinmi jiechu (First Intimate Contact)* on a BBS in 1998, when he was still a graduate student at National Cheng Kung University. *First Intimate Contact* is a popular romance novel dealing with the world of online dating and virtual romance, written in what had by then become a recognizable "online writing style": colloquial language broken down into many short segments.[18] In that same year, the printed version of the novel became a best seller in

Taiwan, while the online version became hugely popular among Internet users in mainland China.[19] A year later, a simplified-character edition appeared in print in mainland China and also became an instant best seller, familiarizing many readers with both web literature and cyber culture and paving the way for the web literature craze that was to follow.

Discussion Forums

A very important technological development facilitating the boom in online writing that took place toward the end of the previous millennium was the emergence of interactive discussion forums (also known as message boards, Chinese *luntan*) on the World Wide Web. Although initially still frequently referred to by the old term BBS, forums are in fact quite different from the old bulletin boards. Forums are web based, feature nice-looking graphic interfaces, and make it very easy for users to generate content. Although in recent years literary forums have had strong competition from literary blogs, forums remain widely popular because they have strong community functions. Whereas blogs typically feature content created by one individual, with other users able to generate only comments, forums typically allow all members of the community to submit their own writing as well as discuss that of others. As will become evident in later chapters, the popularity of forums is showing some signs of waning in China, but they continue to be at the heart of both noncommercial and commercial online publishing, such as the genre fiction websites discussed in chapter 3 and the writings of Chen Cun treated in chapter 2.

Most literary websites host forums devoted to specific genres or themes, often also including classical-style writing, which is undergoing a remarkable revival online. Most discussion forums operate on the principle that only registered members of the site can upload their works to a forum, but that both members and nonmembers can read the works and comment on them. Comments on a particular work are automatically appended to the work itself, creating so-called threads of discussion, which often also involves the author of the original work. This aspect of direct interaction between author and reader constitutes the main distinction between web literature and printed literature in China.

Discussion forums normally appear on-screen as a list of thread titles (*zhuti* or *biaoti*). The title of a thread is identical to the title of the post (*tiezi*) that started the thread. Apart from the thread title, the forum content list normally provides the (pen) name of the author of the original post, followed by some additional statistics, usually the number of hits (i.e., the number of times the thread has been accessed by users), the number of responses or comments, and the date, time, and author of the latest response. In most cases, threads that received recent responses are at the top of the list, and as long as new responses are added, they will continue to receive attention. Once a thread has been pushed off the front page, it tends to be no longer read or discussed, but it will continue to be available for a long time: these works require relatively little server space, and some literary discussion forums have online archives containing literally millions of works.

Most discussion forums are overseen by moderators (*banzhu*), who ensure that works are submitted to the appropriate forums and, if necessary, delete inappropriate or unwanted content, including content that might catch the eye of Internet censors. As is the case with online communities all over the world, including popular non-Chinese sites such as Facebook, moderators on Chinese sites have access to word filtering software that helps them to identify unwanted content, and some communities are more restrictive than others in this respect. How such filters are used to enforce state regulations, such as existing obscenity legislation, and how they are routinely circumvented, is discussed with reference to fiction in chapter 3 and with reference to poetry in chapter 4.

Originally online forums allowed for members to see their contributions on-screen almost instantly, but many moderators now take a more cautious attitude and will screen postings before they are displayed on the forum. Moderators are also responsible for keeping a forum lively and active, for instance by organizing competitions or suggesting specific topics for writing, and by taking an active part in the various discussions. Many sites operate a system whereby community members gain points for making regular contributions, which add up to their popularity (*renqi*) rating. As with most online communities, literary forums usually allow members to create virtual identities that include not only pseudonyms (screen names) but also visual information in the form of avatars

⬆ **Figure 1.2** Front page of *Poetry Vagabonds* webzine, captured by the IAWM on December 9, 2010. http://web.archive.org/web/20101209020227/http://www.wenxue2000.com/mk/xbs001.htm.

that accompany each post. The use of real names is unusual, although normally an existing e-mail address is needed in order to complete member registration.[20]

Moderators are often also involved in selecting the best of the very many works that are posted to the forums for inclusion in special online publications known as webzines (*wangkan*). Most literary websites, especially those operated by small groups of like-minded associates, will publish regular webzines to showcase the best writing published on their forums. Such webzines will normally be carefully designed and edited, with a layout similar to printed literary magazines, and be devoid of interactive functions, that is, they are meant only to be read, not to be commented on.

From the late 1990s onward, discussion forums took the Chinese Internet literature world by storm. For many of their users, the forums are not much more than glorified chat rooms or online meeting places, or simply a place to practice writing as a hobby, but more serious sites try to devote themselves to high-level creation, criticism, and discussion. The web has also produced new avant-garde groups, especially in the genre of poetry, providing space for shocking antiestablishment writing that cannot easily appear in print, most famously on the Shi Jianghu (Poetry Vagabonds) website, which brought forth the phenomenon of "lower body poetry" (*xiabanshen shige*).[21] The typical features of Chinese literature forums in comparison with similar English-language forums will be discussed at length in chapter 4. In the remainder of this chapter, I shall focus on one of the earliest and most prominent providers of literary forums, the Banyan Tree site, and its early achievements.

Under the Banyan Tree

Founded in December 1997 as a personal web page, Under the Banyan Tree has gone on to become, in its own words, "the longest-standing literary website in China, with the most recognizable brand" (*guonei lishi zui youjiu, zui ju pinpai de wenxue lei wangzhan*), as well as "one of the largest archives of original literary manuscripts on the planet" (*quanqiu zui da de yuanchuang wenxue zuopin gaojianku zhi yi*).[22] This record-breaking online phenomenon, too, has its origins in the United States, since its founder, Zhu Weilian (William Zhu), is a U.S. citizen who moved to Shanghai in 1994. All overviews of the history of PRC Internet literature give Banyan Tree a very prominent place and describe the specific business strategy that underlay its success.[23] In 1999, Zhu founded the Shanghai Under the Banyan Tree Computer Company and turned his personal website into a full-fledged online literature portal, billed as "the global website for original Chinese-language works" (*quanqiu Zhongwen yuanchuang zuopin wangzhan*). Right from the start, Zhu engaged in crossover activities with other media. The Banyan label was linked to literary programs on Shanghai local radio as well as to literary columns in newspapers. It organized literary prize competitions and promoted print publications of book series under the Banyan brand, as well as other joint-print ventures with traditional publishing houses. All this activity soon turned Banyan Tree into "a sprawling multimedia business."[24] The site drew the attention of, and was eventually taken over by, the German publishing giant Bertelsmann, which sold it in 2006, by which time it had lost some of its past luster. In 2009 it was acquired by Shanda Interactive Entertainment, which now owns all major literary websites in

↑ **Figure 1.3**   Iconic welcome page of Under the Banyan Tree site, captured by the IAWM on February 1, 2008. https://web.archive.org/web/20080201231630/http://www.rongshuxia.com/.

the PRC, including the large popular fiction sites discussed in chapter 4. In the "About Us" section of its website, Banyan Tree now presents itself as an "independent copyright trading center" (*duli de banquan yunying zhongxin*).

Although it is generally recognized that Banyan Tree discovered a number of authors who went on to great literary fame and considerable critical acclaim (most notably Anni Baobei and Murong Xuecun, both of whom had the print publication of their first novels arranged by the site), scholars have generally paid more attention to its commercial success than to its literary characteristics. Important to recognize in this respect is the fact that when the site went public in 1999, William Zhu had brought together an enthusiastic editorial board, with the established author Chen Cun (see chapter 2) as chief artistic officer (*yishu zongjian*) and general consultant for literary matters. I visited the Banyan Tree site regularly in March 2002, when the takeover by Bertelsmann was on the cards but had not yet taken place, and I noted at the time the editors' attempts to maintain certain literary standards, as well as the tension between artistic and commercial agendas. The following section is an account of my browsing experiences on the site during that period, which I believe are representative of the characteristics of early PRC Internet literature.

Banyan Tree in 2002

As was and is the case with most Internet community websites, there were in 2002 two ways of entering Under the Banyan Tree: as member or as guest. In order to become a member, one needed to register a username (appropriately called pen name [*biming*]) and an existing e-mail address. Upon doing this, one would receive an automated e-mail message including a link to a registration page, where one could complete the registration process. This procedure, commonplace nowadays but still fairly new at the time, constituted a simple security measure, ensuring that prospective members did not submit fake e-mail addresses. No other personal information needed to be submitted in order to register, although one could volunteer a real name, age, and location. As far as was able to be observed, the main difference between members and guest users was that only members could submit their own writing to the main bulletin boards and use the related personalized services.

Once one had decided on the method of entry and clicked on the appropriate button, one would arrive at the main page. The main page contained regularly changing links to featured areas of the site. The main navigation bar at the top provided links to the seven main sections of the site. The navigation bar at the bottom of the main page contained a link to a group of English-language pages introducing the website and the company behind it. The page called "Our Footprints" contained more information about the history of the site, stating that it was founded in July 1999 in Shanghai, with a staff of twelve people. "Our Footprints" made specific mention of the fact that Chen Cun opened his own column on the site in September 1999 and officially joined the site as its "CAO" (chief artistic officer) in April 2000.[25]

While I was carrying out my research in March 2002, Chen Cun's column was appearing less and less frequently and eventually disappeared on March 28, 2002. Although no reason was given, this event was most likely related to a debate unleashed by Chen in July 2001, when he submitted a much-debated piece to one of the site's bulletin boards, stating his disappointment with the development of web literature, announcing that its heyday was already over. Though this may have been the case from his perspective (see also chapter 2), the volume of texts added to Under the Banyan Tree was still staggering. In the eleven days between March 17, 2002, and March 28, 2002, when I visited the site on a daily basis, more than thirty-four thousand articles were published on it. From checking the daily additions to some of the sections, I obtained the impression that this was an accurate figure and that it represented only actual literary works being contributed, not the even more numerous responses to those works that other users submitted.

Apart from Chen Cun's writings, there was another, arguably more important reason why Under the Banyan Tree had achieved such popularity. It published, from August to October 2000, the online diary of a man called Lu Youqing, who was dying of cancer. This unusual event attracted enormous media attention and drew countless users to the site. Although originally submitted through one of the bulletin boards, the diary was later given its own separate area on the site, with parts of the work available in English translation, under the title "Date with Death." In 2002 I did not do a close reading of Lu's work but only registered its significance. A discussion of the work, based on a later reading with the benefit of hindsight, is presented in a later section of this chapter.

In March 2002, the rules for submission to Under the Banyan Tree clearly indicated that anyone was welcome to contribute, regardless of location or nationality, as long as the contribution was written in Chinese. The site appeared to be well supported by advertisers, especially by the Chinese branch of the German Bertelsmann Book Club, which sponsored the annual "Bertelsmann Cup" web literature competition, which by then had already been held three times. Apart from those winning prizes in such competitions and from a number of "contracted contributors" (*qianyue zuozhe*), none of the contributors were paid for their publications.

Already in 2002 it was clear that the company running Banyan Tree was crossing over into other media: collections of works published on the site were available in book form under the Banyan Tree label, and the name of the site was linked to a radio program, which in turn was accessible online through the "Radio Station" (Diantai) section of the site. This section also featured a forum for "texts with sound" (*yousheng wenzhang*). These were literary texts by various contributors, read out by what appeared to be a professional reader: the same voice was used for different texts. This section was the most experimental, in terms of form, of the whole site. In other aspects, however, the formal appearance of Banyan Tree in 2002 remained indebted to the print-culture paradigm. Texts submitted to the forums were visualized on-screen as if they were typed on lineated paper; Lu Youqing's diary was visualized as an open book on-screen.

Banyan Tree catered readily to the need for readers to know more about the authors of literary work. There were a few regular contributors to the site who had their own areas, accessible through the "Special Columns" (Zhuanlan) section. These areas contained much information about these authors' personal lives, as well as links to their writings, pictures of them, and other information they felt eager to share with their readers. One of those areas was devoted to Anni Baobei, who at the time was known mainly to online audiences and not yet the established print author that she is now. The text on the right-hand side of the main page of her section, next to her picture, clearly created the illusion of direct contact between author and reader, as it read, "I write my writings for kindred spirits to read" (*wo ba wode wenzi xiegei xiangtong de linghun kan*), harking back to the traditional notion of the reader as "soul mate" (*zhiyin*). The support of her online fan base has played a crucial role in the development of Anni Baobei's career. [26]

The opposite phenomenon was also visible, that is, print-culture writers accessing web culture on the basis of already established fame. In the "Writers Columns" (Zuojia zhuanlan) section, accessible through a sidebar menu on the front page of the site, readers could access areas devoted to very established writers such as Wang Anyi, Shi Tiesheng (1951–2010), and Shu Ting, as well as the famous Shanghai-based academic Chen Sihe. These areas normally contained a picture of the celebrity in question, some biographical data, and a full version of one of their works, for which Banyan Tree had obtained the right to republish it online.

Apart from well-known writers or contracted contributors, normal contributors to the website, once their contributions became sufficiently regular, also had the opportunity to share biographical information with their readers. Each of the main channels (fiction, poetry, and essay) in the "Literature" (Wenxue) section of the site contained a subsection called "Stars of the Channel" (Pindao zhi xing), where readers could look for information on some of the frequent contributors to the channel. These biographies were generally much more elaborate than those of the celebrities, containing both pictures of the authors and text they provided themselves, signaling their own eagerness to share this information with their readers.

In 2002, Banyan Tree struck me as being involved in community-building practices not dissimilar to those practiced by the literary magazine communities that were active in China roughly a century earlier.[27] The company running the website organized meetings and workshops for readers and prospective contributors, usually in Hangzhou, traditionally the scene of literary gatherings. Banyan Tree had also established at least one literary society, the Under the Banyan Tree Poetry Society, which had its own area on the site, as well as its own online journal, which, once again, was visualized on-screen as if it were a printed publication laid flat on the screen surface. However, what made (and makes) Internet communities like this qualitatively different from print-culture communities was the possibility of almost direct interaction through the various discussion forums. The actual communities were formed on those forums, as authors submitted and published their works and readers (or other authors) commented on them through the website, developing their own critical discourse and values in the process.

There were at the time two distinct types of bulletin board on the Banyan Tree site. In the "Community" (Shequ) section, which was divided into various subsections, members could submit writings on a variety of topics, ranging from ghost stories to classical poetry. Those forums were monitored and writings could be deleted if they contained inappropriate or illegal content. In the "Literature" section, contributions to the various forums for fiction, poetry, and essay were scrutinized by an editor before they were published. Contributors, who must be members, would submit their texts online through the website. Within forty-eight hours, one of the Banyan editors would read it and decide whether or not to publish it, and then communicate the decision to the author's e-mail address.

In order to check whether the system worked in practice the way it was said to work on the website, I registered as a member and, on March 26, 2002, I submitted to the poetry forum a poem I had written in Chinese. Sure enough, two days later I received an e-mail from one of the editors informing me that, regrettably, my poem had been rejected. Although it was considered "sincere" in its emotions, it was deemed in need of further polishing in terms of the actual expression of the emotions. Interestingly, however, the technology of the website did allow me, as a member, to keep an online record of all the writings I submitted, whether published or rejected, and to put them in my own "online collection," where my poorly written poem continued to linger for years until it (and my membership status) finally fell victim to a major site overhaul. The fact that even rejected texts remained available to members wanting to access them online must have meant that there were many more texts in the Banyan database than the one million or so that had been published on the forums at the time. In 2002, two years before the founding of Facebook and three years before the emergence of YouTube, such observations of the sheer quantity of data being stored by online service providers and shared by online communities were still very remarkable.

The main conclusion I drew from the story of my own failed debut as a web literature author was that Banyan Tree was serious about its intention to carry out some form of quality control, no matter how massive the quantity of its output might be. This did not mean that the works that did get published were necessarily all masterworks. It did mean, however, that Banyan Tree at the time refused to acquiesce to being part of "popular culture." From my own readings and observations, I obtained the impression that the majority of writings on the website were creative and original in intent. They did not mean solely to entertain, and the vast majority of contributors did not realize any financial gain. Even though the Banyan Tree company clearly made money from its operations, the thousands who published on the site were predominantly aspiring writers with a pure interest in literature. Their interest was not, however, in a kind of literature that was purely textual in nature but in literature as an act of social communication. As such, they were not just being very postmodern or very popular but also continuing a Chinese cultural tradition, of practicing writing in the context of friendly gatherings, even though the gatherings were now taking place online.

What was especially noteworthy about Banyan Tree in 2002 was its eclectic mix of literary genres. For me at the time this was by far the most innovative element of the site, and of Chinese Internet literature in general. Previously in modern Chinese literature there had been clear-cut distinctions between so-called New Literature, on the one hand, and literature in traditional and popular genres on the other, to the extent that one would scarcely be able to see the products of those three different styles appear in the same space. Literary websites, however, had it all. Banyan Tree had forums for classical poetry, travelogue, and martial arts fiction alongside those for more "serious" or more "modern" genres. The overall impression I took away from the site in 2002 was one of variety and playfulness, none of which could be reduced, however, to specific themes, forms, or formulas, as would be the case with commercial genre fiction. Although Banyan Tree had not become the online equivalent of the leading print literature journal *Shouhuo* (*Harvest*), which was reportedly its founder's original ambition,[28] its literary aspirations were undeniable.

Banyan Tree in 2011

Although it still enjoys widespread name recognition, Banyan Tree is now no longer the leading website in the Chinese online literary landscape. Traffic to the site is considerably less than it used to be.[29] It still features a very sizable searchable archive of writing, some of it dating back to the founding years of the site and including work by well-known contributors, such as Chen Cun, while other work, such as Lu Youqing's diary, which used to have its own section on the site, is no longer available. The site also still has its distinctive logo (a green tree) and color coding (again, mainly green). Occasionally the design of parts of the site is reminiscent of the earlier print-inspired visual form. The main menu of the "Novels" section, for instance, appears on the screen as two small lineated pages in a ring binder.

As mentioned, Banyan Tree was recently purchased by the Shanda company, which also owns all the largest Chinese genre fiction sites and provides membership access to all of them with a single ID, called the Shanda travel pass (*Shengda tongxingzheng*). Like all the Shanda sites, Banyan Tree now devotes much space to the serialized publication of long genre novels, some of them by authors identified as "VIPs," but unlike Shanda's more commercial sites, the novels on Banyan Tree can be read freely without subscription. The site emphasizes its ability to arrange for print publication of online work, and the typical career trajectory of the current Banyan Tree authors is clearly visible by looking at the forum lists. Titles carry little logos that indicate their status, moving from *jian* ("recommended" by the site editors) to *jing* (chosen as "best of" the forum), then to *qian* ("contracted" by the site)and to *ban* ("published" in print). As far as I have been able to ascertain, novels published in print also remain available to read for free on the website.

"Novels" (Changpian xiaoshuo) is the name of one of the three main sections of the site. The second is called "Short Literature" (Duanpian wenxue) and is devoted to short stories, essays, and poetry. The third is called "Rankings" (Paihangbang) and provides access to a wide range of listing methods of all the works in the site archive (*zuopinku*), the total of which exceeded 1.5 million works in December 2011. Works can be listed by title, by length in characters, by date, by popularity (number of hits per day, week, or month; number of comments), and by status (ongoing, finished, published, unfinished). They can also be grouped by the names of the thirty-odd literary societies (*shetuan*) for which the site currently hosts space. These societies, some of which date back to the early years of the site, run their own minisites, including dedicated forums, archives, and so on, some of them with access restricted to members.

All in all, Banyan Tree is still a lively literary site and still relatively less commercial than other sites in the Shanda stable. However, it never regained the popularity and attention it enjoyed in its early years, much of which should be credited to the writings of one man, Lu Youqing, to whose work the chapter now turns.

Lu Youqing's Date with Death

I don't know about others, but personally I have had this picture of death in my mind ever since I was a child. Over the past few decades, whenever I accidentally came to think about the topic of death, that picture, which now seems to me to be like an oil painting, would come to my mind in a very realistic manner:

Winter. A clear, bright lake. The water in the lake is not very clean, but that is just because the frost has set in. Dark earth. White traces in the distance, possibly snow. Around there are some tall, northern trees. They are lonely because of the frost....

On the other side of the lake is a European-style house, probably white. Lights are on in each room. The view is unclear. Its huge shadow cast on the surface of the lake, never stirring, making the lamplight appear even brighter.

> After a while, the lights go out: one, another one, a third one. . . . The lights
> go out slowly but securely, like a ritual. . . .
> When the last light goes out, a person has died.[30]

These are the opening lines of a work called "Date with Death," as they appeared on the Banyan Tree site on August 3, 2000. The author was a man called Lu Youqing, who was a terminal cancer patient determined to leave a public record of the final days of his life. Excerpts of his "death diary" continued to appear online for the next two months, with the final installment appearing on October 23, the diarist's thirty-seventh birthday. He eventually passed away on December 11, a few weeks after his diary had also been published in book form.[31]

The publication of Lu's diary attracted much media attention, to the extent that when he died, it was reported not only in national newspapers but also by the *Guardian* and the BBC.[32] Historians of Chinese Internet literature tend to agree that the success of the diary significantly promoted the reputation of Banyan Tree as the country's most important portal for online writing.[33] The Western media coverage of the event commented on the diary's unusual outspokenness, claiming that Lu's writings "have established a new standard for honesty in a society where reticence and considerations of face inhibit frank discussion of illness and death."[34] They also highlighted the author's criticism of his country's medical system. Yet apart from the social and medical angles, there are other perspectives from which to analyze this event, which, after all, took place in the literary sphere. What interests me here is the exact manner in which both the online and print publication of the diary were managed by a literary website and what Lu Youqing's writing can tell us about emerging styles and genres of Internet literature.

I first learned about Lu Youqing and his diary during my visits to the Banyan Tree website in March 2002, almost two years after it had begun publication. I encountered the diary entries all linked to a separate section of the site, away from the common discussion forums, and with some entries available in English translation. My assumption at the time was that Lu had initially been a normal contributor to one of the forums and that the special minisite devoted to his work was an online archive that had been created at a later date. Now, in 2011, this minisite is no longer to be found on the Banyan Tree site. The Chinese text of the diary is still available on many websites and was also resubmitted to the Banyan Tree archive by an anonymous poster in 2001. The partial English translation is, as far as I know, no longer available. Nevertheless, a more careful examination of the minisite as it existed, with the help of IAWM captures, shows that the story of Lu Youqing's diary is more complex than I originally assumed.

The IAWM captured the front page of the Banyan Tree site on August 18, 2000, just over two weeks after the date of the first diary entry.[35] There is a very prominent link to the diary on the site's front page, and the link is not to any of the discussion forums but to a special section of the site, with the same URL that I first visited in March 2002. The first captured snapshot of that URL in the IAWM dates from October 18, 2000, when Lu was yet to publish his last entry.[36] It shows that the minisite, with its distinctive booklike format that I commented on and reproduced in my earlier article,[37] was already in place while the diary writing was ongoing. Even the English translations of some of the earliest entries were already there. The page has a link to one of the discussion forums where readers can go to discuss the diary, but the diary itself did not originate on any of the forums.

The main page of the minisite, as captured by the IAWM, links to a number of paratexts, including a helpful introduction by two Banyan Tree editors known as Shouma and AVA, under the title "Zui hou de liwu" (The Final Gift).[38] The text explains that the site editors were approached by a woman working for the East China Normal University Publishing House who told them she had a friend who was dying of cancer and wanted to leave a "final gift" to his family in the form of a written account of his final days. The friend wanted to publish these writings on a website and allow readers to comment on them and discuss them, and he had thought of Banyan Tree as an appropriate place to do so. The editors went to visit Lu Youqing the next day, and some further negotiations followed, during which the editors also read parts of the diary already written. Lu Youqing initially asked for a special column called something like "Dying Live" (Siwang zhibo), but the editors considered this to be too "heavy" (chenzhong) and too "cruel" (canku). Instead, they offered to serialize his diary on a regular basis in the "Books and Periodicals" (Shukan) section of the Banyan Tree site, which was a section devoted to the authorized (re-) publication of copyrighted works. They also offered to help Lu Youqing find a publisher for the print publication of the diary. The editors ended the article by explaining that online serialization of the diary would not start until after Lu had granted them authorization and asked readers to keep an eye out for its appearance on the site. In other words, this article was published on the site before serialization of the diary began and was intended to draw attention to the event. When the minisite eventually appeared, it stated clearly that Lu Youqing had granted online publishing rights of the "diary version" (*riji ti*) of his work exclusively to Banyan Tree and that no other websites were allowed to copy his work.

Judging from the language used, the rights granted by the author were only those to the online diary-style serialization. This would, on the one hand, ensure that Banyan Tree had a unique record, while, on the other hand, enabling the author to grant rights to other, offline publications of his prose elsewhere and to an eventual book publication. Moreover, as becomes clear from another paratext, written by Lu Youqing himself, he only ever published 50 percent of his diary online. This was at the behest of his print publisher: if the full text of the book publication was not available online, the book would be more difficult to pirate.[39] This paratext, titled "Gaobie wangyou" (Farewell Online Friends), appeared on the minisite sometime after the last installment of the diary was published and was immediately followed by a piece by Banyan Tree managing director William Zhu himself, in which he pays tribute to Lu Youqing.[40]

In "Farewell Online Friends," Lu admitted that the "gift" he had intended to leave for his family was not just the diary itself but also whatever money could be made from it through book sales. At the same time, as is clear from a conversation between Lu and Zhu recorded in the latter's contribution, the diarist was repeatedly confronted by some representatives of the local media and some online commentators with the claim that he was trying to turn his death into a hype (*chaozuo*) purely for financial gain. In response to this, William Zhu pointed out that his site was offering the diary to its readers free of charge and without any surrounding advertising. Although Banyan Tree is likely to have taken a cut from profits of the print publication, if indeed they helped arrange it as they had promised, and although the diarist himself, for valid reasons, was not averse to profit, the editors' refusal to turn Lu's dying days into a live spectacle and Lu's own fear of being accused of hyping are indicative of the serious intentions by all concerned. The publication of the diary was a managed media event, but it was managed in such a way as to achieve distinction from other media events and best sellers aimed more unabashedly at capitalizing on the exposure of privacy or the challenging of social taboos. We will come across a similar act of distinction in the next chapter, when Chen Cun draws a clear dividing line between his own diary-like online writings about sex and the "sex diaries" of Muzimei.[41]

The serious intent of Lu Youqing's diary is emphasized, both in the text of the diary itself and in the paratext, by means of association with the concept of "literature" (*wenxue*). William Zhu's piece, which recounts a meeting with Lu Youqing, states that literature was always their favorite topic of conversation, whereas Lu refers to himself in the diary as a "young literature enthusiast" (*wenxue qingnian*).[42] In the following lines from the first entry of the online diary, dated August 3, 2000, Lu Youqing places his work quite pertinently in a literary context by discussing his choice of genre, while once again mentioning its lack of commercial potential. In doing so, he harks back to age-old Chinese literary concepts of sincerity and realness.

Why do I use the diary form? I thought about that. I could not possibly produce a scholarly essay [*lunwen*]. Of course I could have chosen some literary prose or essay form [*sanwen suibi*], but I figured since my life is set to become unhappier with every passing day, I might easily end up shunning [the writing] altogether. A diary is better, because it is like a time card: it shows you straight away how hard someone's been working. And anyway, in a diary you can still write scholarly essays, or even poems, and a lot more stories about yourself. Unfortunately my private life won't sell at the box office.

Diaries have another advantage: they are real [*zhenshi*]. It is hard to fake this kind of writing. Indeed, nobody in the kind of state that I'm in could feel the need to say anything fake.

It's real, that's why it's valuable [*zhenshi, jiushi jiazhi*].

This is immediately followed by a statement of his reason for choosing Banyan Tree as his preferred platform, which echoes the same values.

I thought long and hard before choosing Under the Banyan Tree as the first publication outlet for my diary. I felt that the style and aim of this website matched my intentions. More important, its members are not like those netizens who are only after "rankings" or "prizes." They are thoughtful people [*sikaozhe de ren*]. I should like them to be the first to see my writing, and I hope they will chime in and respond. I am really looking forward to reading their comments.

In various places in the diary, Lu writes about the significance of the on-line interaction with his readers at Banyan Tree. Although he was apparently unable to respond much to readers' comments, because he was in too much pain and discomfort to write more than the diary, he occasionally includes responses in the diary entries themselves. On August 13 he notes that his writing is starting to attract more and more attention, not only from the media but also from Banyan Tree members, who are leaving responses and comments. He expresses his gratitude and affection for those readers, some including old friends and classmates he had not heard from for a long time. In the same context, he comments on the time-sensitive nature (*shixiaoxing*) of diary writing. It needs to be "fresh" and "real" in order to be convincing. He assures his readers that, although adjustments to the dates of his diary entries are made for "technical" reasons, all that he publishes is recent and new. He does not expand on the technical reasons other than that they are "inherent" to the characteristic nature of websites and newspapers. Presumably his entries were first read and where necessary adjusted by editors before they appeared on the website.

A third observation about reader response to his writing included in the same entry of August 13 is that he hopes that readers will pay more attention to the written words and less attention to the person writing them. Once again, it is clear that he does not wish the serious nature of the topics he writes about to be undermined by excessive attention to his background and personality. This is the basic aspiration of most traditional literary writers and another indication that Lu Youqing wanted to differentiate his work from that of celebrity authors. The debate about Wei Hui's *Shanghai Baby*, which dominated the cultural media that same year and led to the novel's being banned, is likely to have been a relevant context.[43] In any case, it is clear that the development of the content of this online work was driven at least in part by direct reader response.

This becomes even clearer when, a little over a week later, in the entry dated August 21, Lu refers to reader response again to explain why he is starting to write about his childhood and his family. It is because many readers have expressed the wish to understand him better and know more about him. In this case, moreover, he refers to the readers as "friends" (*pengyou*). As we have seen in the case of Anni Baobei's section on Banyan Tree, the idea that the reader is a kind of soul mate or friend and, conversely, that there is a need to provide readers with personal information about the author so that author *and* work can be better understood is part and parcel of a very traditional Chinese view of literature. The result in this case is some tension between, on the one hand, the author's desire to discourage unsympathetic or critical readers from invading his privacy or casting doubt on his serious intentions and, on the other hand, reaching out to friendly readers and sharing personal information with them. A similar kind of tension is also inherent in the diary as a literary genre: it is private writing for public consumption. Throughout "Date with Death," Lu Youqing does not just record his thoughts and feelings, as all diarists do, but also explains himself to a readership of which he is keenly aware.[44] Moreover, in the parts where Lu writes about his parents, or about his student days, his writing is more akin to the genre of autobiography, although he usually manages to forge some sort of link to the present. (For instance, after having written about his siblings, he comments on the fact that the generation of only children born after the introduction of the one-child policy will never know brotherly and sisterly love and friendship.)

A very special implied reader of the diary is the author's daughter. She was eight years old at the time, and Lu Youqing states repeatedly that he hopes she will eventually get to read his writings, when she is older and he will already have passed away. (Cynical commentators suggested that he could have achieved this without publishing his work.) One of the most moving entries in the diary is that of September 18, when Lu records five "family precepts" (*jiaxun*) addressed to his daughter. He prefaces the precepts with a description of himself as a "traditional Chinese father" who wants to have a say in his daughter's choice of marriage partner. The precepts are meant as instructions to guide her toward choosing the right man. The way he lists and numbers his instructions ("Family Precept One, Family Precept Two," and so on) carries a hint of irony and self-mocking, but with much understated emotion, culminating in the short and simple final precept: "Just do what your mother says" (*Mama shuo le suan*).

Yet this part of the diary, too, appears to have come about at least in part as a result of reader response and editorial intervention. On September 7, Banyan Tree's chief artistic officer, the author Chen Cun, published a short prose piece on the site titled "At the West Garden Hotel."[45] In the piece, he recounts a trip to Yangzhou for the recording of a TV talk show titled "Tell It as It Is" (Shi hua shi shuo), in which both he and Lu You-qing, his wife, and daughter appeared as guests. In simple words, Chen Cun paints his impression of the Lu family. Toward the end of the piece, he expresses regret for not having had the opportunity to ask Lu Youqing a question that had been on his mind: what would he like to say to his daughter? He elaborates by saying that any words that Lu were to leave behind for his daughter would constitute the most solemn advice (*zui zhengzhong de zhufu*), something that would accompany her throughout her life. It is likely that this very special response to his work by an established prose writer encouraged the diarist to record his "family precepts."

The clearest case of reader-response impact on the progress of the diary appears in the entry for August 30, when the diarist explains that his decision to write about his college days and comment on college experience in general resulted from discussions during a special online chat session with Banyan Tree readers a few days earlier. No such prompting was required, however, for the passages where Lu chronicles, sometimes in meticulous detail, the deterioration of his physical condition and his rational and emotional responses to that process.

The diary entry of August 10 deals with the author's physical condition through a classic mirror scene. After mentioning how much weight he has lost in five years of illness, Lu writes,

> The me in the mirror is starting to look more and more like a flat specimen. The only thing that stands out is the tumor on my neck. It has taken a year for it to grow beyond the size of a tennis ball. (That tennis ball is going to be the death of me.) Once as I was standing in front of the mirror I burst out in tears. I felt I should not have become like this. I hated my own flesh. More recently, I have learned to accept the facts.

Despite his frequent use of dry understatement, as with the sentence in parentheses in the quoted passage, there are understandably plenty of passages in the diary expressing bitterness and anger. Lu rarely indulges in self-pity and more typically chooses to revert to using humor with a tinge of self-deprecation to balance his negative emotions. In the entry for September 14, he discusses the effect of recent weather (successive typhoons) on his condition:

[The] clouds and rain and the sudden changes in air pressure that come with the typhoons are making it very hard for me to get through the day. This mixture of depression, wound pain, and oxygen deprivation can barely be put into words. I get angry at times, thinking that if those typhoons keep messing with me, I'll buy myself a plane ticket out of here. I don't care where I'll go, as long as there is sunshine, no crazy winds or rain clouds, and plenty of oxygen.

But the planes were grounded as well.

On September 24, another rainy day, Lu wrote an exceptionally funny and cheerful piece in response to the Chinese women's football team's elimination at the Sydney Olympic Games (they where eliminated at the group stages following a 2-1 loss to Norway on September 20). In the entry, he elaborates on the idea that Chinese athletes' performances are badly affected by the weight of serious expectation on their shoulders. They are perceived as, and perceive themselves as, fighting for the glory of their nation and, as a consequence, they lack enjoyment in their sport. Success and good fortune, he writes, come to those who smile and are happy. "Sports fans throughout the country, myself included, should all agree that at the next match we won't be shouting 'Come on!!' but we'll be shouting 'Cheese!'" He goes on to develop this point into a critique of Chinese people in general: "Is it really that hard for Chinese people to be happy?"

Commenting on the state of China and its people has been a common trope in modern Chinese writing, but it is nevertheless surprising to see it pop up in this kind of private chronicle. Lu himself comes to this realization a few weeks later in the October 4 entry, in which he discusses modern China's obsession with "science," only to end with the comment, "There is a lot more left to say, but I guess for a seriously ill person to discuss affairs of the state might come across as somewhat eccentric [*jiaoqing*]."

One of the most detailed descriptions of his illness appears toward the end of the diary, on October 10, accompanied by an explanation of his reasons not to write about the specific state of his illness too often:

My physical condition is getting worse and worse these days. The tennis ball on my neck has turned into an Olympic shot put ball. There are now also a bunch of tumors of different sizes on my chest, which are diabrotic, so I never feel clean and dry. . . .

> The weirdest thing is that my appetite has improved. I guess the cancer cells have entered adolescence?
>
> Sometimes I think, who cares, I'll just eat whatever I want. But those little buggers are blocking my throat. I even choke on tofu.
>
> You really don't need ink to record the life of a sick man. The feelings themselves are black enough.
>
> The most common way to express concern for a patient is to ask how they are doing. But what the patient fears most of all is his own condition, which is why I write as little as possible about it in my diary. Regular updates like this one are meant as responses to the concerned inquiries of countless friends.

On October 23, Lu Youqing announced the end of the diary, writing the last entry on his thirty-seventh birthday.[46] The last piece typically consists of some reminiscences of past birthdays, a general discussion of Chinese people's changing perception of birthdays in general, and a critique of the younger generation's obsession with celebrating birthdays. But he ends on a brief personal note, barely clinging to his usual understatement. These are his last lines:

> My last birthday has come. I'll be going now.
>
> There are so many junctures in a person's life. Of course I can't bear it, but I really don't dare to dwell on a moment like this, and I am even more afraid of thinking about it too deeply.
>
> Because if I did, my heart would go to pieces.

Commemoration and Legacy

After Lu Youqing's diary had stopped appearing, Banyan Tree published a few more updates on his situation written by his wife, Shi Muyan. Only one more piece written by Lu himself appeared, under the title "Farewell Online Friends," as one of the paratexts on the minisite. The piece is not dated but appears to have been written shortly before his death, just after the publication of the book version of his diary. In it he expresses the significance of his experience of online interaction, friendship, and moral support during the period that he wrote the diary, thanking some of his closest online friends by name. He comments positively on the Internet's ability to connect people and concludes by saying, "If people really have a soul, then I am convinced that contact between this world and the neth- erworld will be first established through the Net." Although such direct communication was to my knowledge never established, Lu Youqing had a significant "afterlife," both online and in print.

The writings of Lu Youqing, who eventually died on December 11, 2000, touched many readers. From the front page of the minisite for his online diary, when it was still online, one could follow a link to an "online memorial" for him, located on the website http://cn.netor.com, which specializes in online memorials. Sponsored by Under the Banyan Tree, this online memorial, which is still in existence, contains pictures of Lu Youqing, information about his life, and links to websites related to him.[47] (There is also still a link to the old URL of the minisite, which obviously no longer works—an indication that the memorial is now no longer maintained.) The main section of the memorial is an online forum where readers can leave comments, wishes, prayers, and the like in mem- ory of Lu. When I visited the memorial on March 28, 2002, more than fifteen months after Lu's death, the forum contained 18,647 messages, 8 of which had been submitted that day, showing that he was still being read and remembered. In fact, when earlier in March 2002 I visited the ranking of "Top Memorials" on the Netor main page, I found that Lu Youqing's memorial was ranked second, eclipsed by only the memorial for Wang Wei, the fighter pilot who was killed in the collision with a U.S. spy plane in March 2001. Nowadays the memorial is of course ranked much lower, and very few messages have been left in recent years. The memorial also has a section devoted to relevant writings about Lu You- qing, most of which date from the period around 2000–2001, with one notable exception: a short commemorative piece written by his daughter, Lu Tianyou, dated March 2007.[48]

After Lu Youqing's death, Chen Cun and others linked to the Banyan Tree website set about publishing the diarist's posthumous literary work, consisting of one novel and a collection of short stories, none of which had been published before. The two books eventually came out in the summer of 2001.[49] As explained by Chen Cun in a text titled "Lu You- qing's Literary Dream," copied onto Lu's memorial site, the manuscript of the novel had been privately printed, but not published, by Lu him- self, whereas the manuscript of the stories had existed only in handwrit- ing. The editors corrected writing and typing mistakes and punctuation

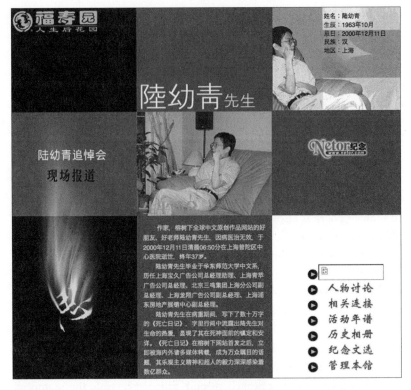

⬆ **Figure 1.4**   Online memorial for Lu Youqing. http://luyouqing.netor.com.

errors but had otherwise left the texts unchanged and in some cases unfinished. Although the swift publication of these books was, to my mind, clearly intended to capitalize on the interest in Lu Youqing before it would dwindle, it seems it was all done tastefully and without much of hype. The books do not appear to have attracted much critical attention.

Lu Youqing's writings not only affected readers but also inspired other writers and arguably created a new genre. On one of the bulletin boards of the Banyan Tree site, other diary-like publications involving disease, suffering, and moral issues were appearing when I visited the site in March 2002. One of these was the online diary of Li Jiaming, titled "Zui hou de xuanzhan" (The Last Declaration of War). On March 28, 2002, the thirty-second installment of this diary had just appeared ten days earlier. During those ten days, it had been visited a total number of 38,632 times and, to quote a more meaningful and reliable number, 417 readers had written comments on it. The twenty-ninth installment of his diary had been visited more than 100,000 times, with more than 1,000 readers leaving comments.[50]

Li Jiaming is a person living with HIV/AIDS, which he claimed to have contracted from a prostitute after a drunken night out. Although some critics doubted, in comments posted on the bulletin board, the veracity of his story, most responses were sympathetic and created an ongoing discussion not only about HIV and AIDS but also about prostitution and alcohol abuse.[51] My impression that texts like this were turning into a genre was based in part on a passage in the very first installment of Li Jiaming's diary, published on August 16, 2001. In the passage, Li carried out an act of distinction vis-à-vis Lu Youqing, saying, "This is not a death diary [*siwang riji*, i.e., the alternative Chinese title of Lu Youqing's work]. I do

🔵 **Figure 1.5**   Forum for Li Jiaming's "The Last Declaration of War," captured by the IAWM on January 3, 2012. https://web.archive.org/web/20120103203838/http://www.2008jiaming.com/article_list.asp?c_id=12.

not have time to show off my eccentricity [*jiaoqing*], nor do I want pity."
Immediately after that, however, he literally quoted Lu (though without
acknowledging it) by saying that his actions and writings were meant to
call for society's better understanding of people who suffer from the same
disease. In other words, Li Jiaming subscribed to the main function of
the kind of writing that he and Lu practiced but at the same time added
to its variety by distinguishing his own work from that of his predecessor.
This is exactly the way in which genres come into being.

For understandable reasons, when Li Jiaming first contacted them
about publishing his writings, the editors of Banyan Tree made a point of
checking Li Jiaming's credentials, including his medical records, before
they agreed to let him contribute to their "Prose Essays" (Sanwen) forum.
As Li started to attract media attention, he was repeatedly challenged to
verify his situation, to the extent that China Central Television had his
blood sample independently tested for the HIV virus before they went
ahead and interviewed him. Unlike Lu Youqing, however, the AIDS suf-
ferer kept his real identity hidden. (Li Jiaming is a pseudonym.) When a
collection of his "notes" (*shouji*)—the term he preferred over Lu Youqing's
"diary" (*riji*)—appeared in print in 2002, it was given the subtitle "Online
Notes by Li Jiaming, China's Most Mysterious Aids Patient."[52] During the
television interview he apparently had his face obscured. When he received a special literary prize for his work from the Barry and Martin's
Trust in 2003, it was given so little publicity that online commentators
accused Li Jiaming, who wrote about it in his notes, of making the whole
thing up. (The awarding of a "Barry and Martin's Literary Prize" of one
thousand pounds to Li Jiaming is mentioned only in the trust's annual
accounts for 2003 but not in the actual text of the annual report, nor on
the trust's website.[53]) Li Jiaming continued to publish new notes irregularly on Banyan Tree until 2005, when he published his fiftieth and last
note. All his writings can still be found in the Banyan Tree online archive.

As pointed out by Haiqing Yu, Li Jiaming also founded his own online community and discussion forum.[54] That forum (http://jiaming.
clubhi.com) was last archived by the IAWM in December 2006 and is no
longer in existence. Li Jiaming moved on to another website, http://ww-
w.2008JiaMing.com, named after his stated aspiration to stay alive and
active long enough to see the 2008 Beijing Olympics. Although at this
writing (January 2012) the front page of that site, which is devoted entirely to information about HIV/AIDS, has been hacked, other pages are

accessible, including a special section devoted to writings by and about Li Jiaming. That section includes a fifty-first episode of his "Last Declaration of War," published in 2008, as well as an update on his situation dated April 2010.[55] On the site's discussion forum, readers are occasionally kept updated about his well-being. The site is also used to market his 2002 book publication to help raise funds for his continued treatment.

In a widely available prose piece titled "Li Jiaming: My Life with AIDS," apparently written in 2009, Li looks back at almost a decade of AIDS activism under his pseudonym. Like Lu Youqing in 2000, Li in this piece also creates a mirror scene:

> Faced with myself in the mirror, I sometimes don't know who I am.
> An AIDS virus carrier called Li Jiaming?
> A son seeking to atone for his sins, hoping to protect his mother at all cost?
> A busy nine-to-five worker in a company?[56]

To the best of my knowledge, Li Jiaming is still alive at this writing, and his true identity remains unknown.

Online Literature: Emerging Practices

To assess the significance of the temporary fame achieved by online chroniclers like Lu Youqing and Li Jiaming it is important to bear in mind that they were active well before the rise in popularity of online blogs. The technology allowing individual users to construct their own minisites devoted to their own writings, to which readers can comment, was scarcely available in China at this time and did not become widespread until the establishment of the Sina blogging portal in 2005. Since the technology became available, the distinction between blogs and forums has become less clear-cut, since some blogging sites, like forums, are run by communities devoted to the discussion of specific topics or practicing specific styles. Generally speaking, however, blogs tend to be driven by the publication of new content, to which readers respond, whereas forums are driven by ongoing discussion in the thread format. What Banyan Tree did when it decided to publish Lu Youqing's diary in the form of a minisite was perhaps to create a blog *avant la lettre*. More important, to my mind, is that the creation of the minisite symbolically raised Lu Youqing's writings to the level of the site's "Special Column" authors, on a par with Chen Cun, Anni Baobei, and others considered important enough to have independent sections devoted to their work. This status came with the privilege to publish outside the normal discussion forums, that is, to have one's texts separated from discussion of those texts. As we have seen, in the online context the removal of commentary and interactive functionalities often represents a form of canonization and a first step toward print publication.

The Banyan Tree editors did not create a similar context for Li Jiaming's work. They did, however, feature links to Li's contributions prominently on the Banyan Tree front page. There are plenty of practical reasons to explain this decision. First, unlike Lu Youqing, Li Jiaming had no clear plan to write a specific number of installments, and his work was therefore less easily "packaged." Second, although both Lu Youqing and Li Jiaming aimed to tell their own stories as well as promote public interest in their situation and that of fellow sufferers, my impression is that Lu Youqing veered more toward the former and Li Jiaming more toward the latter, making direct interaction via the discussion forums the more obvious choice for Li Jiaming. Add to this Lu Youqing's background and habitus as graduate of a famous Chinese department (at East China Normal University in Shanghai) and onetime aspiring author, and it becomes clear why the Banyan Tree editors were better able to promote his writings as a literary event.

In the final analysis, the significance of Banyan Tree's promotion of these writings lies in their awareness that the new media they were involved in favored experimentation with diary-style chronicles as respectable literary forms. This is especially clear in the case of Lu Youqing, where the editors spent considerable effort to promote his diary as a serious publication and not as a personality driven hype. Sure enough, the underlying values of what constitutes "serious" writing continued to be those of the print-culture community, and publication in book form continued to be the long-term aim. Yet compared with earlier literary websites, which were devoted mainly to the online publication of conventional fiction, poetry, and prose, the editors of Banyan Tree had hit upon a new format that was at least partly shaped by the functionalities of the digital interactive media. As we shall see in the next chapter, one of the key figures involved in the early Banyan Tree, the writer Chen Cun, went on to explore the full innovative potential of the online chronicle form.

TWO

Linear Innovations

CHEN CUN AND OTHER CHRONICLERS

▶ **ON OCTOBER 24, 2010,** I met up with Chen Cun in a bookshop in Shanghai. We talked about Chinese literature in general, about the Internet, and about his involvement in Banyan Tree and other literature portals. At some point during the conversation I asked him when he had published his first online work. His response came instantly: "I have never published any works [*zuopin*] online. What I do online is just random writing. My real literary work has all appeared in print."

This chapter represents a deliberate attempt, foolhardy though it may seem, to challenge Chen's opinion about his own work. I have enjoyed reading his online writing, and I feel it has significant literary value, even if it does not represent "work" in the conventional print-era sense of the word. Specifically, Chen's online writing represents a type of literary innovation that makes productive use of the interactive nature of online forums. This is consistent with some of Chen's poetical inclinations from his pre-Internet days, especially his frequently stated desire to undermine the power of the fiction (*xiaoshuo*) genre in favor of a kind of writing that better grasps the fragmentary nature of modern-day existence. In addition, Chen's online writings help to make a theoretical point regarding the study of electronic literature. Whereas most scholars tend to view nonlinearity as a precondition for distinguishing electronic literature from conventional literature, Chen Cun's experiments show us that online linear texts can be given interactive features that make them innovative and unconventional, creating textual worlds that cannot be reproduced in conventional print.

This chapter starts with an overview of Chen's life and literary career, emphasizing his recurrent ability to challenge literary conventions, which I place in the context of debates about the Chinese literary avant-garde. I then show how Chen, unlike others of his generation, has productively carried the avant-garde spirit into the realm of online writing. Toward the end of the chapter, I briefly discuss two very different online writers, both of whom, like Chen Cun, have experimented with chronicle-style online writing but using different types of online media. The celebrity writer Han Han maintains a regular chronicle in the form of an online blog, whereas the relatively unknown author Wen Huajian used the Weibo microblog forum to produce a chronicle that eventually became China's first microblog novel. My discussion of these two authors will acknowledge their innovative ambitions while demonstrating how their work is very different from that of Chen Cun's.

Chen Cun

Chen Cun is the pen name of Yang Yihua, a member of the Hui (Muslim) minority, born in Shanghai in 1954.[1] Like many of his generation he was sent to the countryside (in his case in Anhui) during the Cultural Revolution. He returned to Shanghai in 1975 for health reasons, suffering from a progressive rheumatic disease known as ankylosing spondylitis. The fact that he walks with crutches and is unable to stand upright is mentioned in virtually every article I have read about him. It also plays a role in his recent online work, as we shall see below. His first published work was the story "Liang dai ren" (Two Generations), which appeared in the magazine *Shanghai wenxue* in September 1979 and is mentioned favorably by W. J. F. Jenner in his detailed overview of officially published fiction of that year. It is worth mentioning in our current context that Jenner's reason for being positively disposed toward the story is that it breaks with established narrative conventions.[2]

In 1983, Chen Cun started receiving regular writing stipends (*chuang-zuo fei*) from the Shanghai Writers Association and quit his job as a teacher to live off his writing. Two years later, in 1985, he was employed by the association as a professional writer, a privileged status implying that he received a monthly salary in exchange for maintaining a regular publication record.[3] His online writing does not count in this context and is not included in his annual report to the association, which explains his assertion that his online writings are not really "works."[4]

Chen Cun thus became a member of the literary establishment at the height of its development toward "cliquishness." Before long he started to be identified with the avant-garde style of fiction. Various short stories and especially the 1989 novella "Shaonan shaonü, yigong qige" (Boys and Girls, Seven in Total) have been singled out post facto as belonging to the 1980s avant-garde, partly because of the way in which they break with narrative conventions.[5] In the 1990s, Chen Cun gradually turned away from writing fiction in the traditional sense and moved toward writing other types of prose. His only novel of the 1990s, published in 1997 and titled *Xianhua he* (*Fresh Flowers And*),[6] is acclaimed for its experimental technique, consisting entirely of seemingly randomly recorded prose passages, jotted down in the first person singular by the main character, who is a middle-aged, famous author. At the same time, in the late 1990s, Chen Cun became increasingly well-known for his involvement with web literature. He was one of the first established print-culture authors to make the move to web-based writing, and he has since been one of its staunchest defenders. He became widely known for his involvement with the popular Shanghai website Under the Banyan Tree. More recently he has moved on to a smaller niche inside cyberspace, where he continues to produce experimental work, an example of which will be discussed in detail later in the chapter. First, however, let us have a closer look at the emergence of the contemporary Chinese avant-garde and at Chen Cun's pre-Internet writings.

The 1980s Avant-Garde

The avant-garde in contemporary Chinese fiction is often seen as a phenomenon that belongs exclusively to the late 1980s. Experimental fictional writings by Can Xue, Ma Yuan, Yu Hua, and others are considered to have thoroughly undermined the socialist realist literary paradigm by carrying out the "subversive act" of "the making of a subject without a core who narrates without a purpose," as Jing Wang so eloquently put it.[7] Although the context in which they worked, as pointed out before, was inherited from the socialist system of literary production, the themes they explored in their writings could not be more different from those explored by previous communities active within that system. Probably for that reason, their experiments are usually seen as having been short-lived. By the 1990s, the socialist publishing system was largely dismantled and most if not all avant-garde authors turned away from extreme experimentalism and instead started producing work that was more accessible and more marketable, or simply stopped writing.[8]

In theoretical terms, the development just sketched is somewhat contradictory. Most theories of the avant-garde postulate that its programs or techniques will be gradually assimilated by the establishment, after which they cease to be avant-garde. What was a shock to the system at some point becomes part of the system at a later point. In the case of this particular avant-garde, the opposite seems to have happened: the authors previously belonging to the avant-garde voluntarily adopted establishment techniques. They reduced the shock value of their writing (or stopped writing), thus normalizing their work rather than waiting for it to be normalized. This is exactly why understanding the context in which these authors worked is so important: in the late 1980s, what they wrote shocked the system in terms of its aesthetic beliefs and therefore was avant-garde. But it was part of the system in terms of how it was produced, disseminated, and canonized and therefore represented a cultural elite. This makes the Chinese avant-garde of the late 1980s substantially different from, for instance, the European avant-gardes of the period between the two world wars, because the proponents of those avant-gardes did not generally produce work for mainstream journals and publishers and did not have the kind of material and logistic support that the Chinese avant-gardists had. As a result, the European avant-gardists challenged the literary system from the outside and then gradually made their way in, and saw their methods co-opted and assimilated in the process. The Chinese avant-gardists, on the other hand, started out from privileged positions within the system and then had to adapt when the system changed and became more commercial in the 1990s. For this reason, as well as for nonliterary reasons, such as the ideological inclination of many critics to view the political events of 1989 as the end of an era of cultural liberalism, contemporary Chinese avant-garde fiction is frozen in time and rarely if ever discussed on the basis of texts selected from a later decade.[9] In short: the term "avant-garde fiction" has become a period term, referring almost exclusively to writing of the period 1985–1989.[10] What I hope to show in this chapter is that for at least one author counted among the avant-garde of the late 1980s, the change to the postsocialist publishing system actually represented an opportunity to explore avant-gardism in a more fundamental way, challenging widely held conceptions not only about what literature is but also about where and how it should be produced and disseminated.

In looking at some examples of Chen Cun's work and literary activities, my aim is to show the various ways in which he has attempted to uphold the avant-garde spirit during and beyond its supposed heyday in the 1980s. I hope to convey a sense of the more fundamental (i.e., not merely textual) avant-garde potential of Internet literature as practiced by people like Chen Cun in China today and to demonstrate how this ties in with overall trends in postsocialist publishing.

Chen Cun's Pre-Internet Writings

All biographical sources about Chen Cun mention that the story "Two Generations"[11] was his debut work, but it does not appear to have attracted scholarly interest in China itself. In English-language scholarship, the work was briefly discussed by W. J. F. Jenner. Jenner calls the story "an obliquely written tale—a refreshing change from the usual narrative conventions."[12] It is indeed the case that the story does not employ the omniscient narrator familiar from socialist realist fiction and also from most of the so-called Scar Literature fiction of the preceding years. Instead, Chen Cun's story is told from the perspective of the I-narrator, a teenager called Huanhuan, who describes episodes in his relationship with his father, a once famous author turned editor, throughout the Cultural Revolution and its immediate aftermath. The tone for the story is set on the opening page when Huanhuan describes how, when he was twelve years old, Red Guards raided the family home. Whereas Huanhuan tried to keep them from entering the house and to resist them physically, his father opened the door for them and did not fight back when he was beaten up. Throughout most of the story, the narrator Huanhuan employs a macho tone of voice, boasting about his physical strength, his fighting skills, and his courage and contrasting his character with the fearful attitude of his father. At the same time, his father's connections constantly save him when he gets himself into trouble. At the end of the story, Huanhuan is filled with enthusiasm about the new, post–Cultural Revolution era, but his father continues to err on the side of caution: although his earlier literary writings are once again published, as an editor he continues to turn down submissions that are politically risqué. This leads to a final confrontation, after which Huanhuan decides, in the final line of the story, to leave home.

Throughout the story, references to the political context are minimal. A few words are enough to indicate to the informed reader in which year particular episodes take place. Chen Cun's focus is entirely on the father-son relationship. Apart from the oblique narrative angle, the story is successful in its use of colloquial, down-to-earth language, both in the narrator's voice and in dialogues. This is, however, interspersed with awkward references to Western names and culture of the kind that are typically found in Scar Literature and appear to be meant to symbolize the lifestyle and interests of intellectuals and their families. Thus, when Huanhuan hears the news of the fall of the Gang of Four, he writes,

> I was lying on my bed, eyes wide open. As I thought about it, I became more and more excited. I was tossing and turning, unable to fall asleep. I could not help humming Tchaikovsky's Piano Concerto no. 1.[13]

In terms of content, perhaps the most disturbing aspect of the story is its suggestion that for intellectuals who knew how to "play the game," such as the father character, the return to positions of power was not a question of a sudden rehabilitation in 1976 but rather took place gradually throughout the 1970s. What's more, the ending of the story, when the father figure confirms that a story written by Huanhuan's girlfriend is not publishable for political reasons, indicates that such intellectuals continued after 1976 to have the power to censor the upright voices of the young. In September 1979, so shortly after the closing down of the various Democracy Walls and related publications,[14] this aspect of the story's content must have struck a chord with readers concerned about the renewed controls on freedom of speech. Compared with other works of Scar Literature, which invariably portray intellectuals as victims, Chen Cun's thematic angle is as refreshing as his narrative technique, at least in the context of the time.

Although Chen Cun is not the most famous of the authors whose experimental writing drew attention inside and outside China from 1985 onward, his name regularly appears in recent scholarship on the period, often with the label "avant-garde" (*xianfeng*) attached to it. In chapter 17 of Hong Zicheng's *A History of Contemporary Chinese Literature*, Chen's "Boys and Girls, Seven in Total" is mentioned as one of ten works that signaled a turning point for fiction in 1985. Hong states that innovative writing of those years was customarily divided into two categories, "root seeking" and "modernism" and ranks Chen Cun's work among the latter. Hong writes,

> At the time, Liu Suola's "You Have No Choice" and "Blue Skies Green Seas", Xu Xing's "A Variation Without a Theme", and some of the fiction of Can Xue, Chen Cun, and Han Shaogong, were referred to as "modernist" literature. This was because they shared similar themes with western "modernist" literature: They expressed a sense of absurdity in their worldview, wrote of the solitude of the individual, some had "anti-culture" and "anti-sublime" tendencies, and they often utilized artistic methods such as symbolism, stream of consciousness, and "black humor."[15]

Hong's wording here and later in the chapter indicates that he does not consider the term "modernism" useful, and in later chapters he discards it in favor of the categories "avant-garde" and "new realism." However, he does not mention Chen Cun again, and therefore it is not entirely clear whether or not he considers him avant-garde. A similar lack of clarity marks a 1998 article by Chen Sihe dealing with new work by five authors (Han Shaogong, Li Rui, Wang Anyi, Chen Cun, and Ye Zhaoyan), whom he characterizes as "leading, important authors of the 1980s." Chen Sihe is particularly interested in how, in their work published in 1997 (including Chen Cun's *Fresh Flowers And*), these five authors break with formal conventions of fiction writing yet continue to adhere to their individual styles developed in the 1980s. Although he does not say it, neither in this article nor in his 1999 textbook history of contemporary Chinese literature, Chen Sihe certainly implies that he considers Chen Cun as linked to the avant-garde.[16] Other articles dealing with themes and narrative techniques of the 1980s avant-garde do make specific reference to stories by Chen Cun.[17] All scholars seem to agree that Chinese avant-garde fiction did not survive into the 1990s, although Chen Sihe considers it to have been a catalyst for the emergence of "extremely individualized writing" (*jiduan gerenhua xiezuo*) in the 1990s.[18]

Some of Chen Cun's short stories of the 1980s display avant-garde characteristics familiar from works by Can Xue, Ma Yuan, and Yu Hua: dreamlike settings, seemingly absurd plots, strained human relations, and ample use of metafiction. A case in point is the story "Die" (Daddy), which is included in the 1992 collection *Wuding shang de jiaobu* (*Footsteps on the Roof*) but appears to have been written in the 1980s.[19] The narrator of "Daddy" is a writer suffering from a cold and high fever. After complaining about his colds and blaming them on his deceased father, he goes on to announce his desire to write a love letter and then, for the rest of the story, narrates in a fragmentary and at times surrealistic manner his relationship with a girl who refers to him as "Daddy." Apart from recurring references to illness and colds, the narration revolves almost constantly around animal imagery. In one part of the story the girl falls into the hold of a fishing boat, is observed by the narrator squirming among the fish and compared to a mermaid; in another part the narrator and the girl have a prolonged discussion about his attempt to write a literary story about an elephant and her attempt to write an academic essay about dogs. Despite their obvious intimacy, many of their conversations are by telephone, creating a sense of distance and alienation. Toward the end of the story the narration takes on metafictional characteristics as the narrator contemplates various ways of writing a story about the girl, causing him to comment cynically on how writers will use anything and anyone in their surroundings as "material" and repeating many times that what he really wants is to write a love letter, not a story. Intertextual references appear, including one to another avant-garde author in a passage where the girl announces her decision to move to Tibet. The narrator writes,

> She wanted to go to Tibet and mobilized me to go with her. I told her that Tibet is a great place to die, that sky burial is the noblest and most scientific burial method. However, I did not want to live there. I had a friend called Ma Yuan who went to Tibet and contracted some strange illness, an itch moving outward from his heart, incurable. Ma Yuan made bogus claims about Lhasa being such a wonderful city. Lhasa was also called the City of Sunlight, and from the look of it he was irreversibly poisoned by sunlight. I hoped that she would not become Ma Yuan the Second.[20]

In a similar vein, the narrator refers to one of Chen Cun's own novels, albeit without mentioning him by name. Various binary oppositions are scattered through the story, including that between avant-garde and popular culture, the narrator obviously being a "serious" writer and the girl being a fan of the popular Taiwanese author San Mao and disco dancing. The most important theme emerging from the story, however, appears to be the narrator's inability to understand women and to write about them, causing him to utter the following lament: "The difficulties in understanding a modern woman are just too great. . . . I've written about all kinds of women. I made them all up, including the she in this story." (The use of a metanarrator commenting on the fictional nature of the narration here is reminiscent of Ma Yuan's story "Fabrication," one of the most canonized and paradigmatic works of the 1980s avant-garde.[21]) Eventually, the narrator and the girl part ways, but not before she has once more called him Daddy a few times over the phone, to his great excitement. Prior to that, the narrator has concluded that "evolution" has made lots of simple things difficult for human beings, thus neatly explaining the prior use of animal imagery and foreshadowing Chen Cun's own grander theories about love, sex, culture, and evolution that he has elaborated in his recent web-based writing, to which I now turn.

Chen Cun and Internet Literature

Chen Cun is probably the most prominent Chinese author to have taken an active interest in Internet literature almost from its inception. Despite his claim that he never published any literary work online, the fact that his last major printed work (the novel *Fresh Flowers And*) came out more than a decade ago and that he writes online almost daily makes it clear where his current literary preoccupations lie. Not only has he published writings on the web with increasing frequency since the late 1990s but he has also been involved in managing successful literary websites, especially Under the Banyan Tree, as we have seen in the previous chapter. Moreover, as also alluded to in the previous chapter, he was almost single-handedly responsible for the eruption of a nationwide debate about web literature in 2001. The debate was sparked by a post that Chen Cun submitted on July 3 of that year to the forum that he moderated for the Banyan Tree site. The full text of this now famous post is translated below.

Web Literature Past Its Prime

Submitted by Chen Cun, 2001-07-03, 17:34:53

I go online and I visit Under the Banyan Tree because I want to see what web literature is really like. I have high hopes for it. But web literature these days is starting to make me reconsider. If the highest achievement of web literature is to publish traditional books offline, if that is what qualifies you as a writer and allows you to brag, then is there still a web literature? Its freedom, its randomness, and its nonutilitarian nature have already been polluted. Although I understand these changes, it is still not what I hope to see. Web literature is already past its prime. The period of what Laozi called "utter innocence" [*chizi zhi xin*] has vanished so quickly![22]

This statement is of a more fundamental avant-garde quality than any of the text-intrinsic gestures that we have seen so far. Chen accused web literature authors of selling out to the establishment and to the market rather than remaining faithful to what should be considered the autonomous principles of their practice: freedom, randomness, and nonutilitarianism. He feared that the niche created by web literature would be submerged into the larger literary field at the expense of some of its unique qualities.

This is an often-heard complaint among those who were active in Internet culture in the early stages of its development, and it is by no means exclusive to the Chinese situation, but in 2001 Chen was perhaps the first prominent online personality to voice it so explicitly. According to commentators at the time,[23] Chen's post instantly provoked debate, including thousands of hits and responses on the forum itself, where the site's CEO, William Zhu, came out in strong opposition to Chen's statements. This eventually led to Banyan Tree's deciding it no longer required Chen's services as chief artistic officer.[24] In a piece by Chen titled "Zhuyuan Rong-shu Xia" (Wishing Banyan Tree Well), published on the site on October 25, 2001, and still available in the Banyan Tree online archive, he appears to be saying good-bye to the site, under the guise of commemorating its fourth anniversary. The closing lines of the piece represent a somewhat veiled restatement of his basic argument against commercialization:

Four years down the line, Banyan Tree now has a different look than before. The pressures of commercialization and the realities of existence have

⊕ Figure 2.1   Main page of Chen Cun's Minority Vegetable Garden, captured by the IAWM on June 19, 2006. https://web.archive.org/web/20060619141813/http://bbs.99read.com/index.asp?boardid=18.

brought about its first major changes and new opportunities. This is how trees are different from plants. Trees will survive any setbacks only if they have a tough, weather-beaten trunk.[25] Then they will show off their luscious vitality through layer upon layer of new green foliage.

I wish Banyan Tree many more years.

Chen signed the piece with his name, job title, and the full name of the website (Chen Cun, Art Director, Under the Banyan Tree, the global website for original Chinese-language works). I believe it is not too far-fetched to presume that he did this in order to emphasize his belief that Banyan Tree should promote artistry and originality.[26] As mentioned in chapter 1, Chen Cun's personal space on the site eventually disappeared in 2002. Throughout this period, Banyan Tree vastly increased its con-tracts with print publishers, and the site was eventually sold to the Ber-telsmann conglomerate in 2003. Chen Cun himself started a new online literary venture in 2004 by establishing a separate and restricted space for himself and like-minded web authors: a forum named Xiaozhong Caiyuan (Minority Vegetable Garden).[27]

Minority Vegetable Garden was an online discussion forum with Chen Cun as main moderator. The website hosting the forum until very recently

was 99 Wangshang Shucheng (99 Online Book City, http://www.99read
.com). This is an online bookshop as well as a print publisher and book
distributor founded in March 2004 by a limited company supported by
both state-owned cultural entities (People's Literature Publishing House
and Xinhua Bookstore) and private individuals, including the famous
author and scholar Yu Qiuyu, who functions as honorary chairman of
the company's board of directors.[28] It is a typical example of the kind
of partnerships between the state and private sector that constitute the
"second channel" in Chinese publishing as described by Shuyu Kong (see
chapter 1). Chen Cun was employed by the website as an art director and
general manager overseeing all discussion forums on the site, including
Minority Vegetable Garden, thus he was more than just a forum moderator, who, typically, is not paid. In August 2013, a forum for which he was
responsible was closed down by the authorities after some posts offering
to sell weapons had been detected. Chen subsequently offered his resig-
nation, and most of the past content of Minority Vegetable Garden is, as
a consequence, not available on the live web at this writing (March 2014),
although Chen is trying to reestablish the site elsewhere. References to
URLs in the discussion that follows are to archived snapshots of pages I
saw when doing my research.[29]

Although 99 Online Book City is a commercial site following the Bertelsmann model of linking online literary production to distribution and
sales of printed works (i.e., the model Chen Cun was opposed to when he
worked for Banyan Tree), it is evident that Chen learned from previous
experience and made sure that the space he was in charge of presented
itself as a noncommercial niche. In a manifesto-like opening statement,
originally posted to the forum on September 15, 2004, Chen explained
the name and the aims of the forum.[30] The term *xiaozhong*, here somewhat inadequately translated as "minority," was meant to be opposed to
dazhong ("mass" or "masses"). Chen explained that he and his fellow "vegetable farmers" (*cainong*, the term used for the regular contributors to the
forum) had no intention of selling anything on a mass scale and would
be happy to do their own farming and produce some "organic food." The
forum would accept contributions only from invited contributors. Chen
stated that initially there would be roughly one hundred of his "friends"
involved. After that, he explained, others wanting to join the forum would
be able to do so only if they were introduced by a registered "farmer" and

had submitted writing samples to Chen Cun for consideration. Anyone would be free to enter the forum and read the contributions. As moderator, Chen Cun would have full editorial control over all contributions.

Chen's opening statement showed his awareness of the fact that the closed nature of the forum went against some of the principles of web writing that he previously espoused, namely freedom and tolerance. He defended his new stance by claiming that setting up a few hurdles for potential contributors was meant merely to keep out those who were not serious or who roamed forums to stir up trouble. He also argued that there were plenty of other places for such people to go and that the principle of tolerance should allow for his little "patch" to exist. He ended the "manifesto" with an explicit reference to the principles of randomness and nonutilitarianism, using a familiar and heavily laden term: "Going online is just to do something interesting [*tao ge you qu*]. *He-he*, let's sow some vegetables!"[31]

By using the term *qu* and by references in the text to writers such as the premodern poet Tao Yuanming (365–427), as well as by suggesting the notion of "cultivating one's own garden," Chen Cun's manifesto connected with a long-standing tradition of nonutilitarian writing in Chinese literature, including modern examples such as the prose writing of Zhou Zuoren (1885–1967), whose "poetics of *quwei*" is discussed at length in research by Susan Daruvala.[32]

Some of those same "friends" who were among the early contributors to Minority Vegetable Garden also had their works published in another space controlled by Chen Cun created around this time: the section called "Wangluo xianfeng" (The Web's Avant-Garde) in the print journal *Shiyue*. If the founding of Minority Vegetable Garden indicated that Chen was willing to work with commercial publishers as long as he could have his own "niche," the appearance of "The Web's Avant-Garde" in a highly established literary journal indicated that by this time Chen was no longer opposed in principle to web-based work crossing over into print, as long as it was associated with serious literature and, more especially, with the literary avant-garde. "The Web's Avant-Garde" continued to appear in the journal *October* throughout 2005 and then disappeared for no clear reason.[33]

In Chen Cun's case, the search for *qu* in literature, the occupation of niche spaces, and the promotion of the avant-garde spirit are all linked to what appears to be his increasingly fundamental resistance to fiction as the central genre of modern Chinese literature. As early as 1987, in his essay "Fei xiaoshuo lun" (Not on Fiction), Chen Cun wrote,

> If you've read lots of fiction, you discover that its biggest shortcoming is that it's uninteresting [*wuqu*]. Speaking in a roundabout way is uninteresting. Taking mankind as your only subject is uninteresting. It really is unnatural, from beginning to end. Of course, an unnatural form may well be a good or useful form, but it is not necessarily an interesting form. So-called good fiction is what idle people write for idle people to read. And nowadays, those idle of body and mind are indeed fewer and fewer.[34]

It is statements like these that tie together Chen Cun's late 1970s critique of establishment writers, his 1980s concerns about form and about using animals as subjects, and his interest in web literature. What Chen Cun strives for is an unrestrained writing practice that is as much as possible devoid of formal ("unnatural") restrictions imposed by establishment or market culture, or indeed by human culture in general, and that is, at the same time, in tune with the fast pace of modern life. This, I argue, is avant-garde in the wider, more fundamental sense, and for Chen Cun this has, by and large, been a consistent stance ever since he started writing. It is also a stance that is easiest to adopt in online writing, which is generally short, fast-paced, and, at least in theory, less prone to outside restrictions or at least more likely to provide spaces and niches for all kinds of unorthodox experiments that would not easily make it into the print-based system. All the observations play a role in my reading, in the following, of Chen Cun's chronicle-style writings on the topic of sex.

Random Notes on Sex

In "Xing biji" (Random Notes on Sex), published on Minority Vegetable Garden, Chen Cun displays the full range of his cultural and stylistic concerns.[35] Before going into the content of these posts, I should say a few words about the format of the Minority Vegetable Garden forum and of this particular thread. I visited Minority Vegetable Garden most frequently in early 2006, but I returned from time to time until the site closed down in 2013. During that period, the format of the site underwent very few changes.

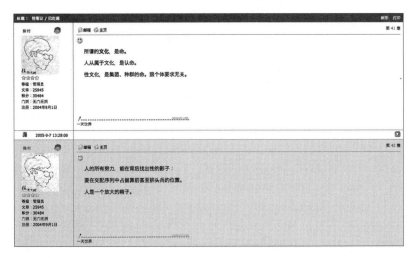

↑ **Figure 2.2**   Page from "Random Notes on Sex," captured by the IAWM on June 25, 2007. https://web.archive.org/web/20070625073030/http://bbs.99read.com /dispbbs.asp?boardid=18&replyid=190863&id=21198&page=1& skin=0&Star=5.

As usual, there were various ways of accessing the forum. When one went to the site, one would see a list of threads that were recently submit-ted or to which new content was recently added. Some important threads or public announcements were kept at the top of the list by default for a certain period, other threads would disappear off the front page unless new content was added to them, in which case they returned to the top. (In online forums in general, causing a thread to be kicked back upward is a phenomenon referred to as *ti* or *dinghuilai*. The mere submitting of these words as a comment on the thread will do the trick.) Some threads were designated as "best of" (*jinghua*), indicated by the image of a stamp of approval on the first post of the thread.[36] Users of the site could choose different views, listing all recent "best of" threads, all "best of" threads started by a particular person, or all threads started by a particular person. Further options were available to registered members of the site, which I was not.

Chen Cun's "Random Notes on Sex" was started with a post published on the forum on September 7, 2005. This was followed by frantic further posting by Chen himself as well as comments by other "farmers" spurring him on in this new project, so that within two days the thread consisted of more than one hundred posts. After one week and 251 posts, most of them by himself, Chen interrupted the series while he was away traveling to conferences and then continued through the period from November 2005 to January 2006. After that his writings became more sporadic, with a final posting on February 24, 2006. Still, the thread was subsequently being kept alive and kicked back to the top of the list by others, reaching a total of 531 posts on April 24, 2006, after which Chen Cun closed the thread and archived it on the site, where it could still be read, but content could no longer be added. Most contributions to the thread are in plain text (disregarding the authors' avatars, various emoticons, and the like), but Chen and others also contributed images and sound files. In fact, Chen's very first post ends with a sound file: the overture to Verdi's *La traviata*, possibly an early indication that the female sex would be the main concern of his writing in this thread.

As with many works of Internet literature, especially those that continue for a long time, it is impossible to give an adequate synopsis of "Random Notes on Sex." During the first days of posting Chen appears to have had a clear idea of how to structure his writings thematically and more or less stuck to it, but at the same time he was inevitably sidetracked by comments on his posts, leading to various other discussions. Moreover, Chen himself intersperses his more serious posts with seemingly unrelated comments. At various stages during the life of the thread Chen directly addresses his fellow "farmers," asking them for comments and criticism, leading to a brief series of responses keeping the thread alive and encouraging Chen to continue. At one point the thread links to another thread on the site, a collection of ministories all on the same topic ("What the Wife Did after Her Husband Strayed") started by one of the "farmers" and continued by Chen with regular new additions, interspersed with comments by readers, with plenty of sexual innuendo. Chen's own contributions are labeled *xiaoshuo* (fiction) when they contain new versions of the story. His posts that do not have that label are comments on the thread. For a short time, this playful thread then becomes known as the supplement (*fukan*) to "Random Notes on Sex" and has likely been read in conjunction with it by some readers. Despite the serious nature of Chen's topic, the tone of the posts is generally light and humorous, at times banal. The vast majority of contributors to the post appear to be male and at least two of them were abroad at the time: one in Japan and one (the scholar Yang Xiaobin, who submitted one post, no. 288) in the United States.

Although not acknowledged, I have no doubt that Chen's decision to start a thread on sex under the title "Xing biji" was inspired by the popularity of various online sex diaries (*xing riji*), most famously those by Muzimei.[37] In other words, Chen takes a theme that appeals to the web-browsing "masses" (female sexuality) and gives it a radically different shape, suitable to the taste of his "minority." Already in his first post, Chen makes it clear that his ruminations on the topic of sex are also linked to his literary practice. He writes,

> I have had the intention of writing something like this for many years, to prattle about what I have seen, heard, thought, and considered about sex. For a professional writer never to have touched upon the theme of sex is a lack and a disgrace, a kind of self-castration. . . .
>
> Write it without method. Write it without belles lettres. Write it with different techniques. It is only an outline or a prompt, the final text will be determined later. . . .
>
> It is only "reading matter" [*duwu*], not "fiction," not a "treatise." It is only "reading matter." It has to do with lust [*se*]. It has to do with passion [*qing*]. It has nothing to do with pornography [*seqing*]. Whether or not these words ever appear on a printed page is not my concern.

In later posts, Chen returns a number of times to the style of his creation, using terms such as "writing at will" (*suibian xie*, post no. 114) and "random writing" (*luanxie*, no. 420) and reminding his readers that he is "not writing fiction" (no. 36). He also repeats several times his statement that the notes are merely a draft and that "the real thing" remains hidden in a drawer, partly because soon after starting the thread he was warned that he should tone down his more explicit references, since those under eighteen might be reading the forum.[38] Perhaps Chen's warnings about the draft status of his text were genuine, but they also happen to be a fantastic metalevel device, radically calling the status of the text into question and confusing those trying to treat it as "literature." This is reminiscent of the 1980s avant-garde experiments with metafiction and consistent with his statements about his online writing not representing literary work. Whether made instinctively or on purpose, these gestures serve to place his online writing outside established conventions.

Thematically, most of the "Random Notes on Sex" revolve around the opposition between nature (often referred to as "God") and culture. Using frequent references to the animal world, Chen muses mostly on how mankind has tried to separate sex from its original reproductive function and created a "sex culture" that is part of a "culture of play" (*youxi wenhua*) and consists of all kinds of symbols and practices that have no real meaning in the natural order of things (or "God's dictionary," as he calls it). He writes about this initially in fairly abstract terms, complaining with barely concealed sarcasm about the evolutionary process that determined that human beings should walk upright (something that he himself is incapable of due to his medical condition), moving on to a lengthy series of posts on women's breasts and their development from having a nurturing function to being a sex symbol. At some point he posts a list of books that influenced his ideas, including a number of popular science works about genes and evolution and works by famous feminist thinkers such as de Beauvoir and by Freud (post no. 146). Although he does employ various styles and techniques in his writing, on the whole his approach seems to be consciously to avoid scientific or academic discourse and to make a literary contribution instead, relying on sudden flashes of brilliance, unexpected turns of phrase, wordplay, funny or outrageous comments, and other things that come under the category of *you qu*. For example,

> Behind all human efforts one can find the shadow of sex: wanting to occupy a forward position, or even the front position, in the mating order.
>
> Human beings are enlarged sperms.
>
> (no. 42)

> Just because one day it was no longer bared, the bosom had to be written about day after day. It's a sad thought: when you bare it, it's nothing special. How many human and material resources have been wasted, just because it wasn't bared.
>
> Only if it is covered will one think about what lies below. Only because it is covered will one use it to write about. Just like those who, in the 21st century, long for "the old Shanghai."
>
> (no. 137)

> Because of that unavoidable "civilization," so many shapes of beautiful bosoms throughout the ages at home and abroad have been sacrificed.

Let us mourn in silence for the sacrificed bosoms.

(no. 139)

I was leafing through *Shanghai Culture* just now. There was an article about bras. It started with Foucault, of course. The author was a graduate student.

What it said (more or less) was that women want a firm bosom because of the pressure from patriarchal culture. What a joke. Firmness is a symbol of youth, as I wrote earlier, it expresses ample reproductive force. To put it bluntly: if you buy vegetables you want them fresh. What does that have to do with whatever culture? Surely not all feminism needs to be done sagging? [*Nandao nüquan zhuyi dou yao dalazhe lai gao?*]

(no. 305)

Clearly, some of Chen's more cynical posts contain heavy doses of machismo. Despite the indebtedness of some of his ideas to feminist thinkers, his point of view throughout the thread is outspokenly that of the male gazing at the female, as is that of most of his audience. He has little to say about male sexuality as such, apart from the occasional joke about Bill Clinton (no. 390, arguing that the "zippergate" scandal made men all over the world empathize with the American president, causing him to quip that "all flesh is equal" or, in Chinese, *rourou pingdeng*). Chen appears unconcerned about criticism of some of his blunter statements and indeed from time to time encourages others to take him to task. Moreover, in post number 187, he submitted the following caveat: "I detest Western 'political correctness.' What is politics, if not opportunism?" Here, too, the author's desire to operate outside established conventions or value systems seems apparent, although I am not so sure that he has positioned himself entirely outside a conventional patriarchal perspective on women.

A more serious theme of his random notes is the relationship between sex and literature. He speaks harshly of the Chinese literary tradition when it comes to writing about sex in a "natural" way. A long debate between various participants in the thread deals with descriptions of sex in Cao Xueqin's (1724?–1763?) *Shitou ji* (*Story of the Stone*) and whether or not its author linked virginity to virtue. Chen also discusses how, as part of the development of "civilization," sex has gradually been displaced by "love," which is another "cover-up," in his view—love is what we came up with in order to get young people to postpone reproducing long enough to finish their education (no. 161). He argues that the two eternal themes of literature are not "love and death" but rather "sex and death." In post number 230, he complains, in terms not dissimilar to those used in his 1980s story "Daddy," that "culture" has made something very simple (the mating of men and women) into something much too complicated. In one of his later posts (no. 474) this line of thinking, in which the development of civilization is deplored, is summed up with striking humor in one famous line, the opening line of the *San zi jing* (*Three Character Classic*), which takes on an entirely new meaning in the context of Chen's work: *Ren zhi chu, xing ben shan,* or "At the beginning of mankind, sex was good."

In addition to his preference for niche activity and his clear thematic concern with deconstructing or escaping established systems, genres, and conventions and exposing them as culturally imposed and unnecessary restrictions, Chen also breaks new ground in terms of form, even in the context of the relatively newly established conventions of online writing. As we have seen in chapter 1, it is not unusual for online writers to produce long works in installments over time, but the normal way of doing this is by submitting each installment as the beginning of a separate thread, often numbered like separate chapters. This has the clear advantage of making sure that each installment starts with the author's text and is followed by some comments, which can be easily removed at a later stage in preparation for permanent publication, whether online or in print. What Chen Cun did with "Random Notes on Sex," however, was to continue to add all his own writings to the original thread, keeping it going for a very long time and creating an indeed quite random structure in which his own jottings are interspersed with commentary by others and cannot be neatly or easily separated out to form installments or chapters of a coherent work. "Random Notes on Sex" thus became an ongoing, multiauthored work that could be "completed" only by a more or less random decision by Chen Cun to move the thread to the archive, where no new contributions could be made. In the archive it remains as it was, including all posts by both Chen himself and his commentators, who are really coauthors in this case, as a single, very long work that, when printed out, makes up hundreds of pages. What this shows is that linear writing, often considered by scholars of electronic literature to represent the essence of traditional print literature, can be used in the service of formal innovation in an online context. The suggestion that linear, non-hypertext writings online "do not provide empowerment to readers" and "fail to use the full potential of the WWW"[39] is simply not true, especially in the era of Web 2.0, where interactivity and online collaboration can, as Chen Cun and his fellow "farmers" have shown, be used to create niche writing that does something genuinely new and is not easy to fit into any existing genre categories.

Fragments

Around the same time that he was working on "Random Notes on Sex," Chen Cun also tried to keep alive a second thread in which he recorded random ideas and observations in (free) verse. He referred to this poetic chronicle by the genre name *xushishi* (narrative poetry). Having started the thread in December 2005, he closed it in April 2006 with a short post stating he found it too difficult to continue writing in this style. Despite a few requests from readers asking him to continue, the thread was locked and archived.[40] Another chronicle in the form of a blog, maintained on the Tianya portal from February 2006 onward, also came to an end in April 2006, with Chen citing ill health for his inability to continue writing it.[41] In the meantime, a thread featuring a personal photographic record of his life in Shanghai started in early 2005 and is still ongoing at this writing, having reached nearly four thousand posts, the vast majority of them by Chen himself, since this is the one thread where he allows little commentary from others.[42] It seems that both the narrative poetry and the blog were initial attempts to start a written chronicle to accompany the photographic one. Finally, in August 2006 Chen found the most suitable format for just a chronicle, namely an ongoing thread under the title "Duankan, duanting, duanxiang" (Fragments Seen, Fragments Heard, Fragments Thought). Unlike the photographic thread, this thread of written fragments plus ample commentary by other members is archived at fairly regular intervals (at the moment once every half year), with the first post in each new thread listing the stable URLs of the preceding ones. When I last visited the thread in 2012, five threads had been archived, one for August 2006–July 2007, one for July 2007–December 2009, one for 2010, and two for 2011. The 2012 thread was ongoing.[43]

The very first post of the "Fragments" thread addresses the by now familiar theme of breaking through established conventions of writing, as follows:

> Ever since I was unable to continue my inferior "narrative poem" and my "Chen Cun blog," I have been without a chamber pot to deposit all kinds of fragments of what I hear, see, and think. Commenting on others' posts is often inconvenient. Today I am starting this thread and recording things one at a time, whether related or not. The artistic tone [*wenyi qiangdiao*] won't come anymore, and I'll no longer think about whether it's pretty or not. Keeping it together, it makes a good backup.[44]

In view of my foregoing discussion, this post represents the end of an ongoing development toward unfettered, fragmentary writing, free of any restrictions imposed by genre, tradition, of mode of publishing. In comparison, "Random Notes on Sex" was a step in this direction in terms of its form, but it still conformed to convention in terms of thematic unity. Conversely, Chen's narrative poem was thematically unrestrained but imposed a specific form. It is only with this new thread that Chen seems to have drawn the ultimate conclusion: that in order to write the way he wants to write, he should sacrifice "art" and beauty altogether. And yet, by comparing his fragmentary chronicle to physical excrements (the things one deposits in a chamber pot), he makes an unmistakable avant-garde gesture, reminiscent of the tradition established by Marcel Duchamp's *Fountain* and many other gestures aimed at destroying "Art" in order to create something new. In my view, what makes Chen Chun's chronicles different from the online diaries discussed in the previous chapter, as well as many other online diaries and blogs produced in China and elsewhere, is exactly his *awareness* of the fact that he is experimenting and trying to break new ground, trying to find modes of writing that are indigenous to the online medium, not borrowed or transplanted from print culture.

"Metaresearch"

The chronicle format employed by Chen Cun and his fellow "farmers" also allows for new ways of interacting with professional readers and critics. This was made clear to me as early as 2006, when I presented a paper on Chen Cun's online writing at the Association for Asian Studies annual conference in San Francisco. Among the audience was Minority Vegetable Garden contributor Professor Xiaobin Yang, who that same evening started a thread on the website reporting on the contents of my talk and showing pictures of me presenting it. He ended with a post containing a classic mise en abyme:

> Michel Hockx correctly pointed out that Chen Cun's writing contains clear elements of avant-garde literature, such as his use of the device of metafiction similar to the style of Ma Yuan. Afterward I said to Michel Hockx, "I will post the pictures on the website tonight, so in the future if you continue to do research on the Vegetable·Garden, you will also be doing research on how you yourself are inside the garden doing research on the garden. Then your research will be 'metaresearch.'"[45]

The appropriation of reviews and criticism into the online work itself is a typical aspect of what goes on in the online literary field in the wider sense. In the preceding example, the result is a playful deconstruction of the normal relationship between text and critic, by forcing the critic into the text. Over the years this has increased my general awareness of the reciprocal relationship between the authors I was researching and the works they were producing.

A typical and arguably paradigmatic example of this occurred in October 2010, when I was in Shanghai and met and interviewed Chen Cun. If more traditional interviews of writers by scholars might end with the scholar asking permission to take the author's picture, my interview with Chen Cun ended with the two of us taking pictures of each other, almost simultaneously. Moreover, while Chen Cun gave me permission to cite what he said during the interview in my work, he clearly assumed that the relationship would be reciprocal and that he could quote me in his work as well. I naturally came to feature in his chronicles, which, after all, are meant to maintain a fairly close record of his day-to-day activities. The day after I met him, his photographic chronicle featured a picture of me taking a picture of him, a picture of the book I had given him as a present, and a link to a new thread where he had copied two Chinese-language interviews with me that had appeared online elsewhere.[46]

The same day, his chronicle of written fragments also mentioned our meeting and my interest in "Random Notes on Sex," adding a link to a related thread ("Ironic Random Notes on Sex," by "habor") from December

↑ Figure 2.3   Excerpt from Chen Cun's photographic chronicle, with a picture of me taking a picture of him.

2006, which I had not been aware of earlier.[47] A few days later I wrote him a follow-up e-mail asking him specifically about his definition of "web literature" and why he did not consider himself to have any "works" published online. He responded to me by e-mail on November 1, 2012, and then proceeded the next day to publish the full text of both e-mails in two posts of the "Fragments" thread.[48] This means that rather than citing "private correspondence" as my source for Chen's statement given in the following, I can cite the actual publication of the correspondence as part of an ongoing online work that I want to research but that I am now also a small part of. In response to my question as to why he did not consider his online writing to be literary work, to which I had added a comment saying that I thought threads like "Random Notes on Sex" had clear literary characteristics and were very innovative, Chen wrote the following:

> As for "Random Notes on Sex" and the "Fragments Seen, Fragments Heard, Fragments Thought" that I regularly put online: The latter is a kind of diary, recording some things and some reflections that can be made public. The former did not have any writing plan, it was also a kind of fragmented thinking. In my opinion, if it were to become a book, there would have to be significant addition, expansion, and revision. Therefore it is not a "work." At most it

is a draft. Such a semifinished product is acceptable on the web, but in other forms it would be difficult.

Another reason is that for my writing [*xiezuo*] I get paid fees [*gaofei*], but on the web there is no remuneration, it is like a game. The words [*wenzi*] I write on the web do not particularly aim at further publication in print or at some sort of paid reading like on the Qidian site. That is why I do not consider myself a "web writer" [*wangluo xieshou*].

What I consider "web literature" should be literary writing that is first published online, that is complete, and that can be transmitted in a nonweb format without harming the expressive content of the text. [49]

Whatever one thinks of Chen Cun or of web literature, his writings show a consistency of purpose that has been overshadowed by widespread assumptions about the difference in Chinese writing of the 1970s, the 1980s, and today. It seems to me that Chen's purpose throughout has been to create a kind of literature that is as free as possible of conventions

⊖ Figure 2.4
My picture of Chen Cun (taken October 24, 2010).

and that is supported by and fostered among small, marginal communities. To be sure, Chen has long joined the ranks of famous authors in China and is often in the public eye, but his work on Minority Vegetable Garden is uncompromisingly experimental, more so than any of his previous work. In its relentless attacks on any and all culture, be it sex culture, academic culture, or literary culture, his work is also recognizably avant-garde, in a much wider sense than the mainly textual innovations of the consecrated avant-garde of the 1980s. The development of Internet technology has helped Chen to develop texts that do not fit easily into any genre norms (including the genre norms for hypertext developed in the field of Internet studies) yet are at the same time indebted to an alternative aesthetics, based on playfulness, randomness, closeness to nature, and individual taste, that has persistently existed throughout Chinese literary history.

Such self-conscious and multifaceted experimentation with the online chronicle form is rare in Chinese Internet literature, but the diary-like nature of many applications favored by online writers (discussion forums, blogs, microblogs) has made the online chronicle a dominant genre, and other types of experimentation with this type of writing are also worth investigating.

Wen Huajian and the Weibo Novel

A more playful and lighthearted type of experiment with online chronicling began in January 2010, when the marketing professional and part-time author Wen Huajian announced his intention to produce the first ever novel to be serialized on Sina Weibo, the hugely popular social media site inspired by the Twitter format.

Twitter is officially blocked in mainland China. Some blocked sites are nevertheless hugely popular with users who know how to scale the Great Firewall. The video-sharing site YouTube, for instance, was ranked by http://chinarank.org.cn as the thirty-eighth most visited website in China in August 2011, despite being blocked. Twitter, on the other hand, has fared much less well in Chinese-language communities, because even those Chinese users who do have access to it generally prefer the Weibo interface. To underscore this point, it is worth mentioning that even in Taiwan and Hong Kong, where Twitter is freely accessible, users demonstrate a clear preference for Weibo, whereas they do not prefer China-made alternatives to YouTube.[50] A formal comparison between Twitter and Weibo is beyond my scope of inquiry, but it is probably safe to say that Weibo appeals because of its built-in additional features, such as allowing users to add pictures to their tweets easily and without sacrificing text content, and the very prominent functionalities allowing users to join all kinds of Weibo groups, clubs, and networks. Wikipedia describes Weibo as "a hybrid of Twitter and Facebook,"[51] which I think is an accurate description and which will help explain some of the features of Wen Huajian's novel.

Apart from the special features of Weibo vis-à-vis Twitter, there is an additional general point to bear in mind before embarking on a discussion of microblog fiction. Regardless of which interface one uses, the 140-character limit applied to individual microblog posts means something entirely different in the case of a character-based language like Chinese compared with an alphabetic language such as English. A detailed technical and linguistic analysis is well beyond my ability and remit, but if we assume that the average length of an English word is about six characters (five letters plus one space), and the average Chinese word length about two characters (no space required), then it is clear that a Chinese-language tweet can contain up to three times as much content as an English-language tweet. This makes it at least relatively easier to serialize a work of microblog fiction in Chinese and ensure that each episode has discrete content.[52]

Wen Huajian's *Weibo shiqi de aiqing* (*Love in the Time of Microblog*[53]) began serialization on January 29, 2010, with a newly established ID (@ wbsqdaq) on the Sina Weibo site. It ended almost a year later, on January 3, 2011, after 405 installments, an average of just over one post per day. By the time it stopped appearing, the Weibo novel had attracted around a hundred thousand followers. The printed version of the novel, which consists of 492 numbered sections divided into seventeen chapters, including two final chapters not included in the online original, came out in March 2011 and gained some media coverage.[54]

Although Wen Huajian started microblogging less than two months before he began serializing his novel, he was certainly no novice to literature, nor to online writing. His first printed novel, *Cry If It Hurts*, was published in Taiwan in 2006.[55] He had been maintaining a personal blog

🡅 **Figure 2.5**   Weibo page for Wen Huajian's *Love in the Time of Microblog*. http://
weibo.com/wbsqdaq (accessible only to registered Weibo members).

on the Sina portal from 2005 onward, which he used among other things
for publishing short poetic texts that he classified as "prose poetry" (*sanwen shi*), and he was active in various online communities devoted to
prose poetry. Not long after he started microblogging, he began to or-
ganize some of his more literary-minded tweets into two genres, using
two separate hash tags, which translate as "Uncle's Meditations" (Dashu
Mingxiang) and "Uncle's Longings" (Dashu Nian). In the early weeks of
January 2010, he posted a flurry of tweets tagged as "Uncle's Longings,"
which all seemed to be addressed to a single beloved, who otherwise remained anonymous, arousing the curiosity of those posting reactions to
his tweets. Shortly afterward, he announced his plan to begin writing a
love story in tweets, based on his experiences in the (micro)blogosphere.
A number of his earlier "meditations" were copied into some of the opening installments of the novel, whereas his predilection for affectedly unconventional (*jiaoqing*) romantic expression was turned into a habit of
the novel's protagonist, leading to some of his "longings" being copied
into the novel as well.[56]

The protagonist of *Love in the Time of Microblog* is a thirty-five-year-
old Beijing resident called Wen Dashu, his given name Dashu a homonym of his nickname "Uncle." He runs his own business, but he has a
college background in psychology, which he puts to good use in acting as

a kind of "agony uncle" to a circle of friends he interacts with on Weibo, most of them younger than him and most of them female. In the opening scenes of the novel, we find Dashu in a restaurant with a young female friend whom he met on Weibo and who has flown to Beijing to have dinner with him. He assumes that dinner will be a prelude to sex, but after the dinner conversation falters and both instead start twittering on their mobile devices, his companion finally asks him to drive her to a nightclub, where she has a date with another Weibo friend. Dashu is upset, drives off, and gets lost. He accesses Weibo again on his mobile, and one of his friends gives him directions. As he approaches home, he is cut off by a speeding police car crossing a double yellow line. He follows and overtakes the police car, blocks it, and confronts the policeman, accusing him of *yanzhong she huang* ("serious transgression of yellow," a pun on "seriously pornographic"). In this and later episodes involving confrontations with the same policeman, Dashu poses as a concerned citizen while constantly employing puns and irony in his speech, helped greatly by the fact that the policeman happens to be called Zhu Dengyan (a homonym of "glaring pig"). The use of Beijing slang, satire, brazen disrespect for authority, and at times very funny puns and jokes is instantly reminiscent of earlier "hooligan fiction" (*pizi wenxue*) as epitomized by the work of Wang Shuo.

The same can be said of the protagonist's penchant for machismo and frequent positive references to the masculine model of the *yemenr* ("real man"). At the beginning of the novel it seems the author at times intentionally goes to extremes in order to provoke responses to his tweets and attract more followers. In the early installments, for instance, he describes at length Dashu's interaction with and sympathy for a female Weibo friend who is the victim of domestic abuse, while a few episodes later he has Dashu advising a male friend to engage in violent behavior toward a woman in order to cure his erectile dysfunction. In both cases the protagonist writes about these experiences on Weibo and quotes some of the responses he receives from other users, which in turn are copies of actual responses submitted to the author by followers of the novel.

Weibo in all its aspects plays a key thematic role in the novel. The characters all know one another through Weibo, they use online slang, which the narrator often helpfully explains, and they function as a mutual support community, such as in an episode where they arrange an event to raise funds for victims of drought in Yunnan. (Again, an actual event like this was organized by the author and his real Weibo friends around the same time.) Eventually, the story comes to focus on the fate of Dashu after he has had a car accident and is left paralyzed in the hospital. Ironically, the only limb he is able to move is his right arm, allowing him to continue using Weibo on his mobile phone. All his Weibo friends, now including the policeman Zhu Dengyan, who has also become a Weibo user, and the female celebrity Dai Man, whom Dashu is in love with, all visit him regularly at the hospital. As it turns out, various unlikely things happening to Dashu while in the hospital, such as his being awarded a huge sum of money for being a "heroic citizen," Dai Man's returning his affections, and surgeons apparently accepting his instructions to carry out a spectacular operation to cure his paralysis are all part of a plot hatched by his Weibo friends to try to get him so agitated and excited that he will indeed be miraculously cured. In the end, he does receive the big shock that makes him sit up and restores the use of his limbs, namely when he is told that Dai Man has suddenly left the country and married a foreigner.

In the online original of the novel, Dashu first goes bankrupt, then founds a new company, which happens to have the same name as the company that Wen Huajian manages in real life, and the story ends when he decides to start writing a novel on Weibo, bringing the narration full circle. In the printed version of the novel, the story goes on longer, and Dashu writing his novel becomes part of the actual novel, as does the ID of another mysterious Weibo user who accompanies and inspires him throughout the writing process and who of course in the end turns out to be none other than Dai Man, who never did leave the country and who really does love him. The anonymous ID used by Dai Man toward the end of the printed novel is identical to an ID used on Weibo in responses to Wen Huajian's "Uncle's Longings" posts from before he started serializing his work.

The original posts of the novel as they appeared on Weibo were all accompanied by images bearing some relevance to the contents of the tweets, some of them pictures possibly taken by the author himself, others copied from the Internet.[57] Instant photo sharing has been a distinctive functionality of Weibo right from the start and is seen by many as one of its main advantages over Twitter, which has only had a (much more limited) photo-sharing functionality since June 2011.[58] Most important in the current context is the fact that Weibo users can add pictures without this resulting in a hyperlink to the picture being included in their tweet, taking up more than twenty characters, which could otherwise be devoted to writing. English-language Twitter novels therefore rarely include images.

It is clear that in his selection of images as well, Wen Huajian from time to time tried to be somewhat provocative in order to attract comments and new followers, selecting many images of intimate couples and of women in various poses, some of them erotic. As a result, some of his tweets (such as no. 52, discussing domestic abuse and masochism, accompanied by a picture of a mud-wrestling couple) are discussed more for their visual content than for their textual content. In comparison, the print version of his novel has less visual appeal, although it is nicely illustrated and has maintained the microblog layout in the form of numbered paragraphs. Clearly, reproducing the images that originally accompanied the text online would have been technically cumbersome and, more important, would have run into countless problems in trying to trace the copyright holders of those images.

As is the case with most online literature, readers' comments (*pinglun*) are an integral part of works like *Love in the Time of Microblog* as they develop over time. In some cases the comments are just short statements of approval or disapproval, but others discuss some of the social issues raised in the story, or comment on the extent to which the author has modified actual tweets sent on his personal account in order to make them part of the narrative. Wen Huajian often responds to the comments and sometimes asks for advice on developments in the plotline. Early on in the development of the work, after post number 11, he sent an unnumbered tweet to the main page, asking how many people were actually reading him, to which he received well over a hundred responses. However, the average number of comments on most of his tweets seems to be around twenty. There are some exceptions, with some tweets getting four or five times as many comments, mainly because they are re-sent by other people to their own account pages. (Each reposting triggers an automatic "comment" on the original tweet.) Apart from those comments that the author worked into later parts of the novel, none of the comments appearing on the original site made it into the paper version of the novel. In fact, even when reading the novel online, the comments are hidden and one actually needs to click on a link to access them.

There are other differences between the online original and the printed version of the novel. These appear mainly in the final part of the novel (after Dashu has left the hospital). Prior to that, that is, in the first 350 tweets or so, there are only minor editorial changes to the printed text, none of which appear to have been inspired by concerns about more stringent censorship of printed publications. All passages where Dashu or other characters engage in satirical discourse about present-day Chinese society remain identical in the printed version, with only one exception. In tweet number 265 of the original Dashu ironically accuses the policeman Zhu Dengyan of *qipian zuzhi, qipian renmin, qipian dang* (deceiving the organization, deceiving the people, deceiving the Party). In the corresponding section of the book (no. 271), the word "Party" has been replaced by the word "society." All other changes that I noticed in the printed version appear to have been straightforward editorial corrections, correcting mistakes, adjusting punctuation, or improving the choice of words. The only other major change involves a plotline late in the novel concerning two new characters, which are introduced very abruptly in the original after tweet number 391, when Wen was silent for nine days and then suddenly announced, in an unnumbered tweet inserted into the text, that there would be a "sudden twist in the plot." In the printed version, the arrival of these two characters is weaved into the plot more subtly. Finally, as mentioned, the printed version is longer, adding another sixty tweet-length sections in which some of the plotlines left unresolved in the online version are given some form of closure: the character Dandan eventually divorces her abusive husband to start a relationship with the policeman Zhu Dengyan, and the protagonist Dashu finally finds out that Dai Man loves him.

Although there is a clear discrepancy between the number of followers of the novel as it developed, which reached well over a hundred thousand, and the number of people actually interacting with the author, which numbered only a few dozen, there is still no doubt that *Love in the Time of Microblog* attracted a reasonable amount of attention and was generally acknowledged as the first experiment of its kind.[59] Already in March 2010, when the novel had been ongoing on Weibo for two months and its author had reposted the first hundred or so installments to two well-known literary websites (Banyan Tree and Tianya[60]), traditional news media started to pay attention to it. On March 17, 2010, the Xinhuanet website reproduced an article from *West China Metropolitan Daily*, interviewing Wen Huajian and discussing the novel's experimental way of weaving real-life stories about ordinary netizens into the narration. The article also raised questions about the provocative treatment of romance in the novel and expressed doubts about its stylistic sophistication.[61]

Most media coverage as well as promotion material for the novel on Weibo and for the later print publication emphasize the fact that Wen's work is the first ever Chinese microblog novel. This claim was contested by Willis Wee, writing on the Tech in Asia website in April 2011.[62] Wee pointed to two other articles making similar claims. One was an item from the Fox News website that reprinted a *Wall Street Journal* article[63] heralding the "influential blogger" Lian Yue's first episodes of a Twitter novel, which appeared on his Twitter account (@lianyue) in March 2010. Forty episodes of the novel, titled *2020* and using the hash tag #ly2020, still appear in Lian Yue's time line, but the work appears not to have been completed. In any case, the first installments of Wen Huajian's novel predate those of Lian's by two months, so the answer to the question of who came first is clear-cut, all the more so since Lian's novel was never finished.

More interesting is the second link provided by Wee, to an article describing what is called "The First Microblog Novel Contest in China," which took place on the Sina Weibo website from October to November 2010 (i.e., still well after Wen Huajian started serializing his work).[64] What this competition was about, however, was not microblog novels (*weibo xiaoshuo*) but "microfiction" (*wei xiaoshuo*), meaning ultrashort fictional texts of no more than 140 characters (i.e., one tweet). This type of fiction was also recently experimented with by well-known British writers at the invitation of the *Guardian*.[65] On Sina Weibo it has proved immensely popular. The format is very straightforward: the organizers announce a time during which anyone can post microfiction using a particular hash tag. The hash tag identifies the posts as entries into the competition. After the set period has passed, a jury goes through all the entries and awards prizes. Weibo has held the competition three times already, and on the dedicated sites for the 2010, 2011, and 2012 competitions, new posts continue to come in, even though they no longer compete for any prizes.[66] According to the article referred to by Wee, the first

competition was couched in some controversy because of the large number of entries featuring gay fiction, presumably of the *danmei* variety,
which is briefly discussed in chapter 4 and has been studied extensively
by Jin Feng.[67] None of this poses any challenge to Wen Huajian's status
as China's first microblog novelist. Wen himself has, in the meantime,
become a great supporter of the microfiction genre. He served as a jury
member on all three competitions, and he manages a fairly active Weibo
community devoted to the genre. Wen also continues to combine his literary activities with his business activities, and on his personal Weibo
site he now identifies himself not only as "the Wen Huajian who is known
as Uncle" but also as the inventor of the concept of "microtrade" (*weishang*) and as "China's first ever microtrade trainer" (*Zhongguo shouxi
weishang jiaolian*).

Comparing Wen Huajian's writings with Chen Cun's work reveals
some similar characteristics. Like Chen, Wen paradoxically uses an interactive platform meant to produce ephemeral, time-sensitive content in
order to create something that lasts and extends over time. Both authors
clearly enjoy the social element of online writing, taking full advantage of
the opportunities for interacting with readers commenting on their posts.
Wen's writing, especially, has a strong community element and hinges
both practically and thematically on the idea of Weibo as a medium that
creates a new kind of tight-knit community that helps people cope and
find support in uncertain times. Wen's writing also contains various references to Weibo slang and Weibo celebrities that are difficult to follow
for the uninitiated reader, although one should modify this by pointing
out that it is highly unlikely that anyone among his readership, even that
of his printed novel, would not be intimately familiar with Weibo as a
social medium and the associated terminology.

Also like Chen, Wen is aware of the fact that he is doing something
new, and he uses various techniques to blur the lines between author,
narrator, and reader. He does this especially, it should be said, in the
printed version of the novel, which goes on much longer after having
reached a point in the narrative where the narrator is starting to write
a novel with the same title as Wen's work itself, leading to earlier comments from readers on Wen's writing being incorporated into the novel
as comments from fictional readers (but with the same IDs) on a fictional
novel (but with the same title).

What makes Wen different from Chen is, first of all, his choice of genre, something of a mixture between romance novel and picaresque novel. Second, what makes Wen different is his relatively stronger need to engage in self-promotion. This can be seen from the way in which Wen copied parts of his ongoing novel to other literary websites in order to increase his readership, from the way in which he actively promoted the print publication of his novel on his various personal blogs and microblogs, and from the sheer fact that he wanted to be published in print in the first place. This clearly shows that Wen is a much less established author than Chen. It also shows that Wen realized early on that his microblog novel was something new and potentially interesting to a wider readership. Whether or not Wen will continue to come up with innovative ideas in his writing remains to be seen.

Han Han

Han Han (b. 1982) is a literary celebrity whose medium of choice is the online blog.[68] So famous are his online essays that he is almost automatically associated with Internet literature in China, and it would seem a book like this cannot possibly leave him unmentioned. Yet it is worth stating at the outset that, like Chen Cun, Han Han clearly separates his literary writing from his online writing. In fact, also like Chen Cun, he became famous well before he went online, by winning the "New Concept" literary prize competition in 1999, famously dropping out of school the same year, scandalously refusing an offer to attend literature classes at Fudan University, and publishing his first best seller (a cynical dissection of the Chinese education system, titled *Triple Gate*) in 2000, when he was still only eighteen years old.[69] Similar to Wen Huajian and many others, he did not start blogging until 2005, when the Sina blog site came online. By that time he was already famous throughout China for his printed novels, and he accumulated half a million followers for his blog in no time. From then on he has gained increasing acclaim (and attracted occasional censorship) for the satirical essays, commenting mainly on current affairs, that he publishes on his blog. His novels, however, continue to appear only in print, and as far as I know he has never published any creative writing on the Internet and has used his blog only for social and cultural critique.

Of course, Han Han's online prose can be considered from a literary perspective, and he has certainly reinvigorated the *zawen* (critical essay) genre of Chinese literature, employing it in a manner not unlike that of the great Lu Xun (1881–1936), who is credited with inventing the genre. Yet compared with the other two writers discussed in this chapter, Han Han neither shows the kind of reflection on his literary choices and methods that we encountered with Chen Cun nor does he engage in any popular genre-based experimentation like Wen Huajian. What makes Han Han interesting in our current context, however, is the way in which he uses his blog writings, and his celebrity status, to reflect on the material and legal conditions of literary production and to create new, independent niches that explore the outer boundaries of what is possible in postsocialist publishing in China. In addition, Han Han's recent move toward distributing publications directly to mobile devices showcases a brand-new publishing strategy that still makes use of the Internet but bypasses the World Wide Web.

By focusing on Han Han's writings about and involvement in the literary and publishing world, I am intentionally not treating his current affairs essays for which he became increasingly well-known around the time of the Beijing Olympics. These essays have drawn much attention and are also available in uncensored English-language editions, both online[70] and in print.[71]

Han Han's blog has always been located on the Sina blog site, where he uses the ID "twocold," presumably because his personal name, Han, literally means "cold," so Han Han sounds like "cold cold," even if the first Han (his family name) is written with a different character. In its current state, the first post on his blog is dated November 2006, and at least one recent commentator has taken this to be the starting point of Han Han's blogging career.[72] However, Han Han was blogging well before that date but has himself removed his earlier posts, for reasons I will speculate on in the following. His very first blog entry was in fact posted on October 28, 2005, and consisted of a single line of text, which read, "Hello everybody! This is Han Han. I will keep a record of my life here. I hope everything will become perfect!" The post was read just under three thousand times and received seventy comments. It was captured by the IAWM only a few days later, on November 2, 2005.[73]

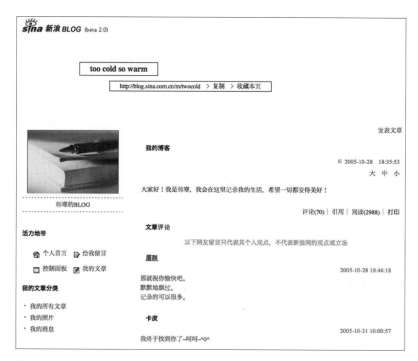

⊕ Figure 2.6 Earliest IAWM capture of Han Han's blog page (November 3, 2005). http://web.archive.org/web/20051103050633/http://blog.sina.com.cn/u/4701280b01000080.

After a hesitant start during the first few days, when he mainly up-loaded texts and pictures about his rally-driving activities, Han started to write longer posts, and by the beginning of December, his blog entries were read by tens of thousands of people. As discussed in detail in an article by Marco Fumian, by spring 2006 Han Han was embroiled in an extended war of words with the critic Bai Ye. Bai had written, on his own blog, that the new generation of writers born in the 1980s (known as *baling hou*, or "post-80") had only entered "the market" (*shichang*) but not yet "the literary scene" (*wentan*). In a blog entry posted on March 3, 2006, under the title "The Literary Scene Is Crap and People Should Stop Acting Like Cunts," Han Han lashed out at Bai Ye's perceived elitism, stating that all literature is individual, that creativity knows no thresholds, and that everybody who publishes anything, even if it is on a blog, has automatically entered "the literary scene." He scoffed at the notion of "pure literature" promoted by Bai Ye as nothing but a form of institutionalized mutual gratification. Or, in Han's rather more direct words,

The literary scene is crap. The Mao Dun Literature Award is crap. Pure literature magazines are crap. It's like a hundred people masturbating so a hundred people can watch. Over here we are all happily doing it in all kinds of positions, but you old-timers are still out there saying, "Look at me masturbating, make sure you copy the exact rhythm of my movements, or you won't be able to enter the wanking scene [*yintan*]."[74]

Han Han concluded the piece by apologizing for his somewhat obscene language, saying he would revise the piece later (he never did) but that right now he was too busy trying to enter the "racing scene" (*chetan*).

In Fumian's thoughtful analysis, the debate between Han Han and Bai Ye illustrates two sides of the present-day Chinese literary field, neither of which is particularly autonomous. Just as Bai Ye's claims to expertise in "pure literature" are tainted by his closeness to official organizations such as the Writers Association, Han Han's claim that his writing is more "pure" because he has acquired a wide readership without any institutional support is questionable in view of his celebrity media status. Fumian demonstrates how, over time, the two positions can be seen to merge, with established writers providing patronage and support to youngsters of the 1980s generation, and some commercially successful younger writers (though not including Han Han) voluntarily applying for membership of the Writers Association, indicating a gradual mixing of social, political, and commercial interests, none of which are particularly conducive to disinterested literary creation. Meanwhile, writes Fumian, Han Han found intellectual (if not literary) autonomy by becoming a respected independent blogger and commentator on sociopolitical affairs.[75]

Perhaps it was this newly found direction for his online activity, away from the literary scene and toward a more direct expression of social engagement, that prompted Han Han to remove his earliest blog posts from the official record. As a result, his side of the debate with Bai Ye no longer survives on his own site but only on other people's sites and in the IAWM archive. Also deleted was a series of posts in which Han Han satirized current Chinese poetry and exchanged rhetorical blows with

Shen Haobo, at the time the most prominent representative of the online poetry avant-garde community known as the Lower Body Poets.[76] I will have more to say about avant-garde poetry on the Internet in chapter 4, but for now I want to dwell on how Han Han's initial clash with Shen Haobo eventually led to the two of them striking up an unusual partnership, which has had important consequences for the state of literary publishing in postsocialist China.

On September 26, 2006, Han Han published a short piece on his blog titled "How Come Modern Poetry and Poets Still Exist?"[77] In it he stated his opinion, with characteristic sarcasm, that modern poetry is nothing more than prose broken into separate lines and that it is therefore a waste of paper. Poetry, he writes, has lost its raison d'être ever since it did away with traditional prosody. If it has any status left, it is as a minor subgenre of popular song lyrics. The only reason why people still want to call themselves poets is because the term has a certain aura that makes it easier for poets than for prose writers to "fool literary-minded young girls" (*pian wenxue nü qingnian*). He ends with a mock poem consisting of a few colloquial sentences broken into many short lines, with some of the enjambment resulting in funny readings.

Although in his post he feigned ignorance of recent events, Han Han was surely aware of the fact that his caricature modern poem capitalized on a major online spoofing campaign ridiculing the work of the female poet Zhao Lihua, which had been gathering momentum online for a few weeks already and which, after Han Han joined in and affected his hundreds of thousands of followers, soon spilled over into the offline media as well.[78]

The spoofing of Zhao Lihua's poetry started on September 11, 2006, with a post on the educational website Liangquanqimei (Best of Both Worlds, http://www.lqqm.com) by someone using the ID "redchuanbo." Titled "The Most Embarrassing Poems in History," the post started with an overview of Zhao Lihua's impressive CV, which included contributions to several established poetry journals, membership of the poetry jury for the Lu Xun Literature Awards, and other laurels linked with the state-sponsored literary system. The poster then asked his readers to "take a deep breath" before copying some of her poems, such as the following:[79]

Lonely Arrival in Tennessee

Without a doubt
my homemade stuffed pancakes
are the tastiest
in the whole wide world

The poster finished with the following lines:

So
poetry
can even be
written
like this
!!!!!!!!!

Within a matter of days, popular online forums were awash with poems spoofing Zhao Lihua's style, and within a week a web domain "zhaolihua. com" was created, devoted entirely to followers of what by then was called (with a pun on the poet's name) the "pear blossom teachings" (*lihua jiao*) producing spoof poems in the "pear blossom style" (*lihua ti*). Apart from hypershort lines and nonsensical enjambments, this "style" was also characterized by the typical preference of Chinese netizens for all kinds of homophones, with the character for "poetry" (*shi* 诗) routinely replaced with the character for "wet" (*shi* 湿) and the character for "reciting" (*yin* 吟) replaced by that for "lewd" (*yin* 淫). One of the most famous spoof poems, also quoted by Han Han on his blog, was the following:[80]

> *yin yi shou shi*
> *bu nan*
> *nande shi*
> *yin yi beizi shi*

Written with the correct characters, this would simply mean "reciting one poem / isn't hard / but what's hard / is reciting a life long of poems." But when written with different characters for *yin*, *shou*, *shi*, and *beizi*, the meaning becomes something like "wanking one hand wet / isn't hard / what's hard / is wanking your whole blanket wet."

As is clear from the post that started the whole affair, as well as from many later contributions, the main issue at stake was the perceived incongruence between Zhao Lihua's status as a high-ranking writer in the official system and the quality of her poetry. It soon became commonplace to refer to Zhao as a "national first-rank poet" (*guojia yiji shiren*), although in reality no such title exists in the official system. The implication was clear, though: here was someone profiting from state resources in order to produce bad writing. Undoubtedly this was why Han Han joined the debate and gave it full endorsement. To him, Zhao must have seemed just another representative of the official literary scene that he had criticized so strongly in his exchanges with Bai Ye.

Han Han would not have expected the strong, hostile reaction he received almost instantly from representatives of the *unofficial* literary scene, especially the leading avant-garde poets Yi Sha and Shen Haobo. I do not think Yi and Shen would have been particularly fond of Zhao Lihua's writing, but as representatives of the "popular" (*minjian*) style of avant-garde poetry, which aimed at desecrating poetry and poeticizing plain, at times vulgar, vernacular language as an aesthetic statement, they were understandably annoyed by Han Han's critique of modern poetry and free verse in general as simply useless.[81] Shen Haobo, especially, did not mince his words in a series of writings on a new blog, hosted on the Sina portal, that he set up solely for the purpose of attacking Han Han.[82] The gist of Shen's criticism was that Han was an uneducated, uncultured nobody: a commercial product, not a person, and definitely not anyone who could be credited with any understanding of modern poetry.

While Han Han's adoring fans proceeded to spam Shen Haobo's new blog, Han himself chose to make fun of Shen and other critics for their inability to produce proper prose in their critical articles or to show some examples of good poetry. The poets, especially those outside the state-supported system, responded by organizing public poetry recitals and gatherings in Beijing, defending their art, while Shen Haobo copied some of his own poems onto his new blog challenging people to imitate or spoof him.

Han Han seemed gradually to develop some respect for Shen, or at least came to understand that he was no government stooge. He even audaciously copied onto his blog some of Shen's more explicit poems, offering him the kind of mass audience that he would otherwise be unable to reach. Although Han was still dismissive of the work as poetry, calling it, not entirely unreasonably, a kind of "performance art," he seemed surprised to find that there were so many different schools of poetry active in the nonofficial circuit. In the end, his most well-considered criticism was of the way in which the poets, despite being divided into so many schools and groups, had pulled together as a collective, finding solace in the idea that they understood the value of their work, even if the rest of the world did not. Han chastised the poets for blaming everybody but themselves for the lack of appreciation of their work. He teasingly called modern poetry a "cult" (*xiejiao*) and stated that, as far as he was concerned, serious literary creation could only ever be a private activity. Writers should stay away as far as possible from any kind of collective or any kind of "association" (*xiehui*).[83] Although his use of the term *xiejiao*, a heavily laden term normally reserved for ideological criticism of religious groups such as Falun Gong, was borderline malicious, Han Han's suggestion that poets like Shen Haobo and works such as "A Handful of Tit"[84] had only "cult status" was not too wide of the mark. Furthermore, his warning against joining any kind of *xiehui* was an obvious swipe at the official Writers Association.

Around this same time, in August 2006, a statement appeared on the front page of Han Han's blog that, despite some small changes over time, has continued to be there until the present. The earliest version of it, first captured by the IAWM on August 5, 2006, reads as follows:

> I don't take part in debates, meetings, or pen clubs; I don't do signings, don't give lectures, don't cut ribbons, don't attend fashionable functions; I don't take part in prize ceremonies or performances; I don't give TV interviews, I don't write on solicited topics, I don't write play scripts, I don't appear in TV dramas, and I don't write prefaces for anyone.[85]

These lines capture Han's intention to establish himself in clear separation from all organized and unorganized social activity that usually surrounds literary creation in China, ranging from participation in official meetings to the conventional habit of exchanging favors by writing prefaces for friends' publications.

In one of the last posts from 2006 that he later removed from his blog, published on November 1, Han Han connects his independent stance directly with a rejection of the Writers Association. Riled, perhaps, by the news that his fellow celebrity and best-seller writer Guo Jingming was about to join the association, Han lashed out at all Chinese writers who rely on the state for a living rather than stand on their own two feet. Comparing Chinese writers and the Writers Association to kept mistresses who perform on demand, he stated that real writers should look after themselves and should prefer to go begging rather than try to gain official favor. He also chastised the association itself for failing to stand up for Chinese writers' legal rights in disputes over piracy or royalties.[86]

Han Han's now-deleted posts from 2006 do not represent Internet literature as such. They are not intended as creative writing, nor do they make any use of the interactive features of online communication. Han posts his texts, and readers comment on them in their thousands, but as far as I can see, he never responded to any of the comments. Nevertheless his early writings are directly relevant to the topic of this book. His critique of Chinese literary institutions and Chinese writers' cliquish behavior aims at the remnants of socialist mentality that remain at the core of the postsocialist literary system. At the same time it is exactly because these remnants exist that Han Han can take his position in such a provocative manner. Despite his aloofness and lack of interaction with his readers, his strong individual stance has turned him into a kind of "cult hero." Reading through the comments on his blog posts, one cannot help but be struck by the amount of readers that comment only in order to declare their love or adoration for Han Han and everything he does.

Less than three years later, on May 1, 2009, Han Han published a blog post that featured another intervention in postsocialist Chinese literary culture. He announced that he would publish a literary magazine, with himself as editor in chief. He stipulated in great detail the fees he would pay for contributions, pointing out that they ranged from ten times to forty times the going rate in the publishing industry. His stated rationale for doing so was simple: the cost of living had risen sharply in China over the past few years, putting much pressure on writers: "If a writer in such a high-pressure society has to worry even about his food and clothing, then in my opinion he is unlikely to preserve his independent personal or literary integrity [*duli de renge he wenge*]."[87] There was again a touch of heroism to Han's announcement, as if he were single-handedly striving to salvage the integrity of China's writers, but the initiative was nonetheless meaningful and consistent with his view that writers should be able to achieve financial independence.

In the months following the announcement of what initially was simply called the journal, expectations soared. Further announcements followed, and by early 2010 the journal was starting to take shape. It was
to be given the name *Duchangtuan*, often translated as *Chorus of Solos*.
The title echoed some of the issues raised during Han's 2006 debate with
the poets. At the time, as we have seen, Han had commented negatively
on the poets' organized response to his criticism, using the term *zutuan*
(getting organized) in a condescending manner. Now he himself had
brought together a *tuan*, but his point seemed to be that all the members
of his collective were still acting as individuals, singing their own tune
(*duchang*).

After the name of the journal was known, several promotional images (*haibao*) for the publication of the first issue were circulated online,
which looked like cover designs. One of them was a now iconic image of a
naked man wearing only black socks and holding a black gun, his private
parts in the center of the image covered by a light-blue circle containing
the characters *duchangtuan*. The point of the image was, as so often, a
pun based on homophones: the words for "covering the center" (*dang
zhongyang*) sound the same as the words for "Party Central Committee."[88] To some observers, these emerging images raised expectations of
Han Han's new magazine being politically provocative, perhaps as a kind
of extension of his independent blogging. When the first issue eventually
came out in the summer of 2010, not all these expectations were met,[89]
but nevertheless over a hundred thousand copies were sold the first day
and well over a million in total.

The cover of the first issue does not carry any of the images that were
previously circulated. To me this seems to have been partly for practical
reasons: Han Han had promised that all authors whose contributions
were featured with their title on the front page would be paid double,
and that at least half of all contributors would be given this privilege. So
it is not surprising that the cover design was quite plain and contained
mainly text. Yet there is a brilliantly subtle political message on the
cover, which surely will not have escaped a readership attuned to puns
and wordplay. Under the Chinese title appears the title of the magazine
in English: *Party*. Han Han had not just founded a magazine, he had
founded a party, something that is quite out of the question in the Chinese political system. Within a few months after publishing the first issue

⬆ **Figure 2.7**   Blog post showing mock design for cover of first issue of Han Han's magazine *Party*. http://news.ifeng.com/opinion/indepth/duchangtuan/a02/detail_2010_07/06/1724009_0.shtml.

of *Party*, Han Han followed up with a new novel, with an equally subtly subversive title. The novel was titled *1988* and would surely have been banned if it had been called *1989* instead due to the blanket ban on any cultural expression hinting at the events of June 1989.

When I arrived in Shanghai in October 2010, copies of *1988* were piled up high in all the bookshops, while copies of *Party* had already become scarce but were still being ardently sought after by customers at magazine stalls. Han Han was everywhere that month, not only in the bookshops and in the media but also smiling at people on advertising billboard posters in subway stations.

The contents of the first issue of *Party* might not have pleased those looking for a political edge, but from a literary perspective it did stand out from mainstream literary magazines. First, in light of my earlier discussion, it is impossible not to notice the fact that there is no poetry in the journal, except for a four-line poem written by a small child: an unmistakable swipe at China's poets. The rest of the content consists of short fiction of uneven quality, including a prepublication of the opening pages of *1988*, and much visual art, including Ai Weiwei's *My Brain*, a copy of his brain scan after he had been beaten by police. Personally I found some of the photography in the first issue most impressive, and it certainly added to creating the impression of a glossy culture journal. According to a discussion on the English-language website Paper Republic,[90] the section of *Party* that Chinese readers liked most was "Everybody Asks Everybody," in which questions from readers on all kinds of topics were answered by so-called experts, although at times with quite a bit of tongue-in-cheek. For instance, questions asked of the authorities and supposedly answered by government offices resulted in the names of those offices (such as "the Prison Police" and "the National Committee for Population and Birth Planning") being featured on the front page of the journal as "contributors."

A second issue of *Party* never appeared. In order to avoid speculation, Han Han described the process of the publishing of the journal in great detail on his blog in December 2010.[91] It constitutes a model case study in postsocialist publishing, its opportunities and its limits. Work on the first issue of *Party* started in cooperation with an investment from a second-channel company that sensed a good market opportunity. While this company's studio (*gongzuoshi*)[92] was starting work on the concept of the journal, the company was bought by Shanda Literature, a culture economy giant that, among other things, now owns virtually all major literary websites in China (further discussion can be found in chapter 3). A Shanda subsidiary company was then appointed as the journal's distributor. Everything was ready to go, all that was missing was an actual publisher that could make the publication legal by giving it a book number. Over the course of almost an entire year, ten different publishers went over the contents of the first issue, and eventually a publisher from Shanxi took the risk. As part of the deal, *Party* was published as a book, the first in a series (*congshu*), rather than as a magazine, since approval for new ISSN numbers is very hard to obtain in comparison with ISBN numbers for books.

After the first issue had appeared and sold extremely well, various media (including state-run media) had drawn attention to the fact that this was a magazine published as a book, and the decision was made to avoid trouble and submit an official application for publication as a journal. The original publisher was unable to help with this, so a new publisher had to be found. This turned out to be, in a truly ironic twist, Beijing Motie Books Ltd., China's largest and most successful private publisher, which operates entirely legally outside the gray area of the second channel, and whose owner is the former avant-garde poet Shen Haobo.[93] Burying old hatchets, Han Han and Shen worked hard to get all official approvals for publication of the second issue of *Party*. Finally, when the first print run had already been printed, approval was withdrawn. In his blog post telling the story, Han Han emphasizes that he is certain that neither the General Administration of Press and Publishing nor the Ministry of Propaganda (the two main censorship offices) were responsible for the ban. Whoever did make the phone call that pulled the plug on the project, he does not know, nor does he know what the reason was.

The partnership between Han Han and Shen Haobo was set to last, however, and together with other prominent publishers and bestseller authors they took on the widespread piracy of Chinese books on text-sharing sites, especially Baidu Library (Baidu Wenku). In an open letter to Baidu's CEO Robin Li, Han Han starts out by painting a grim, almost poetic image of himself and Shen Haobo going together to a paper mill in order to pulp over a million copies of the second issue of *Party*. He details the financial challenges and risks of publishing in China and the meager profits made by writers in order to point out how big an impact Baidu's piracy has on literary livelihoods. He then writes, with a reference to the 2006 debates discussed earlier,

> We don't ask that you close Baidu Library, we only hope that it could voluntarily respect and protect copyright. So when one day in the future today's countless readers will have grown up, perhaps Baidu Library will have become a source of livelihood for Chinese authors, unlike today, where you have become the industry's enemy and target of public criticism.
>
> Because there are no permanent enemies, and no permanent benefits. In 2006 I had a public spat with Shen Haobo from Motie Books. We hurled insults at each other in open letters like there was no tomorrow, over the issue of modern poetry. Yet today we are friends and business partners. Baidu Library could very well become the basis for the wealth of Chinese authors, and not the grave in which they are buried.[94]

After a successful legal challenge to Baidu, the Writers Legal Protection Union (Zuojia Weiquan Lianmeng), founded by Han, Shen, and others, went on to challenge more cases of piracy, including the sale of pirated

⬆ **Figure 2.8** Website introducing Han Han's smartphone app ONE. http://wufazhuce.com.

material on the Apple App Store.[95] Compared with five years earlier, when Han Han had lambasted the Chinese Writers Association for not protecting the interests of writers in disputes over piracy, this new writers union made it clear that Han was no longer forced, as he feared at the time, to face all challenges alone.

Han Han may have attacked the Apple App Store for selling pirated books, but he also sensed the opportunities of the app format for exploring yet another possible channel of literary production. In October 2012 he launched a brand new app called Yige in Chinese and ONE in English, with the promotional slogan "One Is All," again expressing the idea of collective individuality also found in the Chinese title of *Party*. With the launch of this app, Han Han has established a truly new format, making use of the functionalities of Internet connectivity but entirely bypassing the browser-based media of the World Wide Web. Users who have downloaded the free app to their smartphones are provided with daily contents not dissimilar to what was provided in the pages of *Party*. Every day there is one image (artwork or photograph), one text (short story or short prose, no poetry), and one "Question and Answer." Users continue to have access to contents from previous days starting from the day they first downloaded the app, they can store their favorites for quick access, and they are shown unobtrusive advertising that undoubtedly helps to keep the app free.

In a piece published on ONE (and copied onto his blog) on November 28, 2012, Han Han claims that the app format was not designed to circumvent censorship, stating that it would make no sense to invest so much money in a new project if there was substantial risk of being shut down.[96] Yet in terms of employing new technology in order to circumvent existing controls on literary production, ONE undoubtedly represents a masterly move. The format falls entirely outside the scope of any rules for ISBN or ISSN numbers, and it does not involve any publishers in the traditional sense. Unlike most web-based literature, the texts distributed through the ONE platform do not provide interactive features such as user comments. This is consistent with what I noted earlier, namely that Han Han has never been very concerned about direct interaction with his readership.

So far, Han Han has not yet published any new fiction on the ONE platform. It is too soon to tell if the new format will have any impact on his literary writing or if he will continue to draw a clear boundary between his fiction (always published in print) and his prose (published mainly online). Like Chen Cun, Han Han can rightly claim never to have published literary works online. But the work he has done and continues to do for Chinese literary publishing, in terms of shaking up its established practices and exploring new, independent avenues, is innovative and valuable.

In the next chapter, I turn to the world of online novels and genre fiction, where other boundaries of the postsocialist system are being explored.

THREE

The Bottom Line

ONLINE FICTION AND
POSTSOCIALIST PUBLISHING

➔ **"A SHUHAO (LITERALLY BOOK NUMBER),"** writes Kevin Latham in the 2005 *Encyclopedia of Contemporary Chinese Culture*, "is a registration number required to publish any book in China.... Without a book number it is illegal to publish."[1] Nearly a decade down the line, these words remain true but only with reference to printed books. Since 2005 a huge market for born-digital literature, especially popular genre fiction, has emerged in the PRC. Lengthy novels in hundreds of chapters are serialized online for paying customers, none of them carrying ISBN numbers (as book numbers are officially called) unless they are republished in print. This does not mean that the online publishing market is a free-for-all from which state regulators have withdrawn entirely. Although the classic desire of the socialist state to oversee the planned production of literary writing aimed at educating "the masses" has long receded into the background, the state has not completely relinquished its self-perception as arbiter of what is or is not healthy and appropriate for mass audiences to read. This postsocialist tendency to intervene in market forces as soon as they come too close to an ideological "bottom line" (*dixian*) is most clearly noticeable in the regulation of transgressive genres such as erotic fiction. Meanwhile, the landscape of online fiction also includes high-end literary production by self-professed avant-garde groups, seeking to transgress aesthetic rather than moral boundaries.

This chapter starts with a brief overview of the basic features of genre fiction websites, drawing examples mainly from the highly popular Qidian (Starting Point, http://www.qidian.com) site, which is unanimously considered to have pioneered what is now the most common business model for such sites. Since Starting Point and similar sites and their practices have received relatively much scholarly attention, I shall limit myself to a general discussion with reference to existing studies.

In the second part of the chapter I look at issues of regulation and transgression, focusing on state attempts to curb what it considers erotic and obscene content, trying to understand how this is defined and assessed, and looking at examples from the Feilu (Flying Gourd, http://www.faloo.com) fiction site, which regularly featured on blacklists published by the state regulator in 2010 and 2011. Based on interviews with individuals from both sides, I try to pin down what exactly the state's bottom line is when it comes to tolerating this kind of literature, and how the producers themselves perceive their own literary and moral principles. A closer look at excerpts from texts on the Flying Gourd site also demonstrates a certain playfulness at work in the process of circumventing keyword filters, adding an ironic dimension to the works.

In the third and final part I present a short case study of the website Heilan (Black and Blue, http://www.heilan.com) and its various activities and publications. Black and Blue is the online home of a long-standing avant-garde writing community whose preferred genre is fiction. For years they have been active in a remarkably consistent manner, staying largely aloof of official literary institutions while developing their own critical practices and literary assessment mechanisms.

The chapter also provides further evidence of how Internet literature is moving into new, non-web-based media. Both Black and Blue and Flying Gourd, for instance, have recently launched publications on mobile apps, similar to what we have seen in the case of Han Han in chapter 2. The different ways in which both groups use these new apps provide further evidence of their divergent literary orientations while showcasing the commercial and creative opportunities, as well as opportunities for censorship avoidance, offered by the most recent technology.

Online Genre Fiction and the Starting Point Model

According to its own chronicle of major events (*dashiji*),[2] the origins of Starting Point lie with a group of genre fiction enthusiasts who founded the Chinese Magic Fantasy Union (Xuanhuan Wenxue Xiehui, or CMFU for short) in 2001. By December of that year they had set up their own website with the domain name http://www.cmfu.net.[3] By 2002 this had become http://www.cmfu.com, and they had started to include genres other than *xuanhuan*.[4] In late 2003 they started charging readers for access to their most popular serialized works, and by late May 2004 they were attracting so many visitors that they entered the global top hundred websites as ranked by Alexa.[5] Shortly after, they were purchased by Shanda Interactive and became a full subsidiary company in the Shanda family. In 2008 the current domain name, http://www.qidian.com, was adopted. The global ranking of the site now hovers around the five hundred mark, still well above the top website in Alexa's "Literature" category (which includes only English-language sites). Within China, the site continues to be ranked in the top hundred, significantly outranking other literature sites.[6]

The Starting Point business model is simple but effective. On the one hand the site operates as a standard portal for online forums, offering users the opportunity to publish their writing online and receive comments from readers. At the same time, however, they also contract a number of more experienced "VIP authors," whose works appear in serialization, chapter by chapter, initially for free, but usually about halfway through the novel they are moved behind a pay wall. From that moment onward, readers wanting to continue reading the "VIP chapters" have to pay a subscription fee. A typical subscription fee is three "points" per thousand words, with a point equaling one fen (cent) in real money and the initial layout for each reader being fifty yuan, or five thousand points. Income from subscriptions is shared between the authors and the site according to a seventy-thirty split. This means that a typical VIP author receives 2.1 cents per thousand words multiplied by the number of subscribers. Clearly, the brilliance of the model lies not only in its attraction to readers, who are served with regular installments of their favorite genre for a relatively modest amount of money, but also especially in its attraction to aspiring authors. They are lured to the site with promises of

⬆ **Figure 3.1**   Main page of Starting Point website. http://www.qidian.com.

a career trajectory: from submitting work to the normal forums, to establishing a readership, to being discovered by the site's editors, to becoming a VIP author, to making money by producing works counting very many words and attracting very many subscribers. The site, and all others that have by now copied the model, also acts as intermediary for contacts with publishing houses willing to bring out some of the novels in book form.

Sites like these can be seen as cultural translations of business models known in the West from companies such as Harlequin and Mills and Boon.[7] Like those companies, the Chinese fiction websites especially target female readers, with many of them featuring on their main page links to special subsites for women only. Yet whereas the likes of Mills and Boon use their websites only for selling complete books and for social networking, the Chinese genre fiction websites thrive by selling access to work that must be read on-screen in installments and is read that way by millions of readers. Moreover, sites like Starting Point not only cater to readers of romance fiction, as Mills and Boon does, but also address the full range of genre fiction, including martial arts, science fiction, historical novels, fan fiction, and erotica.

Online fiction websites have been instrumental in bringing about a radical redefinition of literary genres, with the word previously used to indicate "literature" in general (*wenxue*) now increasingly used as a genre label for more aesthetically oriented writing. Starting Point, for instance, uses the term *wenxue xiaoshuo* (literary fiction), indicating that *xiaoshuo* is the overarching category and "literature" a subcategory. This is highly reminiscent of practices from the pre–May Fourth period of magazine literature, when journals featuring the word *xiaoshuo* in their titles contained all kinds of creative writing in a dazzling variety of subgenres.[8]

Another attractive aspect of sites such as Starting Point, for both authors and readers, is the opportunity for direct interaction and feedback. As described in detail by Shih-chen Chao in her empirical research on the Starting Point site, there is an intricate ranking system for fiction based on numbers of visits to a particular work, numbers of published readers' comments, numbers of recommendations from readers to other readers, and the number of times a reader added a work to their private collection. There are also separate rankings in all these categories based solely on the reading behavior of VIP members, separate rankings for individual genres, and so on. Readers can even use their online currency to leave "tips" for authors they particularly like. As Chao's research has shown, by far the most popular of the thirteen main genres in terms of production are *xuanhuan* (Eastern fantasy), *yanqing* (romance), and *dushi* (urban), which together make up around half of all the fiction published on Starting Point.[9] Chao also argues that genre distinctions are in fact not as pronounced as they appear to be, with much fiction on Starting Point addressing content that could belong to a variety of genres. What all genres have in common, according to Chao, is their intention to transport readers into a kind of dream world (or a historical world arrived at via time travel) where they can identify with implausible superheroes whose desires for fame, fortune, love, and sex are all fulfilled, often in grotesque proportions.[10] It is this general characteristic of much Chinese online genre fiction that has earned it the nickname "YY fiction" (*YY xiaoshuo*), where YY stands for *yiyin*, or "lust of the mind."[11] Although mainstream sites like Starting Point generally avoid publishing material that is too explicit in its exploration of mental lust fulfillment, other websites have been more transgressive in this respect, thereby challenging the state control mechanisms and, to some extent, forcing those mechanisms to adapt. These processes will be explored in more depth in the following sections.

Innovations and Transgressions

Massively popular genre fiction websites such as Starting Point are doing their share in bringing about literary innovation, specifically in the context of the mainland Chinese literary system. The works they publish are full-length novels without book numbers, read by millions of people. They take shape outside the state-owned publishing system and are not subjected to the same levels of control by editors acting as censors, compared with what would be the case if they were appearing in print. Moreover, these works are so long, are serialized over such long periods, and appear on so many different websites, that it is physically impossible for state control mechanisms to subject them to careful scrutiny.[12] The government has responded by issuing "Internet publishing permits" to some of the larger sites, encouraging them to abide by certain principles of state regulation, such as employing experienced editors and providing links for users wanting to report illegal or offensive content. As Jin Feng has shown, through interviews with staff at Shanda Interactive, which owns most of the largest online literature portals, the leading companies involved are also actively working with the government to close the gap between the print-based and online-based publishing systems.[13]

Nevertheless, it is clear from just browsing the many fiction sites that the relatively unmonitored situation has created considerable room to experiment with a wide variety of transgressive writing, with the government only occasionally intervening through the publication of bans and blacklists of specific works, or through specific instructions to sites to remove specific content. As is well-known from the history of pornography in Europe, transgressive writing plays an important role in, on the one hand, challenging the power of moralistic political (and religious) elites while, on the other hand, spawning debate about the boundaries between "vulgar" and "serious" literature.[14] It is therefore important to look at these "low-end" sites more closely, even though their impact on present-day society might be less significant than that of explicit audiovisual material. Another reason why this material deserves to be studied is that it is largely ignored by Chinese scholars, who tend to shy away from in-depth discussion of the popularity of erotic fiction.

In this part of the chapter I shall look specifically at fiction considered "obscene and pornographic" (*yinhui seqing*). I shall show how the existence of such fiction and a community supporting it exemplifies a widespread challenge to existing obscenity legislation. I shall also point toward textual elements of interest in such writing as it aims to circumvent keyword-based censorship mechanisms and look at examples of what happens when censorship does take effect. As for debate about the boundaries between vulgar and elite literature, although some examples of this can be found, it is on the whole not a prominent feature of the context in which this literature appears, but in my view that only makes it all the more important not to exclude these types of fiction from consideration as part of literary production.[15]

Boys Love and Slash Fiction

The most prominent transgressive genre that has achieved gradual acceptance in recent years and is by now also tolerated (at least online) by the state system is the genre of *danmei*, known as *tanbi* in Japan and as BL (Boys Love) in English. Fiction in this genre features romantic same-sex encounters between male protagonists, often accompanied with more or less explicit yet highly aestheticized descriptions of sexual activity. The Jinjiang portal (http://www.jjwxc.net), partly owned by Shanda Interactive and aimed especially at female authors and readers, is best known for its promotion of BL and related genres. In a recent study, Jin Feng devotes an entire chapter to discussing Chinese BL fiction.[16]

Another popular genre related to BL is "slash," a type of fan fiction focusing on male homoerotic activity between protagonists of well-known movies, TV series, or novels. Fan fiction is called *tongren*, literally "same people," in Chinese. Many fiction sites, including Jinjiang, place BL and fan fiction in the same category. Jin Feng, who devotes a brief section of her study to the phenomenon, prefers the term "*Danmei* fanfic" over the term "slash."[17] A very popular form of slash, both in English and in Chinese, is SS/HP fiction: stories describing romantic adventures featuring Severus Snape and Harry Potter.[18]

Feng's research sheds light not only on the stylistic characteristics of Chinese BL fiction but also, through extensive interviews, on readers' motivations for appreciating this type of writing. She underscores the significance of online publication by pointing out that, up until 2009, any BL fiction circulating in print was illegal, that is, it did not have an ISBN number.[19]

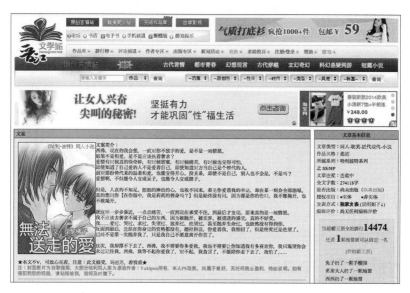

Figure 3.2 Chinese online SS/HP novel. http://www.jjwxc.net/onebook.php?novelid=462139.

Erotic Fiction

BL and slash belong to the general area of erotic fiction, in which online fiction sites are increasingly challenging the limits of state regulation, which can be observed to be shifting.[20] The first thing to notice here is that none of the fiction websites I have looked at actually feature a genre category called erotica or erotic fiction. Works with prominent sexual content appear under the "romance" section or also quite regularly under the "urban" section, but in principle they could appear under any other section as well, including of course the mentioned "BL" and "fan fiction" sections.

The existence of erotic fiction on domestic Chinese websites was highlighted by the publication, on August 1, 2007, of an official statement by the National Office for "Eliminating Pornography and Suppressing Illegality" (Quanguo "Sao Huang Da Fei" Bangongshi), which is housed at the General Administration of Press and Publishing (Xinwen Chuban Zongshu, commonly known as GAPP).[21] The statement was titled "An Urgent Announcement about Strict Action against Online Obscene and Pornographic Fiction." It was addressed to all national and regional offices linked to the campaign to wipe out pornographic illegal publications, and the first lines read as follows:

Taking strict action against online obscene, pornographic, and other harmful material is a necessary requirement for the construction of a socialist
harmonious society and for the purification of a healthy environment for
youngsters and teenagers to grow up in. It is an important element of the
work of "eliminating pornography and suppressing illegality" as well as of the
regulation of Internet publishing, and it is given high priority by the central
leadership. *Recently, GAPP has discovered that some domestic websites have
published novels with obscene and pornographic content. The distribution of
these obscene and pornographic novels disturbs the normal order of online
publishing and it harms the physical and mental health of youngsters and teenagers at large.* Strict action must be resolutely taken against it in accordance
with the law.[22] (emphasis added)

The statement further mentioned a list of forty titles of novels that were to
be banned as well as a list of 348 websites publishing such fiction. These
lists were not made public on the GAPP site, although the titles of the
forty banned works did circulate online, as we shall see in the following.
The GAPP statement ordered relevant offices throughout the country to
take immediate action to make sure any reference to the forty banned
novels was removed completely from the Internet, and to report back
in three weeks' time.[23] In 2008 and 2009 GAPP stayed relatively quiet
on this front, but in 2010–2011 it published regular blacklists of "websites distributing obscene and pornographic content."[24] Interestingly, although the heading does not specifically mention literature or fiction, the
websites singled out on these lists are virtually without exception named
and shamed for providing access to obscene and pornographic fiction, either online or via mobile phones, or both (the arrival of smartphones has
blurred the distinction). The websites in question were not taken offline,
but they were asked to take down the offensive works. Normally websites would comply with such orders, since noncompliance would result
in action taken against the site as a whole. However, as we shall see later,
compliance does not necessarily happen quietly and may result in the
production of informative or entertaining paratexts.

Laws and Definitions

The italicized passage in the quoted 2007 GAPP statement provides useful information about the context in which this particular act of censor-

ship took place. First, it is surprising to find that GAPP did not find out until "recently" before August 2007 that there was erotic fiction on the Chinese Internet. It was certainly there well before that date. Second, the reasons provided for wanting to eradicate online erotic fiction are worth scrutinizing. On the one hand, the statement claims that erotic fiction is harmful to society, especially to young people. This is a fairly common way of arguing in favor of banning pornography, seen also in various Western legislations, such as the U.K. Obscene Publications Act 1959, which defines obscene publications as texts or images likely to "deprave and corrupt" those who encounter them.[25] The idea that young people especially should not be exposed to pornography is even more common all over the world, which is why most countries set age limits to the consumption of this kind of material. The GAPP statement, however, also makes a point of indicating that the publication of erotic fiction has a negative effect on the regulation of Internet publishing. This betrays the regulator's anxiety about loss of control and speaks to the power of pornography to challenge and undermine state authority.[26]

The fact that this particular act of censorship by GAPP was aimed at texts labeled as *fiction* creates an additional complication. Obscenity legislation in most countries makes exceptions for literary or fictitious work. The Criminal Law of the PRC also does this. The relevant article is Article 367, which reads as follows:

> Obscene materials mentioned in this law refer to erotic [*huiyinxing de*] books, magazines, motion pictures, video tapes, audio tapes, pictures, and other obscene materials [*yinhui wupin*] that graphically describe sexual intercourse [*juti miaohui xing xingwei*] or explicitly publicize pornography [*lugu xuanyang seqing*].
>
> Scientific products about physiological or medical knowledge are not obscene materials.
>
> Literary and artistic works of artistic value that contain erotic contents are not regarded as obscene materials.[27]

The text of the law shows something of a struggle with adjectives, which is found also in obscenity legislation in other countries. For instance, U.S. legislation speaks of material appealing to "the prurient interest" or describing sexual conduct "in a patently offensive way" while making exceptions for works of "serious" artistic, literary, political, or scientific value.[28] The difficulties are made even clearer in this case because of problems evident in the English translation of the law (from the English-language database of Chinese laws and regulations provided by Lawinfochina at Peking University). Whereas the text of the law translates the key term *yinhui* as "obscene," an English translation of a later (2004) interpretation of the law that specifically details offenses related to online dissemination translates *yinhui* consistently as "pornographic." Also, the crucial phrase "graphically describe sexual intercourse" in the English text of the law, which sounds very plausible and not dissimilar from definitions of pornography applied in other countries, actually does not appear in Chinese. The Chinese *juti miaohui xing xingwei* means "concretely depict sexual conduct," which widens the scope well beyond the description of intercourse. Finally, the phrase "explicitly publicize pornography" is of course open to many different interpretations.

The exact definition of the key term *yinhui* has been the topic of some discussion in Chinese legal and scholarly circles in recent years. Critics have pointed out the necessity of a more detailed definition and the need for legislation to catch up with current social reality. In practice it seems that legal restrictions on the noncommercial dissemination of pornography among adults are nowadays rarely implemented. Others have advocated removing the notion of "social harm" from discussions of pornography (which is not in the actual text of the law but, as we have seen, figures prominently in official documents). Two later statutes (2004 and 2010) interpreting the law seem to move in this direction, stipulating more severe punishments for disseminating pornography to those under eighteen and for producing and disseminating child pornography (defined as involving individuals under the age of fourteen), which comes close to indicating that there is no social harm in pornography aimed at adults. Yet so far this has not led to the development of a rating system that would make pornography aimed at those over eighteen legal, hence the issue of definition remains an important one.

In a 2005 short article for the *Chinese Journal of Human Sexuality*, Fang Qiang and Hai Yun subject the relevant articles of the Criminal Law to scathing criticism, pointing out that stipulated punishments in the current law are actually harsher than in the previous law (from the 1970s), with severe cases even punishable by life imprisonment. One element of Fang and Hai's criticism is aimed especially at Article 367:

What is "eroticism explicitly publicizing pornography?" What counts as having "artistic value" and what does not? What if one person holds it has "artistic value" and another person does not? And what if something really does not have "artistic value," but it does have "academic value," "value as a historical relic," "research value," "exhibition value," or "collectors value?" Who really has the authority to judge and assess this? How would one apply and implement a law like this (a criminal law containing sentences of life imprisonment!) in different localities, among different nationalities and religions, or under the influence of different literary and artistic trends?[29]

The specific concern expressed by Fang and Hai in this excerpt is the question of whether there can be a nationwide standard for obscenity. In U.S. legal practice, a national standard for obscenity was replaced in 1973 by what is known as the Miller test. The Miller test was formulated by the Supreme Court in 1973 in its verdict on *Miller v. California.* It emphasizes that obscenity must be measured by "contemporary community standards" and that there need not be a national standard of what constitutes an "appeal to the prurient interest."[30] However, according to the Miller test, local community standards are *not* to be applied to the decision as to whether or not the publication in question has "serious" literary or artistic merit, thereby protecting explicit works of widely recognized artistic value from prosecution in the local courts of relatively moralistic or conservative communities. Although this does not remove the difficulty of legally defining what is or is not serious literature (or serious art, or serious scientific research), the Miller test at least specifies when and when not to judge obscenity by local community standards.

In a 2006 article for the *Journal of Beijing Institute of Education,* Zhang Rui and Yang Zhi attempt to defend the need for national standards by proposing a distinction between erotic literature (*seqing wenxue*) and "healthy literature" (*jiankang wenxue*).[31] Zhang and Yang cite affirmatively D. H. Lawrence's famous statement that "pornography is the attempt to insult sex, to do dirt on it," pointing out that even Lawrence, despite once having been accused of being a pornographer himself, was apparently in favor of censoring "genuine pornography." They proceed to sketch the distinction between erotic and healthy literature in partly literary and partly moral terms. First, erotic literature causes social harm through its decadence and depravity; second, it has no artistic value since it appeals only to "certain ugly urbanite mentalities" (*yixie choulou de shimin xinli*) and aims only to make money; third, its descriptions of sexual conduct are overly graphic, focused on the strange and the perverse, and generally sickening.[32] The authors' proposed solution to the popularity of erotic literature online is also twofold. On the one hand, they call for more legislation and better censorship mechanisms. On the other hand, they call for better literary education so as to improve readers' tastes.

Both the need for clearer definitions and the government's wish to promote "healthy" literature were confirmed when I interviewed, in April 2011, a GAPP official in charge of the regulation of online publishing. He explained that the main aim of regulation is to ensure a "healthy" development of online publishing in a way that is beneficial to the country, to society, and to the economy while at the same time satisfying consumers' demands for online access to various types of publications. He acknowledged that much online fiction catered to a modestly educated readership, which would explain the popularity of genre fiction such as romance, martial arts, and science fiction. When asked specifically about erotica, he stated that there was a "social consensus" in China against the promotion (*fayang*) of sex and violence. He emphasized that the blacklists of online erotic content issued by GAPP were not the result of active screening by GAPP itself but were a response to consumer complaints. The GAPP website does indeed offer Internet users the opportunity to file complaints (*jubao*) about specific online material. Some of the larger fiction sites, such as Starting Point, themselves offer such links, which, as we have seen, is one of the conditions they need to fulfill in order to obtain an Internet publishing license. According to the official, any complaints about material that could not be straightforwardly identified as illegal or otherwise were referred to panels of "experts," consisting of academics and industry professionals. Although he admitted that screening for specific keywords also takes place, he strongly denied that any material is ever censored by GAPP solely because of the presence of certain keywords.[33] The official took a neutral attitude toward the question of how to deal with literary, fictional material. As far as he was concerned, anything judged to be legal by the panel of experts, literary or otherwise, was unproblematic. However, referring to the example of film censorship in the West, he acknowledged that it would be helpful to have different levels (*jibie*) of censorship based on age limits, and to have a more specific definition of what does and does not constitute pornography.

Community Response

Whether or not there is indeed a social consensus against pornography in China is difficult to ascertain. What seems to be clear is that erotic content in critically acclaimed literature no longer constitutes a problem, as evidenced by the fact that even opponents of erotica are now comfortable holding up D. H. Lawrence as a positive example, whereas in 1987 a complete Chinese translation of *Lady Chatterley's Lover* was still formally banned despite its claim to literary excellence (and its extensive circulation through unofficial channels).[34] The Chinese translation was eventually legally published in 2004 by the leading People's Literature Publishing House, and the work is now widely available in China, despite the fact that the most detailed official government definition of obscenity, laid down in a GAPP statement from the late 1980s and used at the time to ban Lawrence's book, has not officially been superseded by any other definition. Clearly, the government's own perception of what is or is not "healthy" and what is or is not socially permissible has moved on since 1987. For the serious literary community, that is, the community underpinned by state-owned commercial publishers, literary journals, and university-based critics, there appear to be no obvious restrictions on the treatment of sex in literature. Sex features prominently in many recent works of fiction, and sex-related censorship of work with clearly articulated artistic aims is rare, especially if such work has gone through the established system of editing and publishing.

The problem with online fiction, as mentioned, is that it differs from the established system. This explains why, as we have seen, the censorship of online erotica is based not only on concerns for social harm but also on concerns for disturbance of the regular system of online publishing, a system that, after all, is still in its infancy and that is not easy to regulate. Crucial to the success of regulation of online publishing is the willingness of web editors to ensure that the content they host remains within legal, political, and moral boundaries. In the specific case of erotic fiction, the approach taken so far seems to have yielded the required results. For instance, the forty works of erotic fiction banned by GAPP in August 2007 are not easily found on PRC-based websites, at least not on publicly accessible forums for the publication of fiction.[35] Since the published version of the GAPP announcement did not include the list of forty titles and the subsequent censoring was relatively successful, it is in fact quite rare even to come across the list itself. The later blacklists from 2010 and 2011 also do not mention titles of works but only names of websites where offensive content was encountered and ordered to be removed. I assume this is done so that it makes it harder for Internet users to search for these specific titles, while at the same time "naming and shaming" the websites concerned.

However, responses from some Internet users to the 2007 announcement demonstrate mild amusement, indicating that certainly not all community members feel there is much need for censorship of erotic fiction. These amused, rather than incensed, community responses also warrant the suspicion that the censorship is not overly effective in blocking access to banned works for those who really want to get to them (although I would maintain that it has succeeded in minimizing public exposure of the works in question). One forum moderator of an online file-sharing site copied the full text of the announcement and the list of titles onto the forum and added that if any of these works were to be put on the e-book-sharing section of the site, the culprits would be severely punished! This was followed by a few smileys and more tongue-in-cheek responses from other forum contributors, including a link to a mass file download using the thunder:// protocol.[36] Presumably this particular community was able to share some or all of the blacklisted works privately or had other ways of accessing them and found the whole episode quite funny. Another playful response came from a contributor to an image-based wiki site, who created the wiki item "obscene and pornographic fiction," accompanied by a brief description of the GAPP announcement as well as an image of a scantily dressed woman printed across the pages of a book.[37]

A very clever response came from yet another forum moderator, who copied the GAPP announcement verbatim and then added two images. The first was the list of forty titles, turned into an image so as to avoid automatic keyword detection. The second was an image of ketchup being poured onto a sausage, presented in such a way as to trigger associations

国家新闻出版总署：严查40部网络淫秽色情小说（附名单）

关键词：网络 新闻 出版 色情 小说 ｜ 杂粹 ｜ 推荐：☆☆☆☆ ｜ 来源：cnbeta ｜ 收藏

中国国家新闻出版总署在其官方网站发布通知，要求各地深入开展对网上淫秽色情信息的行政执法活动。严厉查处扰乱网络出版正常秩序、危害青少年身心健康的网络淫秽色情小说。鉴于近日一些网站登载含有淫秽色情内容的小说，国家新闻出版总署下发《关于严厉查处网络淫秽色情小说的紧急通知》，要求各地按照属地管理和"谁主管、谁负责"的原则，对照通知公布的《四十部淫秽色情

⬆ Figure 3.3   Netizens' mocking response to 2007 banning of forty pornographic novels. http://www.u148.net/article/421.html.

with the act of fellatio. Although presumably offensive to some, this particular response very forcefully makes the by now familiar point that the perception of obscenity is subjective: what to some is a ketchup bottle is to others an explicitly erotic image. Moreover, there is no feasible way in which the publication of such an image might be considered illegal, even when it is juxtaposed with the official GAPP announcement and is clearly ridiculing the stated government policy. Other contributors to the forum were equally amused and left equally playful messages, such as, "Wow, I did not know there were so many novels like that out there," or "What an arduous task for the comrades at GAPP to have to read all those novels," and so on. Some even mentioned which novels on the list they had read and which were their favorites.[38]

Flying Gourd: Legal Erotic Fiction

A salient aspect of the blacklists of obscene and pornographic fiction published at regular intervals by GAPP in 2010 and 2011 is the fact that a small number of websites constantly feature in the top five of transgressors. Clearly these sites continually publish transgressive work, pushing the boundaries of what is permissible (to the authorities) or acceptable (to its readers) and taking the risk of occasionally having to remove content that went too far. One of these sites is the previously mentioned Flying Gourd, a medium-size fiction site operating the Starting Point business model and based in Beijing. I visited the site a number of times in 2011 and again in 2013. I also contacted the site owners, a man and woman in their twenties, and met with them over a meal in Beijing, gaining some insight into their business model and their self-perception.

The Flying Gourd front page does not make it look much different from other fiction sites. The main genre categories are also similar to those of other sites and include fantasy, martial arts, romance/urban, youth/campus, BL/fan fiction, historical fiction, and horror fiction. Like Starting Point and other sites, Flying Gourd also has a separate women's section (http://www.feilu.cc), designed with a predominantly pink color scheme. When I first visited the site in 2011, I noticed that there was little distinctive advertising on the main page, but once I followed links to individual novels, the texts tended to be surrounded by ads for Viagra, lingerie, and sex toys, as well as for online adventure games that appeared to feature erotic images. During a second visit in September 2013, there was less, and less explicit, advertising to be seen.

Also like Starting Point, access to the site's VIP works is charged at three fen per thousand words. The site has a certain number of contracted authors and also offers unfamiliar authors the opportunity to serialize their writing. Authors who send in regular installments and manage to cultivate a sizable readership, as well as gain positive comments ("likes") from readers, can make their way up the rank tables, which may result in their being offered a contract.[39] Typically, popular novels on the site will offer around a hundred chapters for free and then switch to VIP mode, a process referred to as *shangjia* ("getting on the perch"). Sometimes novels are serialized for free on more than one site at the same time, but once they become VIP works with one site, the authors are contractually

⬆ Figure 3.4   Main page of Flying Gourd website. http://b.faloo.com.

obliged to discontinue submitting elsewhere. For instance, I found one example of a partial publication of one of Flying Gourd's most popular works, *Mishang xifu* (*Infatuated with the Wife*), on a different site, with an announcement that serialization had been stopped because the work was now under contract with Flying Gourd, referring readers to that site for the latest updates.[40]

In 2011, the site derived its income from four sources: VIP subscriptions, advertising, republication of site content on a mobile (WAP) reading site provided by Baidu, and acting as agent for their authors in arranging print publications. In 2013, the WAP site was no longer available and instead Flying Gourd had launched a reading app for smartphones and tablets containing a small selection of its most popular publications. During our meeting, the site owners claimed that their operation was profitable and provided employment for ten people. They readily admitted to much of their content being "somewhat erotic" (*you dianr qingse*), and they assumed that official requests they received for removing certain content were more likely to be the result of specific reader complaints than of any general policy, since they did not feel that the passages singled out for deletion were necessarily very different from others in the same style. They tended to describe that style with the adjective *aimei* (ambiguous, shady) and with the genre indicator "YY," referred to in the previous section. They emphasized that, as editors, they always strived to ensure that the works they published were beyond legal reproach. As we shall see, later in 2011 they felt compelled to intervene forcefully in order to prevent two authors from straying too far into pornographic territory.

Although there is far too much content on the site to venture a guess as to how much of it is erotic in nature, it is certainly not difficult to find erotic texts, for instance by looking specifically at those that have references to women in the title or that employ vocabulary traditionally associated with the erotic tradition, words like *xiang* (fragrant), *yan* (beautiful, romantic), and so on. None of the works I have seen are consistently erotic in every chapter. Most become explicit only after a few chapters and return to sexual themes every three to five chapters while also employing familiar themes from other genres (especially time travel). This may depend in part on the speed with which the authors update their work. If they post several chapters a day, which is not unusual, they might limit the erotic chapters to one a day, as a kind of regular dosage for readers to get used to and look forward to. Works set in present-day times often feature the seedy world of crime and official corruption, signaled by the high proportion of novels with the word *guanchang* (officialdom) in the title. Based solely on textual evidence taken from the fiction as well as the many paratexts often attached to these works, it seems that depictions of official corruption are not in any way problematic, but descriptions of sexual activity require the application of specific censorship-avoidance techniques, similar to those that have been observed in the study of online political discourse.[41]

The most common way of avoiding drawing attention from censors to erotic work is by disguising sensitive keywords that might trigger alerts. This is commonly done either by writing such words in pinyin or by inserting a symbol, such as an asterisk, in between the two characters that make up a compound. For instance, toward the end of chapter 6 of the novel *Guanchang nü jiaoshi* (*A Female Teacher in the World of Officialdom*), the word *charu* (to enter, to penetrate) is written as 插＊入, whereas in a later version of the same text (by then it has become chapter 7) it is written in pinyin.[42] References to certain body parts, for instance breasts, are also rarely encountered in normal writing, and the same applies to words such as *yuwang* (sexual desire) and *gaochao* (orgasm). These word games are necessitated by keyword-screening software built into the website system, most likely installed by the site editors themselves as part of their efforts to avoid illegal content being uploaded. What this means is that when authors upload their texts, certain sensitive words are automatically refused by the system. Yet in addition to this, the moderators of the site also carry out their own checks and make changes where they deem them necessary.

Either the software or the editors also at times seem to refuse the repetition of certain otherwise innocuous words within too limited a space. For instance, in the same chapter of *A Female Teacher* the word *ruan* (soft) appears twice in one sentence, both times in pinyin. Occasionally this leads to funny results, as in chapter 20 of the novel *Aishang jipin MM* (*In Love with Top-Quality Girls*), where one of the protagonists is cooking chicken for dinner, and the word *ji*, for "chicken" (which can also mean "penis" or "prostitute"), is rendered in pinyin three times in the space of three sentences, making it appear like a transgressive term even though it is not. Similar examples can be found elsewhere on the site and are clearly intentional, that is, once authors realize that certain characters cannot be uploaded without turning them into pinyin, they start using them on purpose in innocuous contexts as a form of humor. This, again, is similar to the kind of phenomena observed by other scholars in the context of political discourse.[43]

Another common mechanism employed to avoid overly graphic writing is to describe sexual activity with recourse to a flowery linguistic register, some of which goes back to language used in traditional erotic fiction, or by employing euphemisms. The following passage, from chapter 18 of *In Love with Top-Quality Girls*, purposefully translated very literally, gives a good impression of the kind of writing that produces the erotic character of these works:

Yang Dong immediately stood up straight on the bed. Liu Li slowly crawled in front of Yang Dong, kneeling by his body, respectfully kneeling with both knees on the bed while she kept her pitch-black eyes fixed on the man. Yang Dong looked down at Liu Li: her fragrant hair, spread out over her snow-white, smooth, jadelike back, looked very sexy. Yang Dong's lower body instantly felt unbearable, so he instantly issued a command to Liu Li, gently using one

hand to press the woman's jadelike head against his own crotch. . . . Liu Li was
startled for a moment, perhaps because that spot of his was too much of a
"magnificent sight" for her. Gently she showed the man her delicate pretty
face, and with an expression of deep emotion she looked at the man. At this
moment, her arched eyebrows, her bright eyes, her thin, high nose, and her
bright red lips all seemed extremely seductive.[44]

Naturally this is clumsy and repetitive writing, but there is more to be
said in this case. *In Love with Top-Quality Girls* is one of two novels that
appear to have gotten the Flying Gourd website into trouble in June 2011.
On June 8 the main editor submitted a post to the site's discussion forum
under the title "Lühua wangzhan huanjing, shuli jiankang xingxiang"
(Create a Green Website Environment and Foster a Healthy Image).[45] He
indicated that two of their regular VIP authors, which they themselves
had cultivated (*peiyang*), had started to include large amounts of "harmful content" (*bu liang neirong*) into their works, thereby showing their
"disrespect" toward their readership, their "lack of responsibility" toward
the site, and their own "betrayal" of their original intentions as writers.
In response, he announced, the website would launch a long-term cen-
sorship/control (*jiancha*) drive. He expressed the hope that all authors
would "stick to the moral bottom line" (*jianshou daode dixian*) and act as
"writers with a sense of social responsibility." As is clear from some of the
terms, this announcement used the register of official language, which is
normally rarely encountered on the site. The shift in register should, in
my interpretation, have alerted readers to the fact that the editor was not
acting on his own initiative. In other words, he was employing a form of
irony not to be humorous but to underline the seriousness of the situation. Two writers and works were singled out as the offenders. Both were
fined part of their wages as VIP authors and instructed to rewrite the
offensive passages within seventy-two hours.

One of the two works, titled *Yünü tianwang zai dushi* (*The King of
Copulation in the City*), was not revised but taken off the site, although a
full version of it remained available on Flying Gourd's Baidu-based mobile phone reading site (presumably Baidu, as a major Internet portal,
was under less pressure from censors). With regard to its publication on
the Flying Gourd site, the author wrote a formal self-criticism that was
published on the site's discussion forum. The other censored work was

In Love with Top-Quality Girls. Its author, who goes by the pseudonym Silent Raccoon Dog (Chenmo de Li), responded very differently and immediately set to work on the revisions, even posting a cheerful, tongue-in-cheek paratext to the area reserved for authors' comments on their own work, which read,

> Brother Raccoon is embarrassed to inform everybody that the uncle from the Internet police has detected a few of my chapters that were written too graphically [*lugu*]. Some chapters are now banned, so you might not be able to read them. Don't be angry with me, okay? I have started rewriting tonight, and I will do my very best to make sure that the ban is lifted as soon as possible.[46]

The next day he published another announcement informing his readers that all banned chapters had been revised. Moreover, he painstakingly indicated in the table of contents which chapters had been revised. At the time, 251 chapters of the novel had been published, and according to the new table of contents, 50 of those were revised. In September 2013, the novel had reached chapter 447. The chapter from which I cited a passage in the preceding was among the ones that were revised, that is, what I cited was the revised text, adjusted to comply with censorship requirements. Although I do not have access to the earlier, unrevised text, I do have a saved version of one chapter of the other novel that was banned, which can provide some indication as to what it is that is considered to cross the line in these cases. The chapter in question employs the various censorship-avoidance mechanisms previously referred to, but it is indeed somewhat more graphic (although still euphemistic) in its description of intercourse, ejaculation, and sexual organs. Referring back to the text of Article 367 of the Chinese constitution, it would seem that the main test of obscenity now revolves around an interpretation of the level of explicitness (*lugu*) of the language employed. As long as a specific register of description is avoided, fiction describing sexual activity is now legal, even if it lays no obvious claims to any artistic value.[47]

For a range of reasons, including editorial pressure, the threat of censorship, or comments from readers, the authors of the novels on Flying Gourd carry out frequent retrospective revisions to chapters already published while at the same time adding new chapters as well as new paratexts. As the case of Silent Raccoon Dog shows, these practices of

constant revision can be presented in a playful way that shows the author deriving pleasure from playing around with the text in order to stay
above the bottom line, and of course avoid further deductions from his
fees. The result is that, to some extent, the fiction on Flying Gourd represents a system of writing that is in flux, with different versions of texts
facing readers depending on when they accessed them as authors adapt
to subtle changes in regulation policies or moral standards and continue
to explore mechanisms allowing them to make some modest profits while
writing the kind of literature they want to write. This adaptive system of
borderline pornography can also be seen to exercise agency by making
use of new opportunities to push the system of regulation into the desired
direction. Flying Gourd did this by making its reading app for smartphones and tablets available through the iTunes App Store, stipulating
that it should be downloaded only by those over the age of seventeen,
thereby self-imposing an age restriction that many in China would prefer
to become official.[48] As we have seen in the previous chapter in the case
of Han Han, the use of apps to distribute literary publications can bring
about innovations otherwise hard to achieve within the established publishing system. The next section, dealing with the avant-garde collective
operating under the name Black and Blue, provides further examples of
the creative use of reading apps for entirely different literary purposes.

Black and Blue

Two things are most impressive about Black and Blue. First, the site has
been around since 2003, operating independently without commercial support and run by roughly the same group of people throughout.
Second is the consistency with which it has brought out new work on a
regular basis. Its webzine, also called *Black and Blue*, has been coming
out once a month since January 2003, never missing a month, making
it one of the longest-surviving and most frequently published unofficial
literary journals in the PRC.[49] Consistency is also what characterizes the
aesthetic vision of the Black and Blue collective, as will become clear. By
ending this chapter with a discussion of this site, I hope to underline the
variety of fiction available online in the PRC, which sometimes goes un-
noticed amid the overwhelming commercial success of the genre fiction
sites. At the same time, as we shall see, Black and Blue forms the perfect

contrast with the work discussed in previous sections, since one of its aims is exactly to ensure that writing about even the most base subject matter possesses redeeming artistic quality. Before going into the style and content of the writings, however, I shall provide a brief description of the history of Black and Blue, and a description of the site as I observed it during visits in 2011 and 2013.[50]

The first thing appearing on-screen when typing in the URL of the Black and Blue site is the word "Heilan" in big black font, with underneath it in small letters the words (in English) "since 1991." As explained in a brief historical overview provided on the site itself,[51] Black and Blue was founded in Jiangsu by Chen Wei (b. 1973) and his classmate Shen Liming. What exactly they founded is not clear, but presumably it was a literary group or society, or perhaps merely the idea for one. By 1995, Chen Wei, who remains the central figure of the group to this day, was in Nanjing, where he teamed up with Wu Haiyan (b. 1975) and Gu Yaofeng (b. 1975), both of whom also continue to be actively involved in the group. In 1996 they came out with an unofficial printed journal called *Black and Blue*. As documented by Maghiel van Crevel, who holds the first issue of the paper journal in his unique collection of unofficial Chinese literary journals at Leiden University, the journal presented itself with the slogan "Gathering Place for Chinese People-Who-Write Born After 1970" (*1970 nian yihou chusheng de Zhongguo xiezuoren jujidi*).[52] In the history provided on the current website, as well as in other sources, Chen Wei is generally credited with having been the first person to propose the designation "post-70" (*70 hou*) as an indication of a distinctive generation of Chinese writers. Later that same year (June 1996), again according to the site's own history, the printed journal was ordered to discontinue publication (*bei leling tingkan*). It is not clear who issued that order and for what reason. In 2001, a website called Black and Blue briefly went online and then disappeared again. It was duly captured by the IAWM, but with no content. The official launch of the site as it exists now took place in the spring of 2002. Its distinctive sixteen-point manifesto, about which more presently, was first captured by the IAWM in February 2003 and has not changed since.[53]

As with most literary websites, the backbone of the Black and Blue site is its forum page. As usual, the forums can be read by anyone, but only registered members of the site can start new threads or leave comments.

The current version of the site has two sets of forums, the first devoted to different genres (such as fiction, poetry, essay, and criticism) and the second set containing subforums devoted to specific authors from the group. The second set also has a forum devoted to "stream of consciousness" (*yishiliu*), while the first group of forums, in true avant-garde tradition, has a forum especially devoted to abusive criticism (*ma*), where established authors in the official system are often their targets of critique.[54]

In September 2013 the number of members stood at just under thirty-six thousand. Although it is difficult to estimate what proportion of the members are active, there appear to be some new submissions of fiction and poetry on a daily basis, and contributors are not limited to those directly involved in moderating the forums. Compared with most forums discussed previously, Black and Blue attracts relatively little general chatter and social interaction. Its interest is clearly in writing as a skill, and the editors encourage criticism that is technical in nature, referring to the writing itself rather than to plot development or context. On Black and Blue one will find no online diaries, no meandering, interactive chronicles, and no serialized long fiction with lots of paratexts. In this aspect, Black and Blue resembles more the kind of online creative writing communities that are common in English-speaking countries (about which more in chapter 4). The group's strong commitment to creative writing as an autonomous art form is also clear from the title of their manifesto ("Fiction Existing as a Thing-in-itself" [*Zuowei benti cunzai de xiaoshuo*]) and appears to be directly influenced by the French *nouveau roman*. Their motto, which displays on-screen immediately after entering the site, cites a famous line by Jean Ricardou (b. 1932): "A novel is no longer the writing of adventures but the adventure of writing" (*Xiaoshuo bu zai shi xushu yi chang maoxian er shi yi chang xushu de maoxian*). It should be noted, however, that the group's stated emphasis is not on the novel as such but on shorter fiction (*duanpian* and *zhongpian*).

Every single month for the past decade, the moderators of the Black and Blue forums have selected the best works on their forums and put them together in a webzine. When I first visited the site in 2011, the one hundredth issue of the webzine had just appeared. In a gesture reminiscent of the visual presentation of online writing as an open book or as lineated paper, which we saw in chapter 1, the *Black and Blue* webzine used to present itself on-screen as an image of an actual magazine, creating

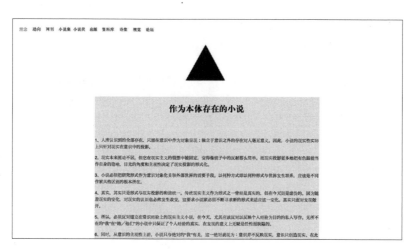

⬆ Figure 3.5 Black and Blue main page and manifesto. http://www.heilan.com/ main.htm.

the impression that the publication also existed in print, but this was not the case. Originally, readers could read the webzine online or go to the forums to download the whole issue. The latter option, however, required payment in "prestige points" (*weiwang*), which members can collect by being active on the site. Since January 2013, new monthly issues of the webzine can be downloaded for free from the e-reader site, http://www. duokan.com, for reading on Kindles or on reading apps for iPhone and Android systems.[55] Unfortunately past issues can now no longer be read online, although they are still downloadable from the forums.

In addition to the webzine, Black and Blue occasionally puts together collections of short fiction or poetry by individual authors, some of which are downloadable. It also occasionally publishes fiction collections in print, as a separate series called Heilan wencong (Black and Blue Series). The books come out irregularly, and the series is described on the website as focusing on short stories and novellas, emphasizing fiction that is innovative on the level of art-in-itself (*zai yishu benti fangmian de chuangxin*). Finally, with again an impressive display of consistency, the group has since 2003 given out the Black and Blue Fiction Award, initially as a quarterly prize for the author of the best story on the site, more recently as a biannual prize for an author's oeuvre on the site, with some oeuvres having been built up over the better part of a decade. All

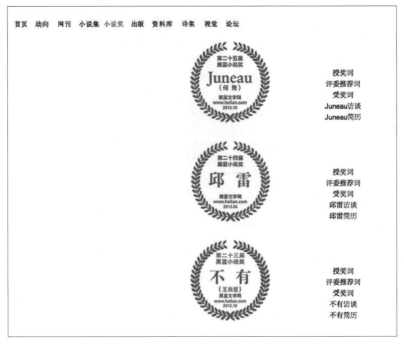

🔼 **Figure 3.6**   Main page for the Black and Blue Fiction Award. http://www.heilan .com/prize.htm.

awards are announced on the website in the same format, with an official citation, copies of the jury reports, an acceptance text by the winner, the winner's CV, an interview with the winner, and links to the prize-winning work. Jury members rotate over time and usually include the previous award's winner. A cash prize is usually given, in some cases using money collected from the group's core members.[56] In short, Black and Blue is a microcosm of the literary field. It is relatively independent from commercial and political structures, and it revolves almost entirely around the accumulation of "symbolic capital." It involves authors, critics, editors, and readers, all of whom subscribe to an autonomous aesthetic whereby fiction is a "thing-in-itself" that requires no external justification. The following points from the group's manifesto best capture how it positions itself vis-à-vis other literary views or trends:

> 8. To emphasize the thing-in-itself means to let fiction return to itself and become itself. Only in this way can fiction change from telling stories to the art

of storytelling. Just as painting is made up of colors and lines, fiction should first and foremost concern narration and language.

9. Fiction is opposed to its subject matter and thematic meaning belonging to a specific era. Fiction opposes Cultural Revolution fiction, rusticated youth fiction, reform fiction, and other such fiction about history that falls outside the "history of fiction." Fiction opposes private fiction that "presents lifestyles." Fiction that is about being "cool," being an "angry youth," about the "body," or "against society" has significance only for establishing the authors' personal image.

10. Fiction opposes morality, and fiction opposes the morals of immorality.

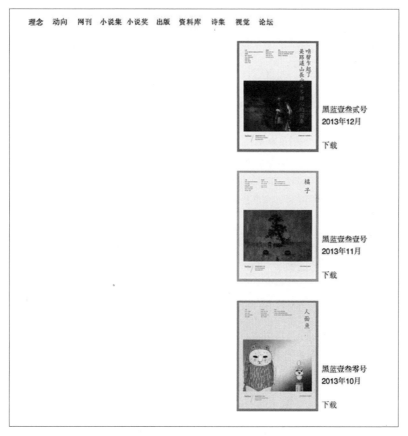

⬆ **Figure 3.7** Black and Blue monthly downloadable e-zines. http://www.heilan.com/periodical_2013.htm.

11. Fiction considers subject matter and theme merely as a component. Only if fiction uses them strictly as material can it possess a naked body.

12. In fiction, a good story is but a pretty outer garment.[57]

The group seems dedicated to maintaining its niche on the Chinese Internet and is making no obvious attempts to become more widely known, other than having updated the method of distributing its free webzine by making it downloadable onto mobile devices. As we shall see, however, this new technology has also enabled it to employ new software features that fit well with its overall aesthetic aims.

The Autonomous Aesthetic and Toilets

In one of the few articles about Black and Blue that can be found in established academic or literary journals in China, a two-page assessment of the group by Tian Er written for *Shanxi wenxue* in 2007, the verdict on their efforts is dismissive. Tian shows himself wary of groups claiming to be "avant-garde," accusing them of posturing. He then describes his brief experience of reading one of the books in the Black and Blue Series, judging that the authors might be good at refined descriptions of objects, magnifying every detail, but that they "cannot create characters" (*xiebuchu renwu*). Then, in the best tradition of abusive criticism, he launches into an extended denigrating metaphor to characterize the group.

> This is a basic fact these days: people without basic skills, lacking basic general knowledge about fiction writing, are calling themselves avant-garde. Avant-garde has become a fig leaf. When you call yourself avant-garde, it means you can pee and poo wherever you want, treating literature as the world's largest toilet. . . . The avant-garde are those who go in front and find new ways. . . . The avant-garde ought to guide everyone onto the great golden road. Otherwise anyone could point at a stinking latrine pit, say, "That's the way to go," and then claim their right to being avant-garde.[58]

Nothing could be further from Black and Blue's literary ideals than this opinion, which postulates the creation of memorable characters as the be-all and end-all of good fiction and considers it the task of the writer to guide others onto the right path. The critic's suggestion that the group is using the "avant-garde" label only to attract attention and gain easy success has proved to be a misjudgment. I can think of few groups in modern Chinese literature that have been satisfied as long with as little public exposure.

The toilet metaphor, however, may serve as a useful entry point into a characteristic short story, found in the opening pages of the July 2013 issue of the *Black and Blue* monthly online magazine. The author, to whose work the magazine dedicated a special issue in June 2013, goes by the pseudonym Lexiaozhu, written in Chinese characters to sign his stories and in pinyin when used as his ID for contributions to the website. The story in question is titled "Lin Xiaohe ruce" (Lin Xiaohe Visits the Toilet). It is a well-written, carefully narrated coming-of-age story featuring a male protagonist, Lin Xiaohe, who grows up in a poor rural community and eventually makes it to the university. Toward the end, the story takes a romantic turn when Lin and a girl from the same village, who also attends the university, travel back to their village by train. She falls asleep on his shoulder, and after arrival they stroll together through the rustic scenery and promise to travel back to school together after the holidays.

The narrative is focused on the inner life of the precocious protagonist, recounted in the third person, as well as on detailed descriptions of his surroundings. What makes the story different from most romantic countryside idylls, however, is the fact that the protagonist's musings and observations, as well as the narrator's description of his progression in life, are dominated by meticulous attention to toilets and the act of defecation. Starting from the various methods that Lin Xiaohe develops as a child to master the technique of wiping his bottom with clumps of earth in the public latrine, to his development of a dislike for the latrine and experiments with defecating in other places, to his observations of his first encounters with toilet paper, running water, and toilet seats, as he moves on in the world, the narration continually provides lavish descriptive detail while managing to maintain a refined narrative style.

The same theme pervades the treatment of Lin Xiaohe's romance with the girl Wang Yanan, whose father's job it was to collect human waste from the latrines to be used as manure. In the idyllic closing scene, Lin Xiaohe and Wang Yanan walk together from the train station to the village:

> After getting off the train, Lin Xiaohe and Wang Yanan walked home together.
> Along the way they had to climb a hill. On the slope of the hill, Lin Xiaohe said

to Wang Yanan that he needed to go to the toilet. Wang Yanan said, "Why don't you go over there?" and pointed to a place behind a small ridge. Lin Xiaohe happily went to the toilet there. The earth of his hometown still had exactly the right firmness. Then he helped Wang Yanan to carry her bag up the hill, and when they said good-bye, Wang Yanan said, "Let's travel together again when school starts." Lin Xiaohe replied, "Absolutely!"[59]

The author's aim in this story is clearly to apply a nostalgic mode of writing about a rural childhood to subject matter undeniably very important to life in the chosen setting yet typically either ignored or employed in other narratives to create images of squalor. In this story, however, despite the baseness of the theme, the overall idyllic sentiment created by the story is maintained, in the best tradition of writing about the native soil, with "soil" taking on a felicitous double meaning in this case. In other words, the story is, more than anything else, an exercise in writing technique, very much in line with the aesthetic program of the Black and Blue group.

Passages from other contributions to the same issue of the magazine may serve to underscore this point. In "Xugou fuyinshu" (The Gospel of Fabrication) by the author "shep," one of the most frequent winners of the Black and Blue Fiction Award, the protagonist is an author who at some point comes to the realization that he has never written fiction about human excretion. This is then followed by a long consideration of how one might write "excretion fiction" (*paixie xiaoshuo*) and ends with a question: when and why did human beings stop publicly exposing their own filth? Here, the Chinese word for "filth" (*huiwu*) partially overlaps with the common term for obscenity (*yinhui*).[60] Another story, written by an author using the pseudonym "cjdxc" and titled "Shui yao dixialai le" (The Water Will Drip Down), includes a description of a discussion among some young, literary-minded intellectuals about the autonomous meaning, independent of the actual object of reference, of the word "horse piss" (*maniao*).[61] Finally, in a translated essay about the photographic art of Joanna Piotrowska, included toward the end of the issue, the text emphasizes that the pictures portraying individuals of different ages and gender in intimate positions are not intended to display incest, homosexuality, or promiscuity, nor are they aimed at promoting "lust of the mind," using the exact same term (*yiyin*) referred to previously in the context of crowd-pleasing popular fiction.[62]

Text and Commentary for Downloading

The emphasis that the Black and Blue group places on technique is also reflected in its penchant for textual criticism. As mentioned, comments on stories posted on the site's forums often attract detailed critique. This practice has now been incorporated in an innovative way into the latest issues of the group's magazine. Because these are now published on an e-book seller's website for downloading straight into e-reader apps on smartphones or tablets (including Kindles), the editors have started to use the "comments" function available on most e-readers to add textual criticism to the magazine contents, typically with two editors each providing separate commentary on each story, and this commentary is then made part of the file that readers download. In other words, the editorial commentary comes with the text and is part of the text, recognizable by small colored signs that the reader can click on to view the commentary. Readers can also add their own commentary and sync it across their devices, but it is only the editors' commentary that is shared with all readers.

The editors' commentary at times consists of normal corrections (of wrong characters, for instance), that is, the kind of intervention that readers normally would not see. However, the editors also add appraisals and interpretive commentary of their own, often highlighting what they consider to be particularly good or particularly infelicitous phrasings or passages. Moreover, in the issue under review here, they have applied the same principle to review an excerpt of famous writer Yu Hua's new novel *The Seventh Day*, which came out earlier in 2013.[63] The commentary (*pizhu*) by two members of the group, using the IDs "Black Talent" (Hei Tiancai) and "X," respectively, focuses on Yu Hua's technique of writing and mercilessly lays bare passages where they believe he has been "lazy" or just sloppy, as well as those parts where he falls back on gratuitous social or political satire (which they refer to as "cheap and consumerist writing"). They are most critical of sentences where Yu's choice of words shows lack of precision, with "X" commenting at one point, "Such methods of expression easily appear in a style of writing that is routine [*shulian*] and careless [*daerhuazhi*]. It is an arrogant method of expression that lacks consideration."[64]

By introducing the very traditional Chinese literary skill of providing commentary on other people's texts and including the commentary in a published edition, the Black and Blue group has found an original way of applying the latest e-reading technologies for aesthetic purposes while at the same time highlighting its consistent stance on the importance of writing technique. This is yet another example of how Chinese online literary communities achieve innovation while adhering to the basic paradigm of linearity.

Coming back to the story of Lin Xiaohe, the use of the classical expression *ruce* (to visit the toilet) in the title also calls to mind a much earlier discussion, of which the author Lexiaozhu may or may not have been aware. In 1922, the young poet Kang Baiqing published a vernacular poem featuring a line about "visiting the toilet first thing in the morning." This drew a furious reaction by the critic Liang Shiqiu and led to a protracted public debate about the appropriateness of using "ugly language" (*chou de ziju*) in poetry.[65] By referring back in its title, whether intentionally or not, to this debate about words and their aesthetic value, Lexiaozhu's story underlines the Black and Blue group stance, evident also from the other passages mentioned, that literature should be judged by its technical achievement and that no word or topic can ever be intrinsically ugly or obscene. This, in turn, brings to mind Article 367 of the Chinese constitution and the exceptional status it awards to "serious" artistic work. Sure enough, as far as I am aware, none of the sometimes very explicit language on Black and Blue has ever been mistaken for obscenity, and keyword filters do not appear to be active on this site. There is no register of language that needs to be avoided, nor is there any playful use of pinyin or other mechanisms to fool keyword filters.[66] The contrast between the different types of fiction and different literary communities presented in this chapter highlights the variety and vitality of Chinese Internet literature, even in the field of fiction, which is traditionally dominated by print publication and the official literary system. It also shows how some very different aesthetic programs share commonalities both in terms of experimentation with new technologies and applications and in terms of exploring and maintaining suitable niches within the Chinese literary world. In the next and final chapter, the discussion turns from fiction to poetry, where we will encounter experimentation, innovation, and transgression on an even wider scale.

FOUR

Online Poetry in and out of China, in Chinese, or with Chinese

➡ **IF GENRE FICTION HAS BEEN** the most successful type of Chinese Internet literature in economic terms, poetry has outperformed all other modes of online writing in terms of variety, experimentation, and critical acclaim. In Chinese Internet poetry we see a range of aesthetic programs being developed, from provocative avant-garde and moral transgression to reappropriation of the social functions of classical poetry. There is also lively interaction between poets working inside and those outside the PRC, while Chinese written characters can also be seen to be incorporated into the work of non-Chinese electronic poets, continuing a modernist tradition that dates back at least to Ezra Pound.[1] With this final chapter, then, this book's focus on the PRC literary system gradually gives way to a discussion of a wider range of writings belonging to the realm of sinophone (or sinographic) literature.[2]

This chapter is divided into three parts. The first deals with online Chinese poetry communities as they have developed both inside and outside China. Similar to the approach I used in chapter 1, part of the analysis in this part consists of descriptive accounts of two separate visits to the same site, the first in 2004 and the second in 2012–2013. Also in this part I compare the practices of Chinese communities with those typically encountered on similar English-language websites, emphasizing the different social functions that online poetry writing appears to have in different literary cultures. The second part continues a line of investigation commenced in chapter 3, focusing especially on ways in which transgressive writing pushes the boundaries of what is or is not considered respectable or legal in the PRC context. Specifically, I compare the gradual canonization of the "Lower Body" (Xiabanshen) group of avant-garde poets, known for their direct engagement with sex in poetry, with the gradual expulsion from the realm of literature of the work of the online poet Datui ("Thigh"). Finally, in the third and longest part of the chapter, I return to questions of formal innovativeness in Internet literature, focusing on online experiments with visual or concrete poetry involving the use of Chinese characters, as carried out by both Chinese and non-Chinese poets. Much of the discussion is devoted to the unique early experiments from the 1990s by the sinophone poet and sound artist Dajuin Yao (Yao Dajun), whose by now almost classic achievements in the genre no longer survive on the live web. I also discuss poetic works by John Cayley and Jonathan Stalling, as well as Chinese translations by Shuen-shing Lee (Li Shunxing) of work by the acclaimed online poet Jim Andrews.

The experimental work discussed in the final part of this chapter can be fully experienced only online. It consists of words that move and change shape, it contains recorded sound, and it features the kind of user interaction that ensures that every "reading" of the works leads to the creation of a new text on-screen. It is hard to quote from such works, or do them justice in writing, nor can they be easily captured in images or screenshots. While I shall do my best to describe the experience of viewing these works, readers of this book are encouraged to follow the links to the actual online versions.

Poetry Forums and Poemlife

Poetry forums (*shige luntan*) are interactive message boards dedicated to reading, writing, and discussing poetry. Such forums exist on websites all around the world, but it is fair to say that in China, where state regulation makes independent niche publishing difficult and where poetry continues to enjoy high cultural standing and relatively strong popularity, these online forums are exceptionally important. Many feel that online forums have taken over the role previously played by underground (*dixia*) and unofficial (*minjian* or *fei guanfang*) print publications, a role succinctly summarized as follows by Maghiel van Crevel in his book-length study of contemporary Chinese poetry:

> The unofficial scene lies at the core of a lively poetry climate that is instru-
> mental for the development of individual poets and the poetry landscape as
> a whole. This is in evidence in literary historiography as well as in poetry's
> general impact, domestic and international.[3]

In a recent interview, the poet and scholar Hu Xudong suggests that on-line forums have also taken over the social function of poetry. Hu says,

> The 1980s was the heyday of modern poetry in China. Poetry was like pop
> culture then—it played the role karaoke has today. Twenty years ago there
> was still no such thing as karaoke, and every small city or town would have
> a place where people would get together after dinner and read poetry. It was
> such an everyday thing, so lively. Every night was like a mini-poetry carnival.
> But now, only twenty years later, and especially in these last few years, you
> hardly ever see this anymore.
>
> These days we have online communities. Every creative group has its own
> online communities—art, film, literature—but the most obvious is in the area
> of poetry, where the internet has had the biggest impact on the community's
> development.[4]

Hu also points out one clear difference between the unofficial communities of old and those currently active online, namely the lack of geographical proximity:

> This community isn't going to be like those of twenty years ago, where a
> group of people gather together in the one city—in a café, or in a university—
> it might be one person in the North of China, another in the South, another
> might be studying overseas. They'll use a particular forum or internet group
> to make this tiny poetry community.[5]

Hu's comments speak to the social aspect of poetry, which is very prominent in the Chinese tradition. Traditionally in China, the composition of poetry took place in the context of social occasions, poetry parties, competitions, and the like.[6] Even in the modern period, although poets moved toward more unconventional uses of language and imagery, the desire to belong to a community and to have one's work understood continued to exist and worked against the spread of excessively involutionary poetics.[7] This convention adds another reason for the popularity of online poetry forums and also lays the basis for our understanding of the cultural differences between Chinese-language and English-language online poetry communities to be explored later in this section.

Compared with the pre-Internet situation in the Chinese poetry world, online forums have brought about at least two important breakthroughs. First, referring back to the comments by Van Crevel and Hu Xudong, online portals have enabled the unofficial scene to bridge the gap between its social activities and its publishing activities. Online, discussion and publication go hand in hand. A good example is the Shi Shenghuo (Poemlife, http://www.poemlife.com) website. Poemlife was founded in 2000 and claims to have been the first poetry site in China with its own domain name and server.[8] The site is registered in Shenzhen, but its official approval was issued by authorities in Hunan. It claims that its contributors come from "all over the world."

Its main forum, simply called Poetry Forum (Shige luntan), describes itself as devoted to "poetry writing and communication" (*shige xiezuo yu jiaoliu*). The term *jiaoliu* has a clear connotation of social interaction and is encountered frequently in the Chinese context, as opposed to similar sites in the United Kingdom and the United States, where the forums are often identified as being devoted to detailed critique of one another's work. For instance, the main forum of the U.K.-based Poetry Forum describes its purpose as "in depth critique," and its site rules add the following information:

> In the critique forum, please specify what kind of critique you are after (for example: serious critique, light critique, about the structure, choice of words, etc.), because it makes it easier for not only you but for the people who reply to your thread. Please only post material here if you feel able to bear peoples [*sic*] frank and honest opinions. DO NOT post here if you are likely to get upset at people finding fault with your writing.[9]

The U.K. forum's statements represent the ethos of creative writing programs and their practices. The forum clearly emphasizes participants' belief that poetry writing is a difficult skill that requires serious commitment and training, and that it should rise above the level of socializing niceties.

Even more typical in this regard is the poetry site Everypoet (http:// www.everypoet.com), which, although registered in Sweden, caters largely to a U.S. audience.[10] Everypoet's most popular resource is the "Poetry Free-for-all" (hereafter PFFA, http://www.everypoet.org), a collection of online forums described on its entry page as "the preeminent interactive poetry community for informed, constructive criticism of your poems." The site has strict rules about the number of posts each member is allowed to upload each day (not more than one poem per day, and for each uploaded poem three constructive critiques of other members' poems must be submitted). Its forums are divided on the basis of the perceived skill level of the contributors and the harshness of critique that can be expected. Its guidelines hammer home the idea that the site is to be seen as an online poetry workshop, not as a social network, as can be seen from these rules:

2. PFFA is not a showcase and it is not a free critique service. It is a poetry workshop. That means your main goal for being here is to improve your work and your critical skills. If that's what you're looking for, you've found it. However, if all you're looking for is a place to share your work, you haven't. Neither of us will be happy campers in that case, and you should go elsewhere.

3. Because PFFA is a workshop that respects the best uses of the English language, not a chatroom, we expect all members, whether poets or critics, to use correct grammar, spelling, punctuation, and syntax in all posts—poems, critiques, and posts alike. Be prepared to find sloppy, borderline-illiterate posts deleted.

(Artistic licence will, of course, be respected. However, don't be surprised if we need convincing that the licence you've taken is, indeed, artistic.)

. . .

5. You're here, we assume, to receive constructive comments to help you improve your work. NOTE: "Constructive" does not necessarily mean complimentary, flattering, or nice like your mom would be; it can also mean negative or even harsh. (Please note also that you are not "entitled" to receive critique or to dictate what kind you will or won't accept just because you post here; no

comment at all can often be the best constructive criticism you'll get.) That is the nature of a workshop—you can't improve if you're just told that you're a good little poet. *At PFFA it's all about the poem, not the poet.* If you can't handle negative criticism, don't post your work here. We mean it.

(While we're on the subject, "criticism" is much more than telling someone their poem "flows" well. If you're unsure of where to begin as a critic, never fear: this thread will get you started.)[11]

This propensity for merciless textual criticism is much less strongly emphasized on modern poetry forums in China, where critique tends to be brief and friendly, or expressed in general terms ("like" or "dislike"), and is often interspersed with socializing comments. A random but representative recent example is a group of thirteen poems posted on the Poemlife forum on September 16, 2011, by the poet Anhuishama, who is an active contributor. The poet followed the post containing the poems with a post stating, "Let's all criticize and communicate!" (*Dajia duo piping! Duo jiaoliu!*), clearly linking criticism and socializing. The comments from readers are limited, however, to short phrases such as "interesting," "noted," or "I like your poems," and each of them is duly followed by a reply from Anhuishama thanking the reader and encouraging them to "communicate more."[12]

For many years, the Poemlife site also published a regular webzine (*wangkan*), appearing as a monthly with some interruptions from 2000 onward, with the final issue being number 83, dated June 2010. The webzine issues appear on-screen as regular magazines: they start with an illustrated cover, followed by some pages of illustrations, and then a table of contents. The individual poems are accessed by clicking on links in the table of contents. It is not possible to browse through the whole issue from beginning to end. The webzine issues contain selections of poems from the forums, with any and all paratexts and comments removed and only the text of the poems remaining. Each issue of the webzine has a named editor, a date of publication, and a copyright statement. Moreover, in 2007 an annual selection of the site's best poetry and critical essays of the preceding year was published in print by the prestigious Huacheng publishing house in Guangzhou.[13] A second annual selection came out unofficially the following year.[14] Also, the website still carries the text of the preface to a very early annual selection, published unofficially in 2001.[15] The annual selections are not available on the website.

The example of the Poemlife website demonstrates the fluidity of boundaries between discussions about poetry and publications of poetry that has been facilitated by the advent of the online forums. Although poetry communities also published unofficial journals and anthologies during the time of the "karaoke-style" poetry salons of the 1980s referred to by Hu Xudong, the main distinction is that in the age of online forums, the contents of community discussions and the earlier versions of the anthologized poems are also publicly available. This draws attention to the fact that selection and anthologizing of online poetry go hand in hand with a process of rigorous decontextualization. As the poems make their way from the forums to the annual selection, all paratexts and comments fall by the wayside, and in some cases the end product (the anthology) does not even appear in cyberspace but only in print, which then becomes the highest form of consecration.

A second innovative element of many Chinese poetry websites is that they contain forums for both modern, Western-style poetry (also known as New Poetry) and classical-style poetry. Ever since the Literary Revolution of 1917, these two styles had been each other's antipodes. Although the literary elite has often attempted to condemn classical-style poetry to the status of historical relic, the classical genres in fact continued to be actively practiced and its prosodies and chanting methods actively transmitted throughout the twentieth century and up to the present.[16] Adherents of the classical style, including many members of the Chinese social and cultural elites, likewise show open disdain for the modern style, consistently attacking its lack of formal beauty and its origins in foreign examples. In Chinese education (not just in the PRC but also in Taiwan) the classical style is given much more prominence than the modern style. As shown in chapter 2, in the context of the debate about Zhao Lihua's poetry, nonspecialist readers in China are also generally mystified by free verse and conceive of poetry mainly in terms of formal regularity. In other words, apart from the distinction between "official" and "unofficial" scenes, the field of poetry in China is also characterized by an important division between the "modern-style" and "classical-style" scenes.

Throughout most of the twentieth century it would have been rare to see both styles appearing together in a single publication. The unofficial scene, especially, generally displayed very little interest in the classical style as a living tradition. It did, of course, acknowledge the significance of, and at times the inspiration provided by, the great poets of the past, especially in the realm of imagery. However, poets identifying with the unofficial scene would hardly ever attempt to create work that would highlight distinct continuities with the formal prosodies and linguistic registers of the classical style. A website such as Poemlife, which has strong ties with the unofficial scene, continues this convention and pays little if any attention to classical-style poetry. However, there are many other poetry forums that break new ground in this respect. A good example is the site Zhongguo Shiren (Chinapoet, http://www.chinapoet.net), to which the discussion now turns.

Chinapoet

Like the Poemlife site, the Chinapoet site, based in Fujian province, claims to be the first poetry site in China with its own independent domain name. A comparison of their domain registration records proves that Chinapoet came first. Its domain was first registered on January 8, 2000, whereas the Poemlife domain was first registered on February 23, 2000.[17] Chinapoet operates a membership system, and the number of members has grown steadily since its founding.[18]

I first visited Chinapoet in 2004 and made some observations about the community's practices, comparing them with those found on the English-language poetry site Everypoet.[19] Here I look at how the site changed over time, drawing on impressions gathered during later visits in 2011 and 2013. I look at practices surrounding the production and distribution of poems as well as practices of valuation (symbolic production[20]). Following the example set in Howard Becker's book on art worlds,[21] I try to take into account all the skills and tools that are needed to bring an online poem into being. I also refer to a more recent essay by Becker about hypertext fiction.[22] In that article, Becker argues that hypertext fiction, being nonlinear writing requiring special software to create, special distributors to sell, and special reading strategies to enjoy, is a truly new art form in the sociological sense. The world of printed literature has no way of accommodating it within the existing forms of organization and cooperation between its producers, distributors, and consumers. This kind of total independence from the print-culture paradigm is not achieved by the poetry forums under discussion here, but that does not make them less interesting or innovative, as also argued with regard to online chronicles in chapter 2.

⊕ Figure 4.1   Main page of Chinapoet website. http://www.chinapoet.net/forum
.php.

The basic material condition for the authors of online poetry is to have
a computer with access to the Internet. For many people in the urban
areas of China, computers are affordable and Internet access is cheap and
convenient. Membership of a poetry website like Chinapoet is free, as is
publication of one's work on the site. This means that most of the cost of
making this kind of literature available is incurred by those who run the
website. Their position combines that of publisher and bookseller in the
print-culture system.

The basic material conditions for hosting a website like this are server
space and software. Large interactive sites like this generate much server
traffic and are generally not hosted for free by Internet service providers.
The software needed to operate the interactive forums is also not freely
available. However, compared with any kind of print-culture venture, the
direct costs of running sites like this is small. In 2004, my impression was
that the site had very few advertisement banners. During my first visit in
April that year, the only advertisement present was for a printed anthology of best works from the site itself. During later visits to the site in September and December 2004 and March 2005, I noticed an increasing

number of advertisements on the front page, presumably an indication of increased popularity. The site also seemed to function as a company offering paid web-hosting services. It was unclear to me to what extent the enterprise was profit making or rather based on generous investment of time and personal funds by enthusiastic individuals. It seems likely that the latter was (and is) the case. The official registration records of the Chinese site, which were linked from the front page of the site in 2004 and have been preserved in the IAWM, place it in the official category of "noncommercial websites" (*fei jingyingxing wangzhan*).[23]

Apart from online poetry, the Chinapoet site also provides copious information about famous poems and poets, this being an indication of its relative closeness to the print-culture tradition. The main attraction of the site, however, is its collection of poetry forums. The forum software appears identical to similar software used for discussion forums around the world, with the first point of entry being a page listing the various available boards and inviting the user to choose which one she or he wants to read or contribute to. These listings also provide some statistical information about the forums, such as the number of posts and threads they contain. The lists also show the screen names of the moderators of each of the forums.

The moderators are the key agents involved in the running of this kind of online poetry forum. Combining the roles of editors and censors in print culture, the moderators decide which posts are and which are not included, but they do so (at least in the forums discussed here) *after* the original post has been submitted. In other words, the moderators' main task is to screen submissions and to ensure that their content is suitable and appropriate for the forum to which they have been sent. The actual work might vary from removing obscene or abusive messages to moving a poem to another forum where it more appropriately belongs. In the case of Chinapoet, the moderators are also responsible for ensuring that submissions do not violate government censorship regulations.[24] As is the case in most Internet communities, the moderators are themselves regular contributors or visitors to the site. It is unlikely that they receive more than token remuneration for their efforts. This is consistent with Becker's model of art worlds: if one wants to do things within an art world that are unconventional (such as publish online rather than in print), one must be prepared to do a lot of the work oneself, since other agents within the community might not be willing (or be trained) to provide the assistance you need.

The key agents in keeping sites like Chinapoet alive are of course the members contributing to the forums, either by submitting their own work or by commenting on others' posted work. As mentioned in previous chapters, contributions to the forums are represented as threads, that is, as a series of individual posts on one topic, normally a poem submitted by one of the members, who, by doing so, starts a new thread. A typical forum list shows the titles of the posts/poems, the screen names of the authors, the number of replies to the original post, the number of times the thread has been visited, the screen name of the last person contributing to the thread, and the date and time when that last contribution was made. Various symbols on the left-hand side indicate various aspects of the status of the thread. For instance, the yellow folder symbol representing a thread might turn into a symbol of a flaming folder if the thread is "hot," meaning it has been responded to or visited more than a certain number of times. As the word "thread" itself indicates, the poems submitted and the responses by other users are organized in a linear fashion, namely in chronological order. In other words, the threads themselves are not hypertexts. Nevertheless, as also pointed out in previous chapters, the possibility of direct interaction between poet and reader/critic is unusual when compared with print culture.

Unlike with most print-culture communities, symbolic production (i.e., the production of the value of the work) in these online communities is not carried out by specialized critics but by other authors (i.e., members who themselves are contributing poetry to the site), presumably because it is difficult to find specialist critics willing (or able) to take on the task. Moreover, it is normal for authors to respond directly to comments on their work, which is a new function not available in print culture. The moderators (themselves also authors and contributors) play a crucial role in attributing recognition to members' works as they decide which posts or threads are selected for inclusion on a special board for the best of Chinapoet. I noted in 2004 that this special board in turn provided material for the editors of the two web journals that Chinapoet strove to publish each month, although in reality they appeared much less frequently: one journal for modern poetry and one journal for classical poetry. These journals were made available for members to download as files to their computers and also appeared online.[25] The web journals were edited by a small group of moderators. The contents of the journals represented only a very small part of what was contributed to the site every month. The works (poems and essays about poetry) were presented on nicely designed web pages that did not have any interactive functions, that is, pages that could only be read and not commented on.

The fact that editors select a tiny proportion of work submitted to them for inclusion in a journal is not dissimilar to the editing process of a print-culture journal. The main difference, however, is that in this case all contributions get published on the site first. To have one's work included in the site's web journal is likely the highest possible form of symbolic recognition that a contributor to Chinapoet can obtain within the site itself. Other literary websites in China have web journals as well, and some of them are important mouthpieces for groups that have little access to, or interest in, official print culture. On the other hand, the format of the web journals is so devoid of interactive characteristics that these publications can also be seen as possible stepping-stones into print culture. These Chinese web journals could be (and presumably sometimes are) simply printed off and enter the offline literary world. Unlike the world of hypertext fiction discussed by Howard Becker, the world of online Chinese poetry on the whole displays no intention to break away from print-culture paradigms, making the boundaries between the two much more fluid. As we shall see later in this chapter, this also means that experimentation with nonlinear forms of poetry is less conspicuous in the PRC than in other communities.

The web journal phenomenon is worthy of further, separate investigation. A useful question to ask is whether or not the editors' selection of works for inclusion in the web journals is influenced by the valuation of those works by contributors to the discussion forums. It is likely that a certain amount of recognition derives from the statistics indicating how often a poem has been read and commented on. In studying these sites, I noticed that, as I was browsing the forums, I was generally inclined to click on threads with high statistics, assuming that they would be more interesting or controversial than others. Naturally these numbers can be manipulated by the author, if he or she simply keeps going back to the thread to add new posts. In 2004 Chinapoet had a rule that members were not allowed to submit more than three posts per day, without stipulating if these should be poems or comments on poems.[26] However, the site did have much stricter rules for the contents of posts, based on government censorship regulations.

The rules for submission to Chinapoet, which I downloaded in April 2004, were in two main parts. One part listed all the content that is not allowed on the site, including "writings violating the PRC constitution, the policy of reform and opening up, and the four cardinal principles," "writings attacking the PRC government, the Chinese Communist Party and its leaders," "writings propagating violence, superstition, and licentiousness," "writings exposing state secrets," and (last) "all other content forbidden by law." The second main part listed all types of screen names that members were not allowed to use, including "names, stage names, and pseudonyms of Party and government leaders or other celebrities" and "names of state institutions and other institutions." Most important and mentioned three times in bright-red font, the site was closed to any and all content alluding to the outlawed Falun Gong movement. The last line stated unequivocally, "This site does not welcome Falun Gong. If we see them, we delete them [*jian yi shan yi*]."

This was not just paying lip service to government campaigns. When visiting Chinese online forums in 2004, I found that Falun Gong members and sympathizers were indeed using freely accessible discussion forums to spread information about their movement and to denounce government oppression. Failure to remove such contributions might in time lead to a website's being closed down. The alternative to outspoken warnings like the one cited would be to renounce the open character of the forums and screen every contribution before publication, a step that Chinapoet obviously was not willing or able to take, since it would place a much heavier burden on forum moderators.

As was the case with Poemlife, the discussions taking place on Chinapoet represent a mixture of criticism and socializing. Detailed discussions of skill and considerations about the right word in the right place are much less prominent than on comparable English-language sites, although they do appear on the forum dedicated to those writing in the classical style, which of course has very strict prosodic rules. Already in 2004 I noted that the feedback on poems in the modern-poetry forums was much less normative and often consisted of one-liners of the type "I like this poem" or "I don't like this poem," without going into much detail.

Questions of content and personality were also often debated, as were issues of gender. In one case, two members responded to a simple poem expressing love for a woman. The first dismissed the poem as romantic rubbish. The second pointed out that this would be the case if the poet had been a man, but since the poet was a woman writing about love for a woman, it was actually much more interesting and gave the reader "food for thought" because the poet created a "contradiction" and a "role reversal."[27] This is exactly the kind of conflation of poet and poem that would be anathema to English-language forums such as Everypoet.

In 2004 Chinapoet had a lively forum devoted to translation. Although the forum rules did not limit the translation to one particular language, all translations I saw were either from or into English. The forum had separate subforums for translation of famous English poems into Chinese and translation of members' poems into English. These forums naturally attracted much normative discussion. The inclusion of translation and the focus on English placed the Chinese site firmly in the margins of the system of world literature, whereas the total neglect of translation places sites like Everypoet squarely in the center. The fact that, according to the Chinapoet site statistics at the time, 95.9 percent of its visitors were from China, and another 1 percent or so from sinophone areas such as Taiwan, Hong Kong, and Singapore, underscores the nature of the predicament.

In September 2011 I renewed my acquaintance with the Chinapoet website. The forums were much the same as before, still with regular contributions coming in on a daily basis, although with seemingly somewhat less discussion about individual poems. The site no longer contained any traces of the early webzines, which I had noted in 2004 and which, as mentioned, remain accessible nowadays through the IAWM. However, the 2011 version of the site did contain a special forum dedicated to the editing and production of an annual anthology, which appears to have been coming out in print since 2003 but which was not very visibly advertised on the site during my earlier visits. In at least one case (the 2010 anthology), the full contents of the printed anthology can also be found reproduced on the forum itself.[28] Print publication of the anthology is facilitated by funds raised among members of the site, and the distribution is done privately.[29] The forum contains records of payments made by members to order copies of the anthology and other publications.

Moreover, the site started a new webzine, the idea being launched in 2009 as a by-product of work on the annual anthologies and given a separate forum on the site. An editorial board was formed, and the first issues of the webzine, simply called *Zhong shi wangkan* (*Chinapoet Webzine*), started coming out in 2010. The webzine is distributed in the form of a compressed file (in .rar format) that can be downloaded by members only. Both the forum devoted to the annual anthologies and the forum devoted to the monthly webzine suggest that, compared with 2004, the site has become more organized. If initially sites like Chinapoet were characterized by a blurring of boundaries between author, reader, editor, publisher, and critic, the establishment of clearly separate groups or individuals carrying out specific tasks (such as editing anthologies, raising funds to publish them, or taking care of distribution) shows the kind of division of labor taking place that characterizes a more developed art world.

The establishment of more standardized working routines is also noticeable from the revised membership rules, as they exist at this writing (February 2013). There is no longer any specific mention of Falun Gong, just general statements stipulating that there must be no submission of posts that break the law, that discriminate on the grounds of race, gender, or religion, or that constitute any kind of defamation or personal attack. The rules further make clear that copyright of all posts remains with the original authors and that no copyrighted material may be posted on the site without permission. Any form of advertising is explicitly forbidden, as is the use of obscene user names, and so on. The site clearly states it accepts no responsibility for user-generated content. Clearly, compared with 2004, the fear that the entire site might be affected by illegal content posted by users is no longer present.

The membership registration process is simple and in line with what is common for most online forums. New members are asked to choose a user name and password and submit a valid e-mail address. There is no request for real-name registration, and when I registered, no confirmation e-mail was sent to my e-mail address, but my IP address was recorded. The site rules stipulate that users' personal information will not be shared with anyone, unless legally requested by judicial or police authorities. As is common practice nowadays in order to prevent automatic registration by spam bots, those registering are asked to type in a verification code shown on an image. In a nice twist, an additional level of verification is added by asking for the answer to a question that consists of the first line of a famous classical couplet, with the person registering having to answer by typing in the second line. (In my case, for instance, I was given a line from the Tang poet Wang Zhihuan's [688–742] "At Heron Lodge." Of course the correct answer could be easily Googled.)

Going over the tables of contents of some of the annual anthologies, as well as the full text of the 2010 anthology, it is clear that Chinapoet's publications continue to feature both modern-style and classical-style poetry. Although the two are kept in separate sections, and the majority of the anthology content is in the modern style, the presence of both in the same context is evidence that this form of border crossing, which has been unusual in mainstream print culture, is gaining more and more currency online. By following the many links to other poetry sites on Chinapoet's front page, it is not difficult to find other sites featuring forums and publications with very similar characteristics, including at least one belonging to the "official" scene: the Chinese Poetry Forum (Zhongguo Shige Luntan), hosted by the Chinese Poetry Study Society (Zhongguo Shige Xuehui).[30] If it is true, as Xiaofei Tian has noted in her study of the old-style Internet poet Lizilizilizi, that Internet publication of poetry is conducive to the emergence of "hybrid entities" that "powerfully demonstrate to us that we cannot disassociate modern Chinese old-style and new-style poetry in our critical discourse,"[31] then the appearance of new-style and old-style poetry in one and the same context, both on forums and in spin-off anthologies, must play a crucial part in this process of hybridization.

Jintian

Xiaofei Tian starts out her "Coda" to the article just mentioned with the following lines:

> Lizi's poetry nicely illustrates the issue of local and global literature. Lizi is a provincial writer who lives in Beijing. Even though he is always at "city's edge," his poetry travels on the Internet, a space bringing together authors and readers across vast regions—even across the Pacific Ocean and to the United States. And yet, his kind of poetry will always lose in translation,

because it affords too much "pleasure of the text"—echoes of classical and modern literature, cultural lore, contemporary colloquialism and slang, exuberant word play, or well-crafted parallel couplets.[32]

In a similar analytical move—confirming the potential of Internet literature to travel around the world but doubting its ability to overcome cultural differences—I concluded my observations about Chinese poetry forums in 2004 by saying that

> these communities foster direct interaction across vast geographical distances, coupled with publication for a potentially huge audience, a combination that print culture practices would find difficult to accommodate. The use of similar software and protocols in different cultural settings ensures that the practices of online communities all over the world have certain elements in common, such as their tendency to rely in part on statistics for recognition and the blurring of boundaries between specialized roles such as author, critic, and reader, which are so crucial to the practices of print culture. . . . At the same time, cultural differences are observable and demonstrate that cyberspace is not the locus of any kind of transnational cultural expression.[33]

A good test case to see if modern Chinese poetry is really not capable of "transnational expression," even when put online, is the history of the famous journal *Jintian* (English title: *Today*). *Jintian* was founded in 1978 by the poets Bei Dao and Mang Ke and first distributed on and around the Democracy Wall in Beijing.[34] Although it was eventually banned from publishing, its "obscure" (*menglong*) poetic style soon set new standards for modern Chinese poetry, and a number of poets associated with the journal (apart from the two founders also Gu Cheng, Yang Lian, and Duoduo) went on to achieve national and international fame. In 1989, when all the mentioned, with the exception of Mang Ke, as well as a number of other literary figures of the same generation were outside China in the aftermath of June Fourth, a decision was made to revive the journal abroad, with Bei Dao as editor in chief and initially published out of Stockholm. For most of the 1990s, the new *Jintian* was considered to represent a kind of Chinese "exile literature," and although its editors aimed to adhere to strict literary standards and published little of a direct political nature, the journal was seen as "dissident" and was for a very long time banned in China.[35] Writers based in China did, however, publish in *Jintian* without fear of reprisal, and copies of the journal were regularly smuggled into the country by supportive sinologists and other travelers.

As time went by and the Chinese government gradually lost interest in dissident poets (with the exception of Bei Dao, for whom the borders of his native country remained regularly closed until quite recently), *Jintian* became more clearly and openly a journal featuring Chinese-language work from a variety of backgrounds, including many contributions from the PRC. The editors reestablished contact with the unofficial scene inside China and included some poets living in China in its editorial board. In December 1998 the journal registered its web domain, http://www.jintian.net, which was for a long time devoted solely to promotion of the printed journal. In February 2004, the website still opened with the following English-language introduction, highlighting the journal's history and previous suppression by the Chinese government:

ABOUT TODAY

Conceived in 1978 and suppressed in 1980, Today became the best-known unofficial literary magazine in China, Bei Dao and Mang Ke as its founding editors. After ten years of silence, in 1990, it was relaunched from Sweden. It is now published as a quarterly and opens its pages to Chinese writers throughout the world. Its reputation continues to grow, that of a literary magazine dedicated to the enrichment of Chinese and world culture, today and in the future.[36]

In 2006 the website was redesigned and made to look more like an online portal than a static site for the promotion of a journal. The new design did away with the English text, which featured so prominently on the old site and was clearly aimed at an overseas audience (and presumably overseas sponsors), and instead switched completely to Chinese. At the same time a poetry forum, called "Poetry Commentary" (Shige dianping), was added to the site. By 2011, the site had twenty-four forums,[37] edited by a mix of PRC-based and overseas-based individuals. It also provides blogging space. Notably, the site now also has a separate section and a dedicated forum for classical-style poetry. Seeing the *Jintian* "brand," with all its connotations of modernism and resistance to convention, open up a space for old-style poetry is genuinely surprising. Moreover, when I last

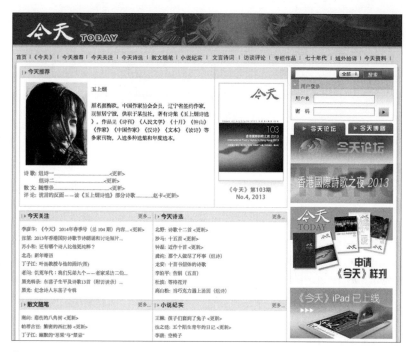

↥ **Figure 4.2** Main page of *Jintian* website. http://www.jintian.net/today/.

visited the site in 2011, the classical-poetry forum was among the site's most popular in terms of activity, as expressed in the number of posts and responses to posts. (Although none of the forums came anywhere close in popularity to the site's first forum, the mentioned "Poetry Commentary," which was receiving around ten times as many contributions as the classical-style-poetry forum and other lower-ranked forums.)

The new organization of the website and the introduction of forums suggests that *Jintian* has successfully reached the audience that eluded it for such a long time when it was an "exile journal," that is, the mainland Chinese audience. The site now has a clear presence among Chinese Internet users, and in 2011 its Alexa ranking for the China region, as well as its domestic Chinarank rating, was more or less as high as that of Poemlife, and much higher than that of most other Chinese poetry websites.[38] The site's own statistics as well as the Alexa statistics revealed that the vast majority of its visitors (80–85 percent according to the site's StatCounter, 95 percent according to Alexa) were now coming from the PRC.

Rather than having crossed boundaries and created new transnational spaces, it seems that *Jintian* has simply come home, having adopted a design and an online editorial strategy that differs little from those of similar PRC-based sites, and having switched entirely back to operating in Chinese and addressing mainly readers in China.

Moral Transgression

Even if Chinese online poetry fails to open up genuinely new transcultural spaces, the discussion so far has shown that it does manage to cross many previously established boundaries, such as those between poet and reader, text and commentary, or classical-style poetry and modern-style poetry. In addition, online poets (as with online novelists, as seen in chapter 3) have taken advantage of the relative freedom of web-based publishing to challenge long-standing moral boundaries for literary creation, especially with regard to the portrayal of sex in texts written by women. Moral, legal, social, and literary conventions all play a role here. General disapproval of explicit portrayals of sexual activity is largely a moral issue: one should not write about sex. In modern societies such general disapproval is usually laid down in obscenity legislation: one is not allowed to write about sex in certain ways. Specific disapproval of poetic descriptions of sex is a literary issue: there should be no explicit sex in poetry (nor anything else that is not conventionally "beautiful" or "meaningful"), but it may occur in other genres; finally, critical outrage at sex in poetry written by *women* is a social issue: women are expected to express themselves differently from men, especially where sex is concerned.

As observed in detail by James Farrer, sex culture has undergone enormous changes in China during the reform era, and this is also observable in cultural production, where "forced romantic rhetoric" has given way to "an ironic appreciation of the problems of free sexual and labor markets."[39] Although Farrer's analysis is based mainly on nonfictional material appearing in popular magazines throughout the 1980s and 1990s, his use of literary terminology ("romantic" vs. "ironic") is helpful in this context. Indeed, the presence of irony has in my view been tremendously important in making explicit sexual descriptions in literature more acceptable in the PRC during the reform era. One of the earliest examples of this process is the 1993 publication of Jia Pingwa's *Feidu* (*Abandoned*

Capital), with its ironic use of empty squares in the text to indicate obscene passages that had been excised. Of course those passages never existed in the first place and indeed the mechanism is classically ironic: rather than "cleansing" the text, the added blocks help to strengthen the *visual* impression of the text's transgressive status. In any case, there was plenty of explicit description left in the novel to warrant its eventual banning, but according to Geremie Barmé, its publication and the ensuing debate also heralded the arrival of a renewed period of intellectual engagement and printed cultural polemic, which had been subdued since the events of 1989.[40]

In poetry, the 1990s saw the emergence of "colloquial" poets, most famously Yu Jian, who made it their business to bring poetry down to earth with the use of plain, sometimes even vulgar, language and a publicly stated resistance to embellishment and metaphor. Theirs was essentially an ironic stance, claiming to be opposed to anything "poetic" while obviously producing poetry.[41] With the emergence of the Internet and poetry forums, the antiromantic stance of this style was trumped by the emergence of a new group of young poets who called their new journal, which had both a printed and an online edition, *Xiabanshen* (*The Lower Body*, http://www.wenxue200.com/mk/xbs001.htm, now unavailable[42]) and who frequently employed explicit sexual reference as a poetic topic. A well-known example is Yin Lichuan's "Wei shenme bu zai shufu yixie" (Why Not Make It Feel Even Better), which, in the translation of Maghiel van Crevel, reads as follows:[43]

Why Not Make It Feel Even Better

ah a little higher a little lower a little to the left a little to the right
this isn't making love this is hammering nails

oh a little faster a little slower a little looser a little tighter
this isn't making love this is anti-porn campaigning or tying your shoes
ooh a little more a little less a little lighter a little heavier
this isn't making love this is massage writing poetry washing your hair your
   feet

why not make it feel even better huh make it feel even better
a little gentler a little ruder a little more Intellectual a little more Popular

why not make it feel even better

In his discussion of the poem, Van Crevel addresses the moral, literary, and social issues that are at play in this context:

> This is vintage Yin Lichuan . . . : derisive, tired, cynical, playful yet tough. The
> effect is strengthened by a dogma that holds everywhere but is particularly
> deep-rooted in China, certainly if one bears in mind a good two millennia of
> literary history: public, detailed description of sexuality is scandalous, espe-
> cially if the author is a woman. To make matters worse, the speaker in "Why
> Not" is an immoral woman, whose carnal ecstasy is not the spin-off of soul-
> mateship or love but emerges in lazy instructions to a man portrayed as a
> tool to satisfy female lust.[44]

In the same context, Van Crevel refers to some critics' equation of the Lower Body school with pornography. He then comments, "It is, however, too frequently ironic and insufficiently focused on sex and sexual arousal to justify this classification."[45] This suggests that, in the literary context, the employment of irony by poets such as Yin Lichuan does not only represent the changed sexual morality of a new generation of Chinese, as Farrer would have it, but also serves as an indication of "literariness," which absolves the text of potential legal challenges on the grounds of pornography or obscenity. In the case of Yin Lichuan's poem, the fact that the text itself refers to "anti-porn campaigning" (*saohuang*) doubles the irony. Although certainly not uncontroversial, Yin Lichuan's poem is now well on its way to achieving a canonized status, as evidenced by regular references to it in PRC scholarly journals, especially those dealing with women's literature or the topic of "body writing" (*shenti xiezuo*).[46]

As discussed in the previous chapter, Chinese criminal law, like that of many other countries, excludes "literary and artistic works of artistic value that contain erotic contents" from persecution on the grounds of obscenity. Also as in many other countries, the law does not specify what "artistic value" is exactly. In many Western countries such issues were famously debated in the courts. In the United States, for instance, the 1957 California trial of Allen Ginsberg's poem "Howl" set an important legal precedent in this context. The legal community in China is also aware of the need to provide further detail to definitions of "artistic value" and of key terms such as "obscene" and "pornographic," but for the moment these do not appear to be forthcoming. When I queried a government official responsible for the regulation of Internet publishing on these issues, he simply stated that decisions about censoring obscenity were referred to a "panel of experts" consisting of academics and industry professionals and that, as far as he was concerned, anything they considered legal was legal, and the rest not.[47] Clearly, the stronger the academic and critical support for and consensus about risqué literature, the better its chances to be spared censorship.

In the context of online literature, however, the question is not so much how to deal with erotic writing that has demonstrable literary value but how to deal with writing that lays no claim to being anything but erotic. Erotic writing can be found all over the Internet, and whereas in most Western countries it is commonly accompanied by an age warning, asking the reader to confirm that they are of a legal age to view such material, the concept of a "legal age" does not exist in China. Instead, the PRC government prefers to carry out periodic attempts at cleansing the domestic Internet through the mentioned antiporn campaigns. As we have seen in the previous chapter, the main literary target of such campaigns is online genre fiction. Chinese online genre fiction will generally find few literary critics willing to stand up for its "artistic value." Nevertheless, the present situation in the PRC appears to be that such work can have explicit sexual content as long as it stops short of employing graphic vocabulary or presenting detailed descriptions of intercourse. When transgression takes place, website owners are instructed to remove the offending passages, and frequent transgressors are "named and shamed" on quarterly lists published by the General Administration of Press and Publishing (GAPP). GAPP's aim appears to be to gently pressure commercial online publishers into falling in line with the norms for state-owned print publishers while at the same time not harming their business and the entertainment they provide for millions of readers.

Whereas the censoring activities deployed by GAPP have attracted wide attention to the online existence of "obscene and pornographic fiction" (*yinhui seqing xiaoshuo*), there appears to have been no concern at all for the existence of pornographic poetry. Yet such poetry does appear online in China and seems to be ahead of online fiction in its willingness to transgress, despite lacking critical or academic support. Specifically, I have in mind work that appeared on various websites in the past few years and that was produced by an author using the pseudonym Datui xianfeng nü shiren, which literally means "Thigh—avant-garde female poet."

In a short autobiographical piece that can be found on the Chinese Internet, Datui traces her own genealogy to the Shi Jianghu (Poetry Vagabonds) website, which was also the home of many of the Lower Body poets.[48] She writes that she registered an ID on that site in 2007 and that the first poem she published there was titled "Cao wo ba, ruguo ni you qian" (Fuck Me, If You Have Money). After Poetry Vagabonds was taken offline in 2008, she remained silent for a while before starting a blog on the popular Sina platform. That blog was quickly shut down, after which she migrated to blogging sites based outside China. Despite the fact that she herself no longer publishes on Chinese sites, her poems can be found on Chinese sites and remain part, however obscurely, of PRC Internet literature.

Datui herself boldly states that her work was even more avant-garde than that written by the Lower Body poets. A comparison of her poems with the quoted Yin Lichuan poem indicates that she is in any case much more graphic in her sexual references. The following poem can be frequently encountered on the Internet:[49]

Put My Cell Phone in My Cunt

I put my phone on vibrate
and sent you a message saying
I put my phone in my cunt
you called my phone like mad
it vibrated again and again
and made me reach
an unprecedented orgasm

Although this poem is lacking in redeeming irony, I would argue it could still be subjected to a sympathetic literary analysis in terms of the impact of modern technology on human relations. But that is beside the point here. The point is that this kind of poem pushes the Lower Body aesthetic into the realm where it did not want to be, namely that of pornography and obscenity. The fact that the author's virtual identity is female (I have no idea of the real-world gender identity of the author, but that is arguably irrelevant to the reception of the work) may well make it even more scandalous. To make matters worse, Datui also has a tendency to comment on national symbols and render them profane, as in this poem:[50]

Birth Control Beijing

Coming to Beijing
to Tiananmen
seeing
the Monument for the People's Heroes
erected there
I always feel that
it's a cock
a Beijing cock
the Nation's cock
tall
thick
and awesome
erected there
I reach into my bag for
a condom
I always want to
make the Monument wear one
so that the Nation
will be safe

In the poem "The East Is Red," she utters the wish to bring Chairman Mao back to life by putting her hand inside his trousers.[51]

Her more recent work, as mentioned, was published on sites outside China and is therefore more difficult to access for readers inside the country, but a poem ridiculing youth idol and Internet celebrity Han Han has been reposted on various domestic sites:[52]

Han Han: Spokesman for the SC

A stupid cunt will never feel that
he himself is a stupid cunt
stupid cunts need a big stupid cunt
to speak on their behalf

When seeing Han Han
doing his best to act like a cunt on TV

豆瓣小组   精选   文化   行摄   娱乐   时尚   生活   科技

《韩寒：SB代言人》from 大腿 先锋女诗人

 来自: 布尔费墨(http://t.sina.com.cn/pourfemme)   2010-05-06 12:27:56

《韩寒：SB代言人》
from 大腿 先锋女诗人 QQ1273688690 by 大腿
《韩寒：SB代言人》

傻逼永远不会觉得
自己是傻逼
傻逼们也需要一个大傻逼
来替他们说话

看见韩寒
在电视上努力地装逼
我真不知道说什么好

韩寒通过他那些傻逼的
装逼的书籍
从广大的傻逼那赚到了钱
赚到了钱
玩他的狗屁赛车

现在又摆出一副
要为广大傻逼出头的姿态
弄得广大傻逼兴奋不已
大呼偶像啊韩少啊
真他妈的
操蛋的傻逼

⬆ **Figure 4.3**   Datui's poem about Han Han. http://www.douban.com/group/topic /11204002/.

I really don't know what to say

Han Han uses his stupid-cunt-like
cunt-acting books
to make money off stupid cunts at large
and when he's got the money
he plays with his shitty racing cars

Lately he's got this air of
wanting to stick his neck out for the stupid cunts at large
making the stupid cunts at large all excited
shouting loud oh idol oh Young Master Han
what a damn
fucking stupid cunt

At least one Chinese forum that reproduced Datui's poetry has added its own age warning by posting a selection of her work under the title "Not Suitable for Minors."[53] The forum post in question only lists the titles of ten Datui poems but has made the files available for download to members of the forum. The way this works, also on other forums, is that one must respond to the original post in order to get to the download. Within a year and a half, over two hundred people responded, and some also left comments indicating their approval. Clearly Datui's work addresses only the smallest of niche audiences. She seems aware herself of the situation when she adds the following postscript to her poem about Han Han:[54]

A real fighter will not
appear in the mainstream media
and even when they do appear on TV
they will not take on the air of acting like a cunt
so my conclusion is that
Han Han is the biggest stupid cunt
the spokesman for the stupid cunts

The Chinese literary system has taken no interest in canonizing Datui's work, as opposed to that of Yin Lichuan and other Lower Body poets, because it has too few redeeming characteristics that might help it escape from charges of obscenity and profanity. Yet at the same time, crude and angry as it may be, Datui's writing demonstrates where the limits for literary recognition lie, especially inside China itself. By reading Datui, we understand better the boundaries within which the successful Lower Body poets needed to operate in order to achieve recognition. Even if critics would *want* to discuss her work, they would probably not be able to cite it publicly without crossing out a few words or reverting to paraphrase or euphemism. As a result, Datui's writing remains situated in the

楼主：烟卷V 时间：2010-05-12 11:27:00   回复 收藏 2楼

转几首大腿的诗，为减少编辑的麻烦和工作量，除了标题外，其他都用明码转：

《对着我的下体开枪》

0438 1034 0006
2053 6008 3061 3127 6226
1417 4192 2053 4104 0007 7555 7030 2847
0936 3634
6719 2508 2053 4104 1129 5207

《相信大腿》

4161 0207 7193 6018 2623 .4161 0207 3156 5902 2623 .4161 0207 5146 1795 7741 .4161 0207 110.
4161 0207 7193 5207 .4161 0207 6389 4787 1166 5116 .4161 0207 7437 4481 .4161 0207 1947 1906 .
4161 0207 7449 3533 .4161 0207 A3651 .4161 0207 1420 1639 0707 .4161 0207 5710 1166 .4161 0207 6699 1314 1152 .4161 0207
6192 6056 .
4161 0207 2590 0645 .4161 0207 4023 4056 5221 .4161 0207 0739 0803 .4161 0207 3662 0098 5974 .4161 0207 7230 2504 4026 .4161
0207 7499 1311 .4161 0207 6226 1390 .
4161 0207 5337 3320 4016 .4161 0207 4148 3739 .4161 0207 1840 7559 3390 .4161 0207 7741 1572 .4161 0207 1178 1166 .
4161 0207 4986 2043 .4161 0207 120.4161 0207 QQ.4161 0207 1136 2814 .4161 0207 2087 3230 .
4161 0207 0063 0934 6663 0520 .4161 0207 0001 1123 1906 .4161 0207 7113 5449 1073 7022 2611 .4161 0207 2293 6892 5887 .4161
0207 3662 6656 .

⊙ **Figure 4.4**   Poems by Datui reproduced in telegraph code to avoid censoring.
http://bbs.tianya.cn/post-187-555040-1.shtml.

literary underworld, so to speak, together with other genres and writings
that do not meet the minimum current requirements for being tolerated.

It is unlikely that, in the foreseeable future, work such as Datui's will
ever appear in print in China. My discussion now turns to a type of online
poetry residing at the opposite end of the literary spectrum but that has
in common with Datui's work its being so unconventional it can never
appear in print.

Textual Morphs: Chinese Language in the Work of John Cayley

The Chinese written language has long fascinated Western literary exper-
imentalists because of its perceived visual and imagistic qualities. These
qualities are especially appealing to those working in the tradition of concrete poetry, that is, poetic creation that emphasizes the visual aspects
of writing as much or more than the semantic or prosodic aspects. In
electronic literature, the work of the Anglo-Canadian author John Cayley stands out for its frequent use of Chinese characters blended in with

other languages constituting nonlinear sequences. Cayley was among the first to experiment with programmable digital media in producing concrete poetry, and although his work is not always intended to be read online, much of it is available for download from his personal website.[55]

The arrival of computers and, especially, programming languages that can make texts do things that print cannot gave new impetus to existing movements in concrete poetry. What computer programming brings to concrete poetry is the ability to make the text move, assume different shapes, or to change from one shape to another much more easily and in many more different ways than can be achieved in print. The poetic experience of this kind of work lies in watching the transformation take place and experiencing an aesthetic response to what appears on-screen.[56] The creative technique introduced by Cayley in the 1990s is called textual morphing, whereby a poem appearing on-screen slowly starts to change, letter by letter, into something else, possibly another poem. Textual morphing can be entirely programmed (i.e., taking place in a predetermined sequence), or it can be "on the fly" (i.e., the trajectory whereby one text morphs into another is randomly generated by software), or it can be interactive (i.e., the user determines what happens to the text and when).

An early and straightforward example of textual morphing uses different versions of the famous Tang-dynasty poem "Deer Fence" by Wang Wei. Each morph involves two texts, including translations of the poem in English and French, a version in pinyin transliteration, and a version in Chinese characters. The reader-user starts the morph by clicking on links, selecting the pair of texts to use, and then moving the mouse pointer across a horizontal bar at the top of the screen. As the pointer moves, the initial text begins to change, on the basis of an algorithm created by Cayley that replaces letters by other letters until, via several intermediate steps, the first text has morphed into the second one.[57] The poetic experience lies in the observation of the process of visual transformation from one text to another.

As becomes clear when one moves the pointer across the screen to let the morphing happen (and as has also been pointed out by Cayley himself[58]), it is not easy to create a form of morphing that allows for the roman alphabet to morph smoothly into Chinese characters. The best that could be achieved in the late 1990s was a smooth morphing into Unicode, which then suddenly (i.e., in a single step without intermediate

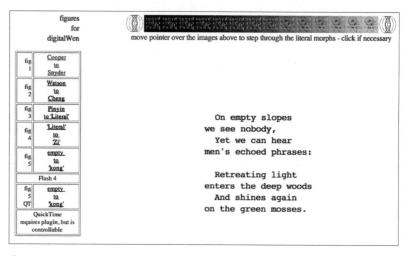

↷ Figure 4.5 John Cayley's textual morphs. http://www.shadoof.net/in/digital Wen/dwframes.html.

transitions) changed into characters. It is worth bearing in mind, also for what follows, that in standard computer software Chinese characters were (and still are) encoded in combinations of letters, numbers, and other symbols within the ASCII character set, whereas Western alphabetic scripts require no such encoding. Cayley's example does include a further link to a short Flash Video clip that shows a single English word (empty) morphing smoothly into one Chinese character (*kong* 空), demonstrating that it is technically possible to create the morphing effect between two radically different writing systems but that it would involve extensive programming if one were to do this for the entire poem.

In the Wang Wei morphing example, the reading process is interactive, but the morphs are not random. The user can only move through the stages provided by the programmer, not unlike the way in which a reader of a printed book can only move through the pages that are bound together. Although the reader is free to decide which page to read when, the specific content that is on each page does not change as a result of any decisions made by the reader.

"windsound," a later work by Cayley, is not interactive but features a long, complex morphing sequence that was entirely software generated and then recorded as what the author calls a text movie.[59] Letters randomly change and move across the screen for a period of roughly twenty minutes, punctuated by the appearance of a number of "nodal" poems written especially for the occasion, including Cayley's own translation of a Song-dynasty poem by Qin Guan. As the words change, a computer-generated voice reads out what is on the screen, regardless of whether or not the letters form recognizable words. This work does not run into the kind of encoding problems just mentioned, but this is clearly because it does not use Chinese original text (nor sound) but only English translation. "windsound" won the 2001 Prize for Poetry of the Electronic Literature Organization (ELO), and a version of the work has been archived on the ELO website.[60]

In one of his later works, titled "riverIsland," Cayley combines sound and image and random textual morphing in a complex whole that involves poems in various languages including Chinese and that is fully interactive. The work is based on a conceptual "map," known only to Cayley himself, that links a multilingual set of translations of Wang Wei poems together in both vertical and horizontal directions. By moving on-screen controls in these directions, the reader can explore the links between these texts, initiating morphing sequences as well as activating sound files that read out the poems in various languages, including Mandarin Chinese. The Wang Wei poem returns in various forms (read in Chinese as well as in a literal English translation, for instance), as does the on-screen morph from the word "empty" to the character *kong*. Contrary to "windsound," "riverIsland" is highly interactive. The sheer endless possibilities for horizontal and vertical movement and the fact that, as soon as one starts interacting, there is no single "straightforward" way of going through the work ensure that every single reading by every single reader of this work is different, not just at the level of interpretation (as is usually the case with literature) but also at the level of perception.

The use of different voices, including a female voice reading in Mandarin Chinese, ensures a fairly seamless integration of Chinese language into this work, yet the integration of characters into the morphing process clearly continues to be problematic, in terms of sheer programming requirements, and is therefore limited to the single morph from "empty" to *kong*, which appears as a kind of stand-alone movie at some point during the work and which has now been expanded to include not only the English word and the Chinese character but also the pinyin transliteration and the English word written in Xu Bing's "Square Word Calligraphy."[61]

Electronic Poetry Turned Chinese

A different type of interactivity in concrete poetry is demonstrated in the work of Jim Andrews, translated into Chinese by the Taiwanese scholar and e-writer Li Shunxing. Andrews's works feature a gaming element that puts the reader-user very much in control of the poem and aims, as before, at eliciting a different set of emotional and cognitive experiences than those usually associated with reading a poem. A seemingly simple example is the work "Enigma n."[62]

"Enigma n" begins with the word "meaning" in the middle of the screen. At the top of the screen is a small menu that encourages users to click on the words "Prod," "Stir," and "Tame." As the reader clicks away, the letters start to move in different directions and patterns, and at different speeds. Further options appear on the menu, allowing the reader to change the size and color of the font and, crucially, to make the letters stop moving. One of the ways in which one might read this work (the way in which I find it most interesting and amusing to read) is to try to stop the letters on the screen at the exact moment that they form the phrase "enigma n," the anagram of "meaning" that is the title of the work.

This work was translated into Chinese by Shuen-shing Lee (Li Shunxing).[63] For obvious reasons, Lee replaced the seven letters of English that are in the word "meaning" (and in its anagram "enigma n") with seven Chinese characters rather than trying to play the game with only two, as the literal translation of the word "meaning" (*yiyi*) would have forced him to do. Lee's choice to translate the work in this way adds a new dimension to it, in that the seven Chinese characters (*wenben zhi wai wu ta wu*, or "there is nothing outside the text") can now be moved across the screen and halted in different positions to make all kinds of funny-sounding, semicorrect complete sentences in classical Chinese. (For instance, *wen zhi wu wu ta zhi ben*, or "the nonmatter of text [is] the essence of him."). It is important to note, however, that if only programming would easily enable it (but the point is that it does not), Lee would have been able to entertain the other option of translating this work, namely to use only two characters (for instance *yiyi*) and have the different components of those characters (the different strokes, or the four corners, or the radicals and phonetic elements) move across the screen and form new and

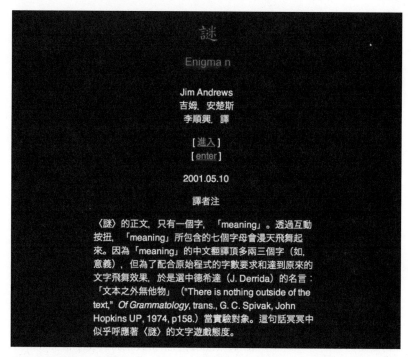

謎

Enigma n

Jim Andrews
吉姆．安楚斯
李順興．譯

[進入]
[enter]

2001.05.10

譯者注

〈謎〉的正文，只有一個字，「meaning」。透過互動
按扭，「meaning」所包含的七個字母會漫天飛舞起
來。因為「meaning」的中文翻譯頂多兩三個字（如，
意義），但為了配合原始程式的字數要求和達到原來的
文字飛舞效果，於是選中德希達（J. Derrida）的名言：
「文本之外無他物」（"There is nothing outside of the
text," *Of Grammatology*, trans., G. C. Spivak, John
Hopkins UP, 1974, p158.）當實驗對象。這句話冥冥中
似乎呼應著〈謎〉的文字遊戲態度。

Figure 4.6   Shuen-shing Lee's Chinese translation of "Enigma n," by Jim Andrews. http://vispo.com/animisms/enigman/chinese/enigmanintro.htm.

interesting combinations.[64] It is precisely because standard computer
software conceives of Chinese characters either as a whole or as a sequence of code that this option is very difficult to carry out. There is no
existing encoding to represent component parts or individual strokes of
Chinese characters, unless such parts happen to be existing characters in
their own right.

The different ways of encoding alphabetic writing and character-based
writing in computer software can be further explored by looking at the
actual language in which Jim Andrews wrote "Enigma n," which is not
the English language but the programming language DHTML. Andrews
cleverly embeds this message in the poem's source code, which can be accessed prior to or during the reading of the work by accessing the source
viewer built into most web browsers. The source code starts out with the
following comment:

```
<!—

Enigma n
Jim Andrews (jim@vispo.com), 1998

Welcome to the 'neath text of Enigma n. Enigma n is a philosophical poetry
    toy for poets and philosophers from the age of four up.
    . . .
—>.
```

And toward the end of the source code we find, hidden among the coding
sequences, the following:

```
<!—

If you're reading this, I don't know really why. You could be reading it to see
    how the piece was done so you can do dhtml yourself or you are looking
    for the true meaning of the piece or you're a habitual source viewer or . . .

I'm not sure whether to talk about the mechanics of the piece here or not.
    Naw, that's technique, and technique is hard won but anybody can do it.
—>
```

In my interpretation, Andrews inserted these comments into the 'neath
text to emphasize on the one hand the complex structure of his work
(there is a whole text underneath it that nobody reads unless it is pointed
out to them) but at the same time, his comment toward the end seems
to suggest that the *art* (as opposed to the *technique*) of his work is to be
found at the surface level. This kind of antimodernist move (discouraging readers from going deeper into the work, encouraging them to stay
on the surface) is typical of much avant-garde electronic literature. Andrews's gesture did not make it into the Chinese translation, however, for
when one accesses the source code of Shuen-shing Lee's Chinese translation of the work, the two passages cited above are still there in English.

A more elaborate example of Andrews's work, which is purposefully
irreverent in its attitude toward poetry, is "arteroids."[65] The point of "arteroids" is to combine the aesthetic experience of viewing, reading, and
using a work of art or literature with the rather different experience of
playing a violent computer game. Words and sentences move across
the screen intent on destroying one another. Users are in control of one
word or phrase or sentence (which users can input themselves) and must

"shoot" other words or phrases or sentences (which users can also input themselves) in order to reach the next level. Complete with sound effects (which users can also change), the work has well over two hundred skill levels. Every time a game ends (when a user's word is blasted by the attacking words), a philosophical phrase shows up on-screen, urging users to reflect upon what it is they are doing.

There is no Chinese translation of "arteroids," but arguably this is not necessary, since all the words that appear on-screen when using the work can be modified by users themselves. The only thing that is constant about this work is the movement of the words on-screen and the way they are controlled via the keyboard. The text itself can be anything the user wants it to be, making "arteroids" an extreme example of the textual fluidity inherent in interactive electronic literature. However, as soon as one tries to copy and paste a Chinese phrase into the text moving on the "arteroids" screen, the result is gibberish (either a row of question marks or a row of blank squares). I presume this means that the work recognizes only standard Western characters and therefore only alphabetic writing, not scripts that require encoding. There may well be a clever way of inputting code and get it to display as Chinese (although I tried inputting Unicode and changing the character encoding of my browser, to no avail), but the point is that it requires much more specialist computer knowledge to enjoy this supposedly completely open and interactive work if one wants it to be written in Chinese than in any of the alphabetic languages.

Jonathan Stalling and Sinophonic English Poetry

A very creative way of poetically blending Chinese and English, relying more on sound than on visual effects, is the poem *Yingelishi* (*Chanted Songs Beautiful Poetry*), which exists both as a printed book[66] and as an online opera.[67] *Yingelishi* consists of short phrases in Chinese and in English, followed by the transliteration of the English using Chinese characters, and a translation of those characters back into English. In the online version, the transliterated version is sung and accompanied by Chinese traditional folk musicians while the text displays on-screen. The aim is to create a poetic experience whereby the reader-viewer-listener can choose whether to receive the text as being in English or in Chinese, or something in between. Most of the text is made up of lines from typical tourist phrasebooks, and the inspiration for the transliterations comes from the way in which such phrasebooks (and also English-language textbooks published in China) use the sounds of Chinese characters to approximate the sounds of English words. Stalling's creative transformation of these conventions reminds us that the Chinese sounds also have meanings separate from their function as transliteration. However, Stalling does not use the same standard set of characters for transliteration all the time but instead varies the characters in order to achieve specific translation effects, which are often poetic, and sometimes can be comical, as in this brief example:[68]

哦，我的天啊！

oh my god!

'ō mài gāo de

噢！卖糕的！

Oh! a cake peddler!

Despite the presence of humor, Stalling's purpose in writing sinophonic English, which he has been using to write poetry since the late 1990s, is a very serious one, as explained in the introduction to the printed version of *Yingelishi*:

> Even if one does not understand the characters, it is important to acknowledge them because we must remember that every line's assumed intelligibility (as English) comes as a result of the reader's cultural imposition upon the sounds, which house meanings that English consciousness doesn't have access to. I am hoping that such an experience will create a sharp contrast between the sense of superiority that manifests as humor ... and the realization that profound meanings exist elsewhere in another language that speaks with the same voice. For this reason, I have chosen to write the Chinese poems in this book in a distinctly melancholic register that further heightens the distance between the desire to reduce these sounds to a kind of mockery and the realization that it is the English speaker who has imposed external linguistic and cultural meanings upon these sounds.[69]

A good example of this method of distancing the phonetic from the semantic can be seen in the following phrase, from the section titled "Customs":[70]

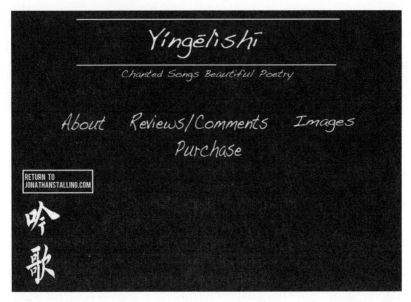

⬆ **Figure 4.7** *Yingelishi*, by Jonathan Stalling. http://jonathanstalling.com/yinge
lishi.html.

你将在这里呆多久?

how long will you be staying?

Hào làng wéi'ōu yǒu bì sǐ dāi yǐng

浩浪围鸥游

闲死

呆影

Vast waves play encircling gulls

sunken eyes fall dead

stiff shadows

The addition of traditional Chinese instruments and singing voices in the online version of the poem adds a further contrast, especially for the listener who recognizes the English line as English while hearing it sung in Chinese.

As we have seen, the fact that computers were not originally designed to display Chinese writing directly, rather than through encoding, makes merging the Chinese language into electronic works relatively more difficult. This might explain in part why such work is not so popular in China, although, as mentioned, conventional expectations about what poetry should or should not be also play an important role in discouraging formal experimentalism of this kind.[71] One very notable exception is the ongoing poetic experiments of Dajuin Yao (Yao Dajun), which started out online as early as the mid-1990s. Yao has in common with Cayley and Andrews a preference for concrete poetry, whereas he shares with Stalling a desire to engage with Western perceptions of the Chinese language. A discussion of Yao's highly original and constantly evolving work concludes this chapter, and the main body of this book.

Dajuin Yao

If the boundaries crossed by the poetry forums discussed in the preceding were mainly those between different scenes and between the different stages of the process of literary publishing, by looking at the work of Dajuin Yao we move toward more intrinsic questions of border crossing between text and image, sound and poetry originating in the Chinese language. That is not to say that Yao has not crossed more conventional boundaries. Geographically, he was born in 1959 in Taiwan to parents who had come from mainland China; he did his graduate studies in art
• history at the University of California, Berkeley, and he now teaches at the China Academy of Art in Hangzhou. In terms of literary publishing, he has consistently produced works that are not easy to reproduce in print, and he has therefore, in his own words, always been "outside the system" (*tizhi wai*).[72]

On June 4, 1996, Yao registered the web domain http://www.sino-logic.com to create a website to promote his company selling Chinese-language-learning material. In February 1997, together with Jerlian Tsao (Cao Zhilian, b. 1969), herself now also a well-known Internet artist and novelist, he opened a section of the Sinologic site for the publication of avant-garde poetry, under the name "Wonderfully Absurd Temple" (Miao miao miao).[73] In 1999, Yao added another section to the Sinologic site, this time featuring only his work and titled "Wenzi Concrete" (Wenzi juxiang). Drawing inspiration from the Western tradition of visual or concrete poetry and indulging in what he called auto-exoticism in playing with the presumed visual nature of Chinese characters, Yao created a number of works that have by now obtained canonical status in the field

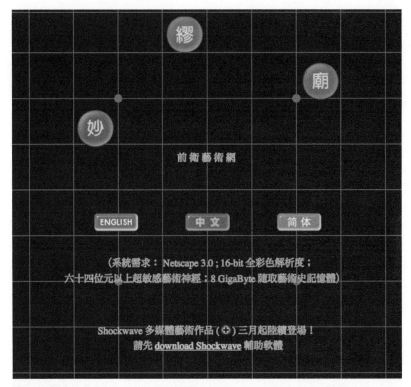

繆

廟

妙

前衛藝術網

ENGLISH　中文　简体

(系統需求： Netscape 3.0 ; 16-bit 全彩色解析度；
六十四位元以上超敏感藝術神經；8 GigaByte 隨取藝術史記憶體)

Shockwave 多媒體藝術作品 (⊕) 三月起陸續登場！
請先 download Shockwave 輔助軟體

⊕ Figure 4.8 Main page of Wonderfully Absurd Temple, captured by the IAWM on June 13, 1997. https://web.archive.org/web/19970613210434/http://www.sino logic.com/webart/menu.html.

of Chinese Internet literature, even though they are no longer to be found online.[74]

An integral element of Yao's work is that it frequently comments on the lack of attention to formal experimentation and visual effect in the Chinese poetic tradition. The work "Xinbian quan Tang shi (di si juan)" (English title: Complete Tang Quatrains), for instance, displays four vertical lines that each consist of five squares, which are constantly changing color.[75] In my interpretation, the work drives home the message that, for a visual poet, there is little diversity in the time-honored genre of the five-word quatrain or *wuyan jueju*. Different words are put into the right positions in the standard-length lines but, visually speaking, they are but blocks of ink with slightly different appearances.[76]

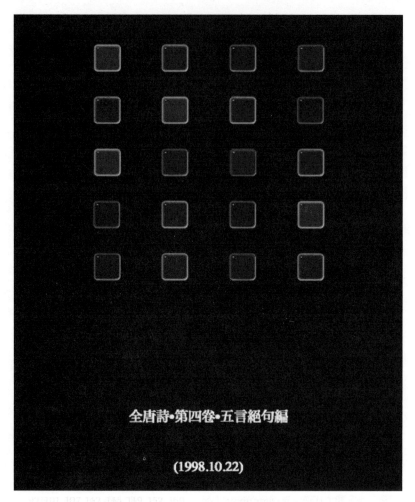

全唐詩•第四卷•五言絕句編

(1998.10.22)

⬆ **Figure 4.9** "Complete Tang Quatrains," by Dajuin Yao, captured by the IAWM on May 14, 2008. http://web.archive.org/web/20080514034832/http://www.sino logic.com/webart/jueju/jueju.html.

Another work featuring a more complex comment on traditional po-etry is "Duoshengbu wuyan jueju—lan jing" (English title: Multiphonic Quatrain: Looking into the Mirror 1 Day Before Autumn).[77] When the poem starts, the only instruction given is not to start interacting until it is fully downloaded. This serves the function of hinting to the reader-user that interaction is possible. On the second screen appears a poem by the Tang poet Li Yi (748–829), with again the instruction to wait before interacting, indicating that interaction is possible. The voices that speak when the various characters of the classical poem are clicked represent different dialects and different registers of the Chinese language, and when clicked in rapid succession, they create a sense of noise, confusion, and polyphony that, in my interpretation, is meant to be the exact opposite of the Chinese poetic tradition in its relation to practices involving formal regularity, memorization, canon building, standardization, and so on. At the same time, however, the appearance of the classical poem on-screen reminds us of the fact that, despite all the different voices, registers, dialects, and regional languages, there is something that all these speakers have in common: a cultural tradition in which poems like this play an important role. As is appropriate for a work of concrete poetry, the actual semantic meaning of Li Yi's poem is, at least in my interpretation, less important to the overall meaning of Yao's work.

Some of Yao's early work was created using a software that he refers to as Poetry Design Assistant (PDA) and similar software used to create "random" poetic lines on the basis of specific algorithms based, presumably, on word class and function. A very early work of this kind, dated 1994, is "Chengshi luoji jiqi shi—yi" (English title: Algorithmic Poetry—One), translated as follows:[78]

Algorithmic Poetry—One

lotus flowers turning to dust in a periscope burst open
crazy thoughts of the border

a dangling tenor
ancient undying angry fire scaling the void
the custom of the passer-by

because the unforgettable touch for an instant at the lake's center   ·
the forgotten rhythm

is the striking of the past

is the deep red ocean

just as an apparition in a mirror

In my interpretation, this poem may well be mistaken by many readers for a "normal" poem of the "obscure" (*menglong*) variety referred to earlier in this chapter. The fact that it was written by a machine (or rather, the author's *claim* that it was written by a machine) is what sets in motion some pondering on questions of originality and poeticality. Note that we have no evidence, other than the author's claim, that such a thing as a "Poetry Design Assistant" ever existed. Although it is perfectly conceivable that such a piece of software might be designed, the poem perhaps obtains a yet more interesting layer if we bear in mind that the poet's statement might be ironic.

Yao also created sound poetry on the basis of such algorithmic work, as in "Zhendang de manzu" (Satisfaction of Oscillation), which is a nine-minute sound file containing sounds generated by a computer on the basis of a Mandarin recitation of five syllables of one of Yao's algorithmically generated poems (or so he claims—I have no doubt that the sounds are computer generated, but there is no evidence that the sounds were taken from a poem, nor that the poem itself was computer generated). This work is still available online and appears among other avant-garde sound works by other artists on the website Archival Vinyl.[79]

A very specific textual concern expressed by Yao in his work from his early experiments onward is the blurring of the boundaries between horizontal and vertical Chinese writing. In a work tellingly titled "Xuanyan" (literally, "Manifesto"; English title: Autoexoticism Manifesto), Chinese text is arranged on-screen in square blocks of 320 (20 by 16) characters each.[80] The blocks themselves constitute a visual reference to the Chinese language, since Chinese characters are all presumed to fit into perfect squares. The text in each block is in fact the same, but in the blocks on the left-hand side it is written horizontally and in the blocks on the right-hand side it is written vertically. Also, in the second, fourth, and sixth blocks in each column, the text is written backward, that is, horizontally from the bottom right corner and vertically from the bottom left corner. The text itself is a description of another poem by Yao, titled "Made! Wo de Quan Tang shi diaodao taikongcang waimian qu le" (Damn! My Complete Tang Poetry Has Fallen out of the Space Capsule), which features a visual representation of myriad Chinese characters dumped into space, where they form new "constellations" of form and meaning that do not make conventional sense. And this, the text concludes, is what is called auto-exoticism (or "self-estrangement," in Chinese *ziti yihua*, with a nice, perhaps intentional, homophone of *ziti* 自体, "self," with *ziti* 字体, "type font").

In more recent work, Yao has focused mainly on sound art, but he has not moved away completely from textual work, and he continues to pay attention to visual aspects of language and to the random nature of the connection between words and meaning. He developed a vertical writing software called Verticalis, which produces hard-coded vertical writing that can be copied and pasted across programs and platforms and which, among other things, he recommends for the production of concrete poetry and for the publication of texts that cannot be found by search engines or censorship keyword crawlers. I tried using it to input hard-coded Chinese into Jim Andrews's "arteroids," but it still failed to display. Nevertheless, this is clearly an example of a Chinese poet attempting to find ways around the problem of encoding noted in the previous section of this chapter.

The Verticalis software also comes installed with a tool called Funky Funkey that claims to use "artificial intelligence algorithms" to change any inputted text into poems in a variety of genres, ranging from five-character and seven-character classical style to modern free verse.[81]

On his new website, now called Post-Concrete, Yao maintains an irregular blog that has the following statement on the front page, providing further evidence of his continued interest in alienating language from its conventional meaning and in playful pastiche of orientalism and exoticism:

This site is half written in semi-classical Chinese with excessive hyphenation, name dropping and meta-referencing and therefore remains untranslatably (un)Chinese, defying all machine translation.

(Dis)Orientally yours, Dajuin[82]

Finally, Yao has recently presented a new software and video installation called IdeoRhythm that showcases what he refers to as algorithmic calligraphy, aiming to break the link between calligraphy and handwriting by projecting specially created calligraphic computer fonts. In other words, he has created a kind of calligraphy that is produced by typing on a keyboard rather than holding a brush. I have not yet seen the installation, but its description, cited in the following, clearly draws on many of the concepts and ideas discussed previously.

IdeoRhythm is the artist's unique homage to the Chinese script system, exploring the ideographic writing's extreme possibilities in expression in this

"post-handwriting" era of global culture. IdeoRhythm is a real-time software algorithm system projecting animated Chinese characters on large
projection screens or gallery walls. With the pervasiveness of computer inputting, the ideographic writing system is already much removed from the
motor memory and practice of our hands. In future Chinese calligraphy of the
"post-handwriting" era, the art will be executed via the agent of fonts, software and algorithm, instead of traditional writing instruments. The recontex-
tualization and indecipherability of Chinese characters seen in this series
signify the alienation and auto-exoticism of Chinese culture in this and future
centuries.[83]

Summing up, it seems fair to say that Dajuin Yao's work burns as many
bridges as it crosses. He moves freely between poetry, visual art, sound
art, and software promotion and in doing so has created a number of
works that make very creative use of the typical characteristics of the
World Wide Web: hyperlinking and user-machine interaction. Moreover
he has done so at a very early stage of the development of the Internet,
joining the ranks of a global avant-garde experimenting with the literary
and artistic potential of programmable digital media and the web environment. At the same time, the main bridge he has burned (and other
similar experimenters with him) is that of linearity. In the examples given
in the preceding, his only works that developed in a linear fashion and
that were therefore open to conventional readings and interpretations
were those he claimed were written by a computer program instead of
a human being. His work is definitely transgressive when set against the
poetic norms perpetuated by the online forums discussed in the earlier
sections of this book. Due to its visual qualities, it also travels well across
geographical and cultural borders, although in the PRC, in my experience, there are still very few who are willing to accept that his visual poetry is indeed poetry. However, similar experiments are widespread in
the PRC art world, and it is not surprising that that is where Yao has now
found his professional niche. Clearly, Yao's work is much less adept in
crossing the boundaries between online publishing and print publishing,
simply because too much of his work features either movement or interaction, or both and therefore cannot be printed.

This chapter has focused on showcasing the variety of online sinophone poetry that can be encountered on the Internet today. As in previous chapters, I have tried to show that even mainstream work, produced on a daily basis on countless literary forums, is not devoid of innovative value. At the same time, I have demonstrated that some types of online poetry are either forced to, or choose to, remain largely outside the system. The work of Dajuin Yao, which literally disappeared from the web one day while I was trying to do research on it, epitomizes the precarious existence of much online writing. Taken in its entirety, however, as an art world steadily developing its own standards and conventions, Chinese online poetry provides Chinese poetry lovers with many of the aesthetic, cultural, and social functions that they enjoy, overcoming many of the limitations and boundaries inherent to the print-culture system.

⮕ **AT THE BEGINNING OF THIS BOOK** I cited statistics showing that prior to 2012 more Chinese people went online to enjoy literature than to do online shopping. Since that year, the growth in numbers of users of Internet literature applications has slowed down, prompting the following pessimistic comments from the China Internet Network Information Center, here quoted in the original English:

> As a new form of literature, the online literature was popular in the earlier stage of its development due to its low threshold when a vast number of works were written and distributed on the Internet to a vast number of readers, which led to the rapid development of online literature. However, the online literature is now in a predicament. On one hand, the low threshold resulted in a large number of low-quality works; on the other hand, in order that the online literature could be updated and distributed rapidly, it was written in such a way that it was less like the works of literature; and to adapt to the taste of the readers, the online literature became stylized. The low quality, lack of innovation and stylizing are the problems existing in online literature and prevent the development of online literature.[1]

Hidden among the many pages of a largely statistical annual report on the development of the Internet in China, these lines bear the unmistakable traits of postsocialism. Here we have a bureaucratic entity expressing concern about the stylistic quality of a novel kind of literature. Even more saliently, this entity, undoubtedly linked in some way to the Communist Party, couches its worries about literary quality in a warning against writers' adapting to the taste of their readers. Giving the people what they want, apparently, can only lead to low quality, making literature seem less like literature, and eventually causing the same people whose tastes are provided for to turn away and go in search of some other form of entertainment. (The subsection of the report dealing with online literature is part of a larger section on online entertainment, which also comments on online games and online videos.) The passage is a perfect example of how, in the wonderful world of Chinese postsocialism, a distinction can be forged between what the market seems to want and what "the masses" really want, and articulated through a concept of style more commonly encountered in the writings of literary critics.

The passage also shows to what extent in recent years the term "online literature" (*wangluo wenxue*) has become synonymous with online commercial fiction. To be fair to the report's authors, this limiting definition was partially imposed on them by the nature of the statistics they are collecting. They look at the use of specific applications designed for specific purposes. Genre fiction sites such as Starting Point or Flying Gourd have special characteristics, especially the VIP subscription system, which make them clearly recognizable and distinguishable from, for instance, online shopping sites. Moreover, when commercial fiction sites set up their web domains, they register as providers of literature, whereas noncommercial literary communities typically do not have their own domains and are therefore not individually registered. It would frankly be undoable for anyone to gather complete statistics on all literature created on the Chinese Internet.

Others in China worry about the future of online writing as well. In her textbook history of Internet literature, referred to at length in chapter 1 of this book, Mei Hong paraphrases some pessimistic comments by experts, all of which are couched in terms of economic capital. The main problem they perceive is that only martial arts and fantasy fiction are selling well online, but that even the big sites continue to struggle to make decent profits.[2] As we have seen, however, some of the longest lasting literary websites in China, such as the Black and Blue site and the two poetry forums discussed in chapter 4, do not pursue profit at all, nor do they receive stipends from the Writers Association, yet they continue to thrive. If one looks beyond the profit principle, the outlook for online literature might be less gloomy. I shall provide my own speculations about the future of Internet literature in China shortly, but first I want to look back at some of the main points put forward in the previous chapters and address some areas I did not cover.

It has been the first and foremost aim of this book to show that there has been and still is a wide variety of Internet literature in China. Conscious of the fact that no comprehensive introduction to the topic had appeared in English before, I have tried to provide as much as possible basic knowledge. What is Internet literature? What is a discussion forum? What are threads and posts? What are VIP chapters? No scholarly audience in China would have required this kind of explanation. Long before the commercial business model now most commonly associated with *wangluo wenxue* was created, Internet literature was already widely discussed in the Chinese media, and printed reproductions of online work were widely available in bookshops, where they were clearly identified as a separate category of literature. As described in chapter 2, the first nationwide debate about Internet literature was sparked around the year 2000. The same year also saw the publication of the first of many printed anthologies of born-digital literary work. By 2005, Chen Cun was editing a special section on Internet literature for the highly established print journal *October*. By 2010, the fact that the Lu Xun Literary Prize was *not* awarded to a web author required a public explanation by a spokesperson of the Writers Association.[3]

The descriptive overview of the first decade and a half of Chinese Internet literature provided in this book has been much less comprehensive than the overviews that have come out in China in recent years. There are some very important areas that I have not included in my study. One of these concerns the mentioned highly popular genres of martial arts and fantasy fiction, which could be fruitfully approached from a range of different perspectives, including their traditional roots in premodern literature and their convergence with film productions and video games.

Although I have frequently pointed at examples of overlap or interaction between the online and print-based literary worlds in China, the
role played by online publication and online fandom in the blossoming
print-based careers of highly successful authors such as Murong Xuecun
and Anni Baobei has not been discussed. Not dissimilar to the case of
Han Han, discussed in chapter 2, both Murong and Anni have capitalized on their popularity, rooted in large part in their early careers as Internet writers, to push the boundaries of the Chinese publishing system.
Murong has done this by making outspoken public comments both on
Weibo and in the Western media on issues of freedom of speech, while
Anni has tried to launch and sustain an independent, glossy literary magazine, with the English title *Open*, which published two issues in 2011
before being discontinued, most likely for similar reasons that caused the
closing down of Han Han's *Party*.

I have not discussed online literature that aims to make straightforward political statements, such as for instance the poetry written by the
sinophone Tibetan blogger Woeser (http://woeser.middle-way.net/). The
problems of political expression in China are well-known and have been
widely studied and are generally not unique to literature. When dealing with the political side of the postsocialist mix, my focus has been on
issues that are more directly linked to literary production, such as the
relationship between online writers and the Writers Association, the
regulation of online publishing, and the moral and legal debates about
the balance between artistic quality and obscenity. Nothing is more consistently censored in China than pornography, and few things are more
typical of the postsocialist mind-set than the government's insistence, for
purely ideological reasons, that its citizens should be allowed access only
to "healthy" culture. The government insists that its view not to make
pornography available to anyone, not even adults, represents the consensus opinion of the Chinese people. Ironically, as standards applied to
moral censorship increasingly veer toward banning only the most explicit
forms of pornography, less-explicit types of erotic online culture become
automatically available to all ages. This has many parents in China wor-
ried and, as we have seen, has also caused the online industry to start
self-regulating, as in the case of Flying Gourd, which makes its iPhone
app available through the Apple App Store, allowing for the setting of
age limits. The same Flying Gourd novels that only adults can download

from the App Store are available to readers of all ages on the Chinese Internet, excepting the most explicit passages.

The increasing popularity of mobile applications for the distribution of literature via the Internet, but circumventing the World Wide Web, represents a technological innovation that will make it even more difficult than before for the Chinese authorities to check the health of its nation's culture. At the same time, as we have seen in chapter 3, these applications have also allowed groups such as Black and Blue to come up with creative innovations in literary form itself. The addition of little editorial footnotes to literary texts downloaded straight onto e-readers is a small, but fascinating, innovation, bringing to mind the age-old Chinese literati tradition of reading texts with commentaries. The creativity of Chinese Internet writers when it comes to doing new things while staying within the linear paradigm is one of the things that has impressed me most over the years. Partly responsible for this is the very large extent to which Internet literature in China has often been a social activity. This can be seen from early examples such as Lu Youqing's "death diary," when the dying author amid his suffering obtained some solace from his interactions with his online reading community. It is also apparent in the playful interactions between Chen Cun and his fellow "gardeners," not to mention their enthusiastic incorporation of me, the researcher, into their collective writing environment. A special case is that of the online poetry forums discussed in chapter 4, where the plentiful social interaction surrounding the composition and discussion of poems recalls the tradition of "poetry parties" of premodern times and appears to go hand in hand with an online revival of classical-style poetry writing. As I have shown, all these linear writings can easily be seen to possess innovative qualities and to challenge the ways in which we normally read and research literature. This innovative potential of what one might call interactive linearity has been greatly underestimated in the critical debate about electronic literature, for which the pursuit of nonlinearity in writing has been axiomatic.

It is tempting to suggest that the relative lack of formally experimental electronic literature in the PRC has something to do with the post-socialist condition. After all, writers and translators with Taiwanese roots, such as Dajuin Yao and Shuen-shing Lee, have enthusiastically practiced this kind of writing, as shown in chapter 4, so its relative absence in China cannot be explained by pointing to unique qualities of the Chinese language or literary tradition. (Although, as I have shown, the English-language origins of computer programming do make it more difficult to achieve some of the desired effects when working in Chinese.) One possible explanation might lie in the overall regulation of the Chinese Internet, where setting up a personal web domain is not as easy as in other countries. The higher the barriers for establishing one's own site are, the more Internet users will be likely to settle for using standard applications (personal blog, microblog, discussion forum) offered by commercial portals. And the more standard the applications used, the less likely it is that online writers will be able to experiment with the shape and design of their writings. Another likely reason for the lack of formal experimentation in poetry especially is conventional literary education in the PRC, which tends to de-emphasize modernist experimentation in favor of memorization and appreciation of classical work, promoting widely held conservative views about what is, or is not, poetry. As we have seen in chapter 2, even otherwise unconventional literary figures such as Han Han are prone to condescending views of, for instance, modern free verse, considering it simply "not poetry." Whenever I presented the material in chapter 4 to PRC audiences, I was met by similar reactions: the crowd was entertained by the dancing letters on-screen, but inevitably someone at the end would stand up to proclaim that all of this really was "not poetry." I do believe that this will change. The fact that creative individuals like Dajuin Yao are now working and teaching in the PRC, albeit in an art school rather than a literature department, seems to suggest that changes are under way. Although the glorious tradition of Tang poetry is part and parcel of the stories about Chinese culture that feature in "soft power" initiatives, I do not believe that the state has any intentions to prevent, or declare "unhealthy," other forms of poetry as they develop (with the exception of sexually explicit poetry such as the work of Datui).

It would be nice if, by writing this book, I have made some contribution to the more frequent inclusion of online material into the teaching of modern Chinese literature. As I hope to have shown, the material I have looked at, and much more like it, lends itself to discussions about the aesthetic, commercial, and political aspects of current Chinese writing, preferably considered simultaneously rather than in isolation. I would also be greatly pleased if some of this material would find its way into electronic literature syllabuses, which tend to be dominated by conventional lists of clearly delineated works by prominently named authors, no matter how unconventional the works themselves might otherwise be. Finally, I hope to have done something to support the emerging popularity of world literature curricula. If the study of literature that travels the world does not include the study of literature on the World Wide Web, then surely there is something wrong. Plenty of barriers are in place to make it difficult for Chinese Internet literature to be put on the curricula of U.S. and U.K. universities. The texts are often ephemeral, you do not always know where they begin or end, what is part of them or not, and translating them can be difficult if they include nontextual elements. Yet perhaps the identification of such barriers can itself be the stuff of fruitful discussions with students about what literature is and what kind of conditions and support structures are needed for it to travel in the first place.

There is no denying the fact that Internet literature has made a contribution to the development of Chinese literature as a whole. New writers have emerged, new niches have become available, and existing restrictions have been overcome. The question is: will it last? Although I do not share the bureaucrats' concern about Internet literature losing its quality and its mass appeal, I think the specific practices of online interaction that created much of the literature studied in this book are undoubtedly in decline. As literature sites start to act more and more as publishers, and publishers invest more and more in e-publications, more and more literary work is becoming available for direct download onto mobile devices, where it can be consumed in very much the same way that one traditionally consumes a book, that is, by sitting on a sofa, or on a train seat, and looking at text, even if the text is now on a screen rather than on a printed page. The habit of going online to join communities where texts are written, read, and discussed will not disappear but may well become an activity of a minority of enthusiasts for particular genres or subcultures. Experimental authors or groups will continue to use the Internet to find their own spaces, but they, too, might choose to provide less content publicly on the web, where they might feel constrained by the need to use conventional applications. The rise of the mobile application definitely offers new opportunities for creative individuals wanting to combine literary writing with software development. Even long-standing online writers with no particular interest in formal experimentation beyond the textual, such as the Black and Blue writers, can be seen to go in this direction, with their magazine now no longer available on the World Wide Web. In future, websites are likely to function more as places where one finds information about writers and their publications and links to where these can be downloaded rather than as the actual spaces where reading and discussion take place.

Perhaps the poets will stay active on public forums, spurred on in part by enjoyment of social interaction in the context of poetic life. The poets might continue to bring out low-cost publications, displaying a preference that dates back to the time of hand copying and sharing underground writings during the 1970s. For chroniclers like Chen Cun, the web continues to be a perfect environment as well, allowing him to share the textual and visual fragments of his life with his friends and colleagues and leaving a public record. Public figures like Han Han, too, will continue to find use for web-based applications, especially blogs, although his longing to escape the confines of the postsocialist publishing system has already pushed him toward using customized mobile applications as well.

Whether or not the postsocialist publishing system will last, disintegrate, adapt itself into disappearance, or simply be abolished is anybody's guess. Many have been expecting to see, sooner rather than later, the end of the state-owned publishers' monopoly on book numbers, assuming that it would be more profitable for the state to sell book numbers directly to private publishing companies. Similarly, the state may decide at some point that there is no more need to subsidize and support official literary organs such as the Writers Association. Already the distinction between the "official" (*guanfang*) and "nonofficial" (*fei guanfang*) literary communities is highly blurred as the two are melting together in the postsocialist mix. Many are also expecting age limits for pornography to be introduced soon, although as Western countries, notably the United Kingdom, are considering expanding their own censorship mechanisms for pornography, it will be interesting to see to what extent the Chinese censorship system will function as a positive, rather than a negative, example. The least likely to change is the principle of the "bottom line." As long as the CCP continues to take its ideological function seriously, it will want to have the final say about what can or cannot appear in the public sphere, and there will always be the possibility of that one phone call coming from somewhere to pull the plug on a publishing project, without giving a reason. But most likely there will be so many technologies, spaces, and means of communication available to find different ways of continuing the same project that it will matter less and less.

Even if in a decade from now all the literary websites are deserted and the World Wide Web has become entirely obsolete, I believe that the material discussed in this book, ephemeral though it may be, deserves to be remembered and from time to time reconsidered. The questions it raises about how to read and analyze unstable, interactive literary texts, how new literary genres and literary fields come into being, how professional and amateur writing communities interact, and how governments regulate literary production are relevant to all countries and all eras. Whether or not writing a book about a form of literature that has moved beyond books was a good idea remains to be seen. If nothing else, I hope that I have contributed to the preservation and understanding of a tiny sample of a huge display of creativity.

INTRODUCTION

1. http://www.chinadaily.com.cn/dfpd/shizheng/2011–10/26/content_ 13977518_5.htm. For a discussion of the usage of subjectless predicates ("Perfect . . . Maintain . . . ") in Chinese propaganda language, see Perry Link, *An Anatomy of Chinese: Rhythm, Metaphor, Politics* (Cambridge, Mass.: Harvard University Press, 2013), 17.

2. The term *wangluo wenxue* can and has been translated in a number of different ways. Since *wangluo* is the standard word for a (computer) network, the translation "Internet literature" is plausible, but the fact that *wang* means "web" and can refer to "the web" means that the translation "Web literature" is also possible. Some scholars prefer more general terms such as "cyberliterature," whereas in the English-language academy, as will be discussed, the term "electronic literature" is used to indicate a new scholarly field of inquiry. Since all the works I discuss in this book are transmitted through the Internet, but not all of them appear on the World Wide Web, I have decided to use "Internet literature" throughout, occasionally alternating it with neutral terms such as "online literature" or "online writing."

3. *Statistical Report on Internet Development in China* (Beijing: China Internet Network Information Center, January 2013), 38, http://www1.cnnic.cn/IDR/ ReportDownloads/201302/P020130312536825920279.pdf.

4. Ibid., 50.

5. No such category exists, for instance, in the U.K. statistics about Internet activities. See http://www.ons.gov.uk/ons/rel/rdit2/internet-access---house-holds-and-individuals/2013/stb-ia-2013.html.

6. I borrow this term from Jing Tsu, who uses it to describe the "soft power" exercised by literary elites promoting specific state-driven or nation-driven understandings of what Chinese literature should be and what does or does not belong to it. See Jing Tsu, *Sound and Script in Chinese Diaspora* (Cambridge, Mass.: Harvard University Press, 2010).

7. http://collection.eliterature.org/.

8. http://elmcip.net/knowledgebase.

9. The quoted phrases are part of the definition of what Espen J. Aarseth, in an influential early study, calls ergodic literature, i.e., any kind of literature that requires its readers to do more than just move their eyes and turn the pages. Espen J. Aarseth, *Cybertext: Perspectives on Ergodic Literature* (Baltimore: Johns Hopkins University Press, 1997), 1–2.

10. N. Katherine Hayles, *Electronic Literature: New Horizons for the Literary* (Notre Dame: University of Notre Dame Press, 2008), 1–42.

11. Howard Becker, "A New Art Form: Hypertext Fiction," n.d., http://home.earthlink.net/~hsbecker/articles/lisbon.html.

12. A good example is Ouyang Youquan's study of the "ontology" of Internet literature, which provides a very long list of Chinese websites in the bibliography but analyses very few actual examples of mainland Chinese work. See Ouyang Youquan, *Wangluo wenxue benti lun* (*An Ontology of Internet Literature*) (Beijing: Zhongguo wenlian chubanshe, 2004).

13. To some extent this is also a problem of definition. Much work that deconstructs language by emphasizing the visual rather than the semantic nature of Chinese script is found in avant-garde art circles in China and therefore not considered to be part of the literary.

14. Hayles, *Electronic Literature*, 3.

15. Ibid., 4.

16. Statistics provided by David Kurt Herold on the basis of 590 scholarly publications about the Chinese Internet published between 1990 and 2013 show that U.S. and U.K. academics in this field publish predominantly on political issues related to the Chinese Internet, and that over 85 percent of those publications deal with the question whether or not the Internet will bring democracy to China. This obsession appears not to be shared by scholars working in continental European countries, in Australia, or in Asia, even if their language of publication is English. David Kurt Herold, "Through the Looking Glass:

Twenty Years of Research into the Chinese Internet," 2013, 10, http://repository.lib.polyu.edu.hk/jspui/bitstream/10397/5789/1/Herold_Through_Looking_Glass.pdf. In an even more comprehensive survey carried out by Jack Linchuan Qiu and Wei Bu, who in addition to the 500 or so English-language publications discussed by Herold also looked at more than 1,200 Chinese-language publications, the preference of English-language publications for dealing with political questions is confirmed. At the same time, Qiu and Bu note that English-language and Chinese-language publications are similar in their lack of diversity and their overemphasis on national-level phenomena at the expense of studies of smaller or marginal online communities. Jack Linchuan Qiu and Wei Bu, "China ICT Studies: A Review of the Field, 1989–2012," *China Review* 13, no. 2 (2013): 123–52.

17. Herold, "Through the Looking Glass," 11. Herold himself has been among the first to promote a different approach to Chinese Internet studies, focused more on the rich variety of online expression in China than on its repression. See David Kurt Herold and Peter Marolt, eds., *Online Society in China: Creating, Celebrating, and Instrumentalising the Online Carnival* (Abingdon, U.K.: Routledge, 2011).

18. A detailed study of Internet censorship in China is contained in Rebecca MacKinnon, *Consent of the Networked: The World-Wide Struggle for Internet Freedom* (New York: Basic Books, 2012). The shortcomings of the term "Great Firewall" as a metaphor for Chinese Internet censorship are discussed in Lokman Tsui, "An Inadequate Metaphor: The Great Firewall and Chinese Internet Censorship," *Global Dialogue* 9, no. 102 (2007), http://www.worlddialogue.org/content.php?id=400.

19. According to the Chinarank site, YouTube was ranked as high as thirty-one on June 30, 2011. The IAWM has preserved a snapshot of the page in question: http://web.archive.org/web/20110630112353/http://www.chinarank.org.cn/top100/Rank.do?page=2. In October 2013, YouTube's ranking had gone down significantly, below the thousand mark, which is most likely an indication that blocking has become more effective.

20. Geremie Barmé and Sang Ye, "The Great Firewall of China," *Wired* 5, no. 6 (1997), http://www.wired.com/wired/archive/5.06/china_pr.html.

21. Similar observations were recorded by Perry Link in his study of the socialist literary system in China and the way in which it controlled print publications, depending not on formal institutions but on "the private calculation of risks and balances in the minds of writers, editors, and those who supported them." Perry Link, *The Uses of Literature: Life in the Socialist Chinese Literary System* (Princeton: Princeton University Press, 2000), 81. Under postsocialism,

the risks are much smaller than they used to be and increasingly balanced by the potential for commercial profit, but a calculated approach toward publishing is still essential.

22. http://harvardmagazine.com/2013/09/reverse-engineering-chinese-censorship. See also Gary King, Jennifer Pan, and Margaret E. Roberts, "A Randomized Experimental Study of Censorship in China" (paper prepared for the annual meetings of the American Political Science Association, August 31, 2013, Chicago), http://papers.ssrn.com/sol3/papers.cfm?abstract_id=2299509.

23. Other scholars have recently called attention to the ongoing changes in Chinese print culture as a result of the impact of online publishing. See Guobin Yang, "Chinese Internet Literature and the Changing Field of Print Culture," in *From Woodblocks to the Internet: Chinese Publishing and Print Culture in Transition, circa 1800 to 2008*, ed. Cynthia Brokaw and Christopher A. Reed, 333–52 (Leiden: Brill, 2010). See also Daria Berg, "Consuming Secrets: China's New Print Culture at the Turn of the Twenty-First Century," ibid., 315–32. Daria Berg's work also highlights other forms of online culture, such as online reality shows, that are driving change in present-day Chinese culture as a whole. See Daria Berg, "A New Spectacle in China's Mediasphere: A Cultural Reading of a Web-Based Reality Show from Shanghai," *China Quarterly* 205 (2011): 133–51. Finally, the work of Heather Inwood presents fascinating interaction in the field of poetry across different media, including print, TV, Internet literature, and online video. Heather Inwood, "Multimedia Quake Poetry: Convergence Culture After the Sichuan Earthquake," *China Quarterly* 208 (2011): 932–50.

24. For a general discussion about how to study censorship as part of literary production, see Michel Hockx, "The Literary Field and the Field of Power: The Case of Modern China," *Paragraph* 35, no. 1 (March 2012): 49–65.

25. Guobin Yang, *The Power of the Internet in China: Citizen Activism Online* (New York: Columbia University Press, 2009), 85–102.

26. Xiao Qiang, "The Grass-Mud Horse Lexicon: Translating the Resistance Discourse of Chinese Netizens," n.d., http://chinadigitaltimes.net/space/The_Grass-Mud_Horse_Lexicon.

27. The underlying reasoning here is best summarized in a phrase from the "Language Log" at the University of Pennsylvania, describing terms like "grass mud horse" as "Chinese netizen language designed to avoid the censors and to poke fun at the political system." http://languagelog.ldc.upenn.edu/nll/?p=6538.

28. Arif Dirlik, "Postsocialism? Reflections on 'Socialism with Chinese Characteristics,'" in *Marxism and the Chinese Experience*, ed. Arif Dirlik and Maurice Meisner, 362–84 (Armonk, N.Y.: M.E. Sharpe, 1989).

29. Ibid., 380.

30. Ibid., 364.

31. Ibid., 374.

32. Sheldon H. Lu, "Postscript: Answering the Question, What Is Chinese Postsocialism?" in *Chinese Modernity and Global Biopolitics: Studies in Literature and Visual Culture* (Honolulu: University of Hawaii Press, 2007), 204–10.

33. Paul G. Pickowicz, "Huang Jianxin and the Notion of Postsocialism," in *New Chinese Cinemas: Forms, Identities, Politics*, ed. Nick Browne et al., 57–87 (Cambridge: Cambridge University Press, 1994).

34. Chris Berry, *Postsocialist Cinema in Post-Mao China: The Cultural Revolution After the Cultural Revolution* (New York: Routledge, 2004).

35. Xudong Zhang, *Postsocialism and Cultural Politics: China in the Last Decade of the Twentieth Century* (Durham, N.C.: Duke University Press, 2008), 10.

36. See Xudong Zhang, *Chinese Modernism in the Era of Reforms: Cultural Fever, Avant-Garde Fiction, and the New Chinese Cinema* (Durham, N.C.: Duke University Press, 1997).

37. Jason McGrath, *Postsocialist Modernity: Chinese Cinema, Literature, and Criticism in the Market Age* (Stanford: Stanford University Press, 2008).

38. For an overview and discussion of such approaches, see Susanne Brandtstädter, "Transitional Spaces: Postsocialism as a Cultural Process," *Critique of Anthropology* 27, no. 2 (June 1, 2007): 131–45.

39. Lydia H. Liu, "Beijing Sojourners in New York: Postsocialism and the Question of Ideology in Global Media Culture," *positions: east asia cultures critique* 7, no. 3 (1999): 772.

40. Andrew Kipnis, *China and Postsocialist Anthropology: Theorizing Power and Society After Communism* (Norwalk, Conn.: Eastbridge, 2008). Most of the points summarized here are made in the introduction.

41. Ibid., 73–74.

42. Nancy Fraser, *Justice Interruptus: Critical Reflections on the "Postsocialist" Condition* (New York: Routledge, 1997), 1.

43. Ibid., 5.

44. An important exception is Robin Visser's magisterial study of 1990s Chinese urban culture, which references postsocialism in the title yet frames its argument around aesthetic responses to the onslaught of neoliberalist forces. However, other than in the title of her book, Visser rarely employs the term "post-socialist," nor does she provide it with a definition. Robin Visser, *Cities Surround the Countryside: Urban Aesthetics in Post-Socialist China* (Durham, N.C.: Duke University Press, 2010).

45. He does, however, employ several terms that can be seen as hinting at similar ideas, such as "consumer socialism" (xvi), "corporate communism" (251), and "the Sino-socialist person" (281).

46. Geremie Barmé, *In the Red: On Contemporary Chinese Culture* (New York: Columbia University Press, 1999), 285.

47. Ibid., 311.

48. Ibid., 363.

49. Zhang, *Postsocialism and Cultural Politics*, 15.

50. As mentioned, Barmé did discuss the Chinese Internet in other publications. Apart from the article with Sang Ye already referred to, he also coauthored a typically skeptical assessment of the significance of online debate in China. See Geremie R. Barmé and Gloria Davies, "Have We Been Noticed Yet? Intellectual Contestation and the Chinese Web," in *Chinese Intellectuals between State and Market*, ed. Edward X. Gu and Merle Goldman, 75–108 (London: RoutledgeCurzon, 2004).

51. Another example is the Danish National Library, which also harvests websites on the basis of legal deposit legislation, under the slogan "collects and preserves the Danish part of the Internet." See http://netarkivet.dk/in-english/.

52. Jin Feng, *Romancing the Internet: Producing and Consuming Chinese Web Romance* (Leiden: Brill, 2013).

1. INTERNET LITERATURE IN CHINA

1. Shao Yanjun, *Qingxie de wenxuechang: Dangdai wenxue shengchan jizhi de shichanghua zhuanxing* (*The Inclined Literary Field: The Commercial Transformation of the Contemporary Literary Production Mechanism*) (Nanjing: Jiangsu renmin chubanshe, 2003), 23. For statistics on literary journals in circulation between 1915 and 1949, see Liu Zengren, *Zhongguo xiandai wenxue qikan shilun* (*An Overview of Modern Chinese Literary Journals*) (Beijing: Xinhua chubanshe, 2005).

2. See Perry Link, *The Uses of Literature: Life in the Socialist Chinese Literary System* (Princeton: Princeton University Press, 2000), 118–22.

3. Paul Clark provides useful detail on the quantity of literary publications during the Cultural Revolution but is misleading on the topic of the pre-1976 revival of literary magazines. He writes that "from the early 1970s" literary publishing houses at central and provincial levels were producing books and journals again, and then adds that "periodical titles" were up to 194 in 1972 from 21 in 1970, without specifying that this statistic is for all periodicals, not just literary ones. See Paul Clark, *The Chinese Cultural Revolution: A History* (New York: Cambridge University Press, 2008), 223. Shao Yanjun simply states that "the vast majority" of literary magazines ceased publication during the Cultural Revolution. See Shao, *Qingxie de wenxuechang*, 25. A full text

search of the *People's Daily* for the expression "literary magazine" (*wenxue zazhi* or *wenyi zazhi*) returns no hits for the period 1965–1974.

4. Xudong Zhang, *Chinese Modernism in the Era of Reforms: Cultural Fever, Avant-Garde Fiction, and the New Chinese Cinema* (Durham, N.C.: Duke University Press, 1997).

5. Shao Yanjun, "Chuantong wenxue shengchan jizhi de weiji he xinxing jizhi de shengcheng" (The Crisis in the Traditional Literary Production Mechanism and the Emergence of a New-Style Mechanism), *Wenyi zhengming*, no. 12 (2009): 13–14.

6. Shao, *Qingxie de wenxuechang*, 129.

7. Ibid., 158–86.

8. For a succinct overview of changes in the PRC publishing system from 1949 to the present, see Christopher A. Reed, "From Woodblocks to the Internet: Chinese Printing, Publishing, and Literary Fields in Transition, circa 1800 to 2008," in *From Woodblocks to the Internet: Chinese Publishing and Print Culture in Transition, circa 1800 to 2008* (Leiden: Brill, 2010), 1–35. For a longer discussion of the second channel, see Shao, *Qingxie de wenxuechang*, 112–30. A very detailed study of the second channel can be found in Shuyu Kong, *Consuming Literature: Best Sellers and the Commercialization of Literary Production in Contemporary China* (Stanford: Stanford University Press, 2005), 65–94. A very comprehensive overview of the Chinese publishing industry as it exists today, including information about changes that took place after the developments studied by Shao and Kong, as well as much information about legal and political backgrounds, is provided in Xin Guangwei, *Publishing in China*, trans. Li Hong et al., 2nd ed. (Singapore: Cengage Learning Asia, 2010). I consulted Xin Guangwei's work in the Kindle edition, which has no page numbers. References therefore include chapter and section numbers instead.

9. Kong, *Consuming Literature*, 65.

10. Ibid., 73.

11. Xin, *Publishing in China*, sec. 1.1.3.

12. Kong, *Consuming Literature*, 73–75.

13. Ibid., 180.

14. See Howard S. Becker, *Art Worlds* (Berkeley: University of California Press, 1982).

15. Lei Shiwen, "Xiandai baozhi wenyi fukan de yuanshengtai wenxue tujing" (The Landscape of Primitive-State Literature in Literary Supplements to Modern Newspapers), *Zhongguo xiandai wenxue yanjiu congkan*, no. 1 (2003): 159–60.

16. See "Hua Xia Wen Zhai—The World First Chinese E-Magazine," n.d., http://www.cnd.org/HXWZ/about-cm.html. A very useful, textbook-style overview of the past and present of Chinese Internet literature is Mei Hong et al., eds., *Wangluo wenxue (Internet Literature)* (Chengdu: Xinan jiaotong daxue chubanshe, 2010). A brief historical overview in English is provided by Guobin Yang, "Chinese Internet Literature and the Changing Field of Print Culture," in *From Woodblocks to the Internet: Chinese Publishing and Print Culture in Transition, circa 1800 to 2008*, ed. Cynthia Brokaw and Christopher A. Reed, 333–52 (Leiden: Brill, 2010). There is also a very detailed, book-length history edited by Ouyang Youquan, which provides copious statistics and tables of websites, as well as a helpful chronology of "main events" in Chinese Internet literature from 1991 to 2008. See Ouyang Youquan, ed., *Wangluo wenxue fazhan shi—Hanyu wangluo wenxue diaocha jishi (A History of the Development of Internet Literature: Research Notes on Chinese-Language Internet Literature)* (Beijing: Zhongguo guangbo dianshi chubanshe, 2008), 351–87.

17. Mei Hong et al., *Wangluo wenxue*, 39–40.

18. Kong, *Consuming Literature*, 181. Mei Hong describes the same style as typical of the work of PRC Internet fiction celebrity Anni Baobei, who rose to fame in 2000. Mei Hong et al., *Wangluo wenxue*, 17.

19. Cai Zhiheng, *Di-yi ci de qinmi jiechu (First Intimate Contact)* (Beijing: Zhishi chubanshe, 1999).

20. Despite repeated suggestions that real-name registration should become compulsory in order to "develop a better Internet culture," the PRC government has been unable to implement this widely. An important exception is the so-called anti-indulgence system (*fang chenmi xitong*), which is installed in most popular online gaming software. The system enables access to the game only after submission of the user's state ID (*shenfenzheng*) number. If a check on the ID number identifies the user as underage, the game playing time is restricted to three hours. See "Fang chenmi xitong" (Anti-Indulgence System), http://baike.baidu.com/view/1054473.htm. Interestingly, according to a short article on *China Digital Times*, some PRC citizens' rights activists, including prominent individuals like Ai Weiwei, have actually campaigned in favor of using real names online, arguing that it is a first step toward eliminating fear of censorship. See "Radical Real Name Registration Campaign," http://china digitaltimes.net/2010/06/radical-real-name-registration-campaign/.

21. For more on the Lower Body group, see Maghiel van Crevel, *Chinese Poetry in Times of Mind, Mayhem and Money* (Leiden: Brill, 2008), 305–44. See also chapter 4 of the present volume. For an extensive treatment of avant-garde online poetry groups, featuring a detailed case study of the "School of Rubbish" (Laji Pai), see Heather Inwood, "On the Scene of Contemporary Chinese Poetry" (Ph.D. diss., SOAS, University of London, 2008).

22. "Guanyu women" (About Us), http://www.rongshuxia.com/about/aboutus .html.

23. Kong, *Consuming Literature*, 178–80; Mei Hong et al., *Wangluo wenxue*, 58–60; Yang, "Chinese Internet Literature," 348. A collection of reminiscences, photographs, and recordings related to the early years of Banyan Tree has been archived online by the blogger Xisai Shanren, under the title "Rongshu xia de gushi" (Stories of Under the Banyan Tree), http://www.txtplus.com/ blog/?cat=519.

24. Kong, *Consuming Literature*, 180.

25. "Our Footprints," http://web.archive.org/web/20071123181151/http://www .rongshuxia.com/channels/english/footprints.htm.

26. The significance of Anni Baobei's online fan base and her gradual development into a respected print author is discussed in a recent article by Shao Yanjun. Shao points out that, although Anni Baobei nowadays no longer publishes online, she takes care to continue to cultivate her readership through online means, notably through her blog. According to Shao, the fact that Anni Baobei built her career gradually and maintained close contact with her fans distinguishes her from one-off sensations such as Wei Hui, who had one print best seller but no stable fan base and therefore no staying power in the literary field. Shao, "Chuantong wenxue shengchan jizhi," 16–17.

27. See Michel Hockx, "Links with the Past: Mainland China's Online Literary Communities and Their Antecedents," *Journal of Contemporary China* 13, no. 38 (2004): 105–27.

28. Ouyang, *Wangluo wenxue fazhan shi*, 30–31.

29. Mei Hong claimed in 2010 that Banyan Tree had never left the top 400 of worldwide websites as ranked by alexa.com, but that statement must by then already have been outdated. See Mei Hong et al., *Wangluo wenxue*, 59. In 2011 the site's worldwide Alexa ranking fluctuated between 10,000 and 20,000, and its Alexa ranking for the .cn domain was between 1,500 and 2,000.

30. Lu Youqing, "Yu sishen xiangyue" (Date with Death), August 3, 2000, http:// web.archive.org/web/20080913213230/http://www.rongshuxia.com/chan-nels/zl/100/100_0803.htm. Further quotes from this text are identified solely by the date of the diary entry, without additional footnoting.

31. Lu Youqing, *Shengming de liuyan: "Siwang riji" quanxuan ben (Words Left-over from a Life: The Full Text of "Death Diary")* (Beijing: Huayi chubanshe, 2000).

32. John Gittings, "Last Testament," n.d., http://www.guardian.co.uk/technology /2000/dec/19/healthsection.lifeandhealth; Duncan Hewitt, "Cancer Diary Man Dies," *BBC*, December 11, 2000, http://news.bbc.co.uk/1/hi/world/ asia-pacific/1066203.stm.

33. See, for instance, Ouyang, *Wangluo wenxue fazhan shi*, 31.

34. Gittings, "Last Testament."

35. Rongshu Xia, http://web.archive.org/web/20000818173925/http://www
.rongshu.com/index.htm.

36. "100days," http://web.archive.org/web/20001018114338/http://www.rong
shu.com/shukan/100/100index.html.

37. Hockx, "Links with the Past," 118.

38. The IAWM does not have a complete capture of this text, but it can be found
attached to most copies of Lu Youqing's diary available on the Internet.

39. Nevertheless, in the weeks between the publication of the book and Lu's
death, pirated copies had already appeared on the market, as was reported
in the media at the time. According to Gittings's piece for the *Guardian*, Lu's
wife withheld this information from him since it would have deeply saddened
him. See Gittings, "Last Testament." This also explains why the book publication carries the subtitle *The Full Text of "Death Diary"* (*"Siwang riji" quanxuan ben*).

40. Lu's text was not captured by the IAWM but is widely available online. The
text is not dated, but given the chronological listing of all texts and paratexts on the minisite, it must have been written after the last installment of
the diary (October 23, 2000) and before the piece by William Zhu, which is
dated October 27. William Zhu's piece, titled "Wu shi wu you Lu Youqing" (My
Friend and Teacher Lu Youqing), was captured by the IAWM on April 1, 2001,
at the URL http://web.archive.org/web/20010401003557/http://www.rong
shu.com/article/20001027/89265.htm.

41. For a detailed analysis of the hype and controversy surrounding the 2003
publication of Muzimei's sex diaries, see James Farrer, "China's Women Sex
Bloggers and Dialogic Sexual Politics on the Chinese Internet," *China Aktuell:
Journal of Current Chinese Affairs*, no. 4 (2007): 1–36.

42. The term *wenxue qingnian* literally means "literary youth." It tends to be used
to describe young(ish) people who have a confessed interest in literary and
artistic matters without necessarily making a living out of it.

43. For an overview of this debate and the development of the standard negative
view of Wei Hui and other "glamlit" writers as capitalizing more on their looks
and private lives than on their talent, see Aijun Zhu, *Feminism and Global
Chineseness: The Cultural Production of Controversial Women Authors*
(Youngstown, N.Y.: Cambria Press, 2007), 137–39.

44. For a brief discussion of modern Chinese writers' diaries, see Michel Hockx,
ed., *The Literary Field of Twentieth-Century China* (Honolulu: University of
Hawai`i Press, 1999), 65–67.

45. This piece, which later also became one of the paratexts on the "Date with
Death" minisite, is still in the Banyan Tree archive. Chen Cun, "Zai Xiyuan bin-

guan" (At the West Garden Hotel), http://www.rongshuxia.com/book/63534
.html.

46. The full diary (i.e., including those entries not published online) covers exactly
    one hundred days, being the period between his daughter's birthday, when he
    started writing, and his own. His intention to write for exactly one hundred
    days had been announced from the start and was also related to his life expec-
    tancy, which he eventually exceeded by about two months.

47. "Lu Youqing xiansheng jinianguan" (Memorial Hall for Mr. Lu Youqing),
    http://luyouqing.netor.com.

48. Lu Tianyou, "Nü'er de jinian—gaobie shengming" (A Daughter's Commemo-
    ration: Saying Farewell to Life), http://article.netor.com/m/jours/adindex.as-
    p?boardid=3376&joursid=79078. Unlike most of the articles available on Lu's
    memorial site, this piece by his daughter appears not to have been published
    elsewhere.

49. Lu Youqing, *Weiwei kafeiwu* (*VV Coffee Shop*) (Shanghai: Shanghai wenhua
    chubanshe, 2001); Lu Youqing, *Huan cheng* (*Happy City*) (Shanghai: Shang-
    hai wenhua chubanshe, 2001).

50. Mei Hong refers to the publication of Li Jiaming's diary as another "major
    event" in the history of the Banyan Tree website. See Mei Hong et al., *Wangluo
    wenxue*, 59.

51. For a brief but informative analysis of Li Jiaming's story and the huge extent
    of media attention it received in 2001–2002, see Haiqing Yu, *Media and Cul-
    tural Transformation in China* (London: Routledge, 2009), 64–66.

52. Li Jiaming, *Zui hou de xuanzhan: "Zhongguo zui shenmi de aizi bingren Li
    Jiaming wangluo shouji"* (*The Last Declaration of War: "Online Notes by Li
    Jiaming, China's Most Mysterious AIDS Patient"*) (Tianjin: Tianjin renmin
    chubanshe, 2002). The same epithet had been given to Li Jiaming when he
    appeared on CCTV; see Yu, *Media and Cultural Transformation*, 65.

53. Barry & Martin's Trust, "Seventh Annual Report and Accounts: Period 1 Jan-
    uary–31 December 2003," 14, http://www.barryandmartin.org/annual%20
    reports/2003.pdf.

54. Yu, *Media and Cultural Transformation*, 66.

55. Only members of the community can read the contents of these pieces. The
    information given here is based on my browsing the list of titles in the section
    as it appeared in 2012. The page has since disappeared from the live web.
    A snapshot can be found at https://www.zotero.org/groups/252231/items/
    TXRKSC37/file/view (change character encoding to Chinese Simplified GB
    to view).

56. "Li Jiaming: Wo de aizi shenghuo" (Li Jiaming: My Life with AIDS), available on
    various websites, here cited from http://www.99.com.cn/azb/kags/85372.htm.

2. LINEAR INNOVATIONS

1. Biographical information about Chen Cun was taken from various online articles about him and interviews with him. I found the most useful information in Guyun, "Chen Cun: Tangzhe du shu qilewuqiong" (Chen Cun: Reading While Lying Down Gives Endless Pleasure), http://blog.tianya.cn/blogger/post_show.asp?idWriter=0&Key=0&BlogID=102&Post ID=2889814. This article is no longer available but was archived by the Digital Archive for Chinese Studies, Leiden Division, at the following URL: http://leiden.dachs-archive.org/archive/citrep/vancrevel_tan_hockx_2009/guyun.html. Additional biographical information was obtained during my interview with Chen Cun in Shanghai on October 24, 2010.

2. W. J. F. Jenner, "1979: A New Start for Literature in China?" *China Quarterly* 86 (1981): 293.

3. It is an indication of Chen's status as a writer in 1985 that the then president of the Shanghai Writers Association, Ru Zhijuan, awarded the only available professional writer contract that year to him, rather than to her own daughter, Wang Anyi, who eventually joined the ranks of professional writers in 1987.

4. His online writings are also not listed in the section devoted to him on the association's website, http://appl.eastday.com/lit/zuojia/zuojia.asp?zuozhe=%B3%C2%B4%E5.

5. See, for instance, Hong Zicheng, *A History of Contemporary Chinese Literature*, trans. Michael M. Day (Leiden: Brill, 2007), 280–81.

6. As the novel itself explains in the first chapter, the term "cow dung" (*niufen*) is left out of the title.

7. Jing Wang, *China's Avant-Garde Fiction: An Anthology* (Durham, N.C.: Duke University Press, 1998), 4.

8. The paradigmatic example of an avant-garde author who went on to write much more commercial work is definitely Yu Hua, whose less experimental novels of the 1990s and beyond, such as *To Live* and *Brothers*, made him a household name well beyond the previous audience for his experimental stories. The paradigmatic example of an avant-garde author who stopped writing after the 1980s would be Ma Yuan.

9. It is worth mentioning in this context that Chen Cun himself, during our interview, expressed the opinion that in the 1980s writers in China had more freedom than they have now.

10. The use of narrow period terms ("the High Tang," "the late Qing," "May Fourth," "the 1980s," "the Fifth Generation," etc.) is pervasive in the study of Chinese culture and often results in the neglect of larger trends and continuities. Idema and Haft's *A Guide to Chinese Literature* is one of few textbooks attempting a different form of periodization, based on the material context

of literary production: the invention of paper, the spread of book printing, and the introduction of Western printing methods. For further discussion of periodization and the historiography of modern Chinese literature, see also He Maixiao [Michel Hockx], "Wenxue shi duandai yu zhishi shengchan: Lun 'wu si' wenxue" (The Periodization of Literary History and the Production of Knowledge: On "May Fourth" Literature), *Wenhua yu shixue* 6 (2008): 109–20. For a general discussion of the use and significance of period terms in literary history, see Micah Mattix, "Periodization and Difference," *New Literary History* 35, no. 4 (2004): 685–97.

11. Chen Cun, "Liang dai ren" (Two Generations), *Shanghai wenxue*, no. 9 (1979): 17–24.

12. Jenner, "1979," 293.

13. Chen Cun, "Liang dai ren," 22.

14. For a detailed first-hand account of the Democracy Wall movement and its aftermath, see David Goodman, *Beijing Street Voices: The Poetry and Politics of China's Democracy Movement* (London: Boyars, 1981).

15. Hong, *A History*, 281. The title of Liu Suola's "Lan tian lü hai," being a reference to a line from the Beatles song "Yellow Submarine," is perhaps better translated as "Sky of Blue and Sea of Green."

16. Chen Sihe, "Lun 1997 nian xiaoshuo wenti de shiyan" (The 1997 Experiments with the Form of Fiction), *Wenxue bao*, July 9, 1998, 4. In the brief author biographies appended to his 1999 textbook history of present-day Chinese literature, Chen Sihe describes Chen Cun as an author whose later works are "experimental." See Chen Sihe, *Zhongguo dangdai wenxueshi jiaocheng* (*A Course in Contemporary Chinese Literary History*) (Shanghai: Fudan daxue chubanshe, 1999), 387.

17. The story "Yi tian" (A Day) is discussed for its avant-garde narrative technique in Mao Keqiang and Yuan Ping, "Dangdai xiaoshuo xushu xintan" (A New Inquiry into Narration in Contemporary Fiction), *Dangdai wentan*, no. 5 (1997): 10–14. The story "Si" (Death) is discussed for its theme and linked with the 1980s avant-garde in Xu Fang, "Xing'ershang zhuti: Xianfeng wenxue de yizhong zongjie he ling yizhong zhongjie" (The Metaphysical Subject: A Conclusion and an Ending for Avant-Garde Literature), *Wenxue pinglun*, no. 4 (1995): 86–96. The same story is discussed in detail in chapter 10 of Chen Sihe's history, not for its avant-garde qualities but for its treatment of the trauma of the Cultural Revolution. See Chen Sihe, *Zhongguo dangdai wenxueshi jiaocheng*, 198–201.

18. Chen Sihe, *Zhongguo dangdai wenxueshi jiaocheng*, 294–95.

19. I do not know when and where the story was first published. That it makes a number of references to the popular Taiwanese author San Mao without mentioning her suicide suggests that it was before 1991.

20. Chen Cun, *Wuding shang de jiaobu* (*Footsteps on the Roof*) (Wuhan: Changjiang wenyi chubanshe, 1992), 46–47.

21. Ma Yuan, "Fabrication," in *The Lost Boat: Avant-Garde Fiction from China*, ed. Henry Y. H. Zhao, trans. J. Q. Sun, 101–44 (London: Wellsweep, 1993).

22. The original post did not survive on the Banyan Tree site. The full text of the post as well as related posts could still be found on Chen Cun's later site, Minority Vegetable Garden, in a 2004 thread in which Chen reminisces about the events of 2001. The URL was http://bbs.99read.com/dispbbs.asp?boardid=18&id=1978&page=&star=4. A snapshot of the page can be found at the following: https://www.zotero.org/groups/252231/items/QPPBBFM4/file/view#. The post appears as part of number 38 in the thread.

23. See, for instance, "Wangluo wenxue mingrihuanghua?!" (Is Web Literature Outdated?!), http://www.china.com.cn/firbry/2001-10-12/2001-10-12-14.htm.

24. In my interview with him, Chen Cun insisted that he was not fired but that he was simply not offered a new contract and did not oppose the decision.

25. The phrase *baojingfengshuang de zhugan* can also be read to refer to "a strong backbone" and might be a comment on his CEO's yielding to commercial capital.

26. Chen Cun, "Zhuyuan Rongshu Xia" (Wishing Banyan Tree Well), http://www.rongshuxia.com/book/787129#0.html.

27. Archived by the IAWM on June 27, 2009, https://web.archive.org/web/20090627153845/http://bbs.99read.com/index.asp?boardid=18.

28. Information provided on the site's "About Us" page, http://www.99read.com/company/aboutus.aspx.

29. Information based on interview with Chen Cun.

30. Chen Cun, "Ruhe dang cainong" (How to Be a Vegetable Farmer), http://bbs.99read.com/dispbbs.asp?BoardID=18&ID=19919. Snapshot preserved at https://www.zotero.org/groups/252231/items/7T3DV24K/file/view.

31. Chen Cun, "How to Be a Vegetable Farmer."

32. Susan Daruvala, *Zhou Zuoren and an Alternative Chinese Response to Modernity* (Cambridge, Mass.: Harvard University Press, 2000), 138–51.

33. When asked by me for the reason why the section did not continue after 2005, Chen Cun responded by saying that the journal editor simply no longer asked him to do it.

34. Chen Cun, *Bainian liushou* (*Custodian of a Century*) (Beijing: Qunzhong chubanshe, 1995), 21.

35. Chen Cun et al., "Xing biji" (Random Notes on Sex), archived by the IAWM on June 8, 2007, https://web.archive.org/web/20070608232636/http://bbs.99read.com/dispbbs.asp?BoardID=18&ID=21198.

36. I am not sure if the rise to "best of" status happens automatically (i.e., depending on the number of visitors to or comments on a thread) or if the status is assigned by the moderator (i.e., Chen Cun himself).

37. For a detailed study of the Muzimei phenomenon and other so-called sex bloggers, see James Farrer, "China's Women Sex Bloggers and Dialogic Sexual Politics on the Chinese Internet," *China Aktuell: Journal of Current Chinese Affairs*, no. 4 (2007): 1–36.

38. This is remarkable since in China there is no legal age for viewing pornography.

39. Ananda Mitra and Elisia Cohen, "Analyzing the Web: Directions and Challenges," in *Doing Internet Research: Critical Issues and Methods for Examining the Net*, ed. Steve Jones (Thousand Oaks, Calif.: Sage, 1999), 193.

40. "Wei cunzhang zhi xushishi" (The Village Head's Pseudonarrative Poem). Original URL: http://bbs.99read.com/dispbbs.asp?BoardID=18&ID=27211. No longer available online.

41. "Chen Cun zhuanlan" (Chen Cun's Column), http://blog.tianya.cn/blogger/view_blog.asp?BlogName=chencun.

42. "Chen Cun paizhao" (Chen Cun Snaps), archived by the IAWM on September 1, 2011,https://web.archive.org/web/20110901085756/http://bbs.99read.com/dispbbs.asp?boardid=18&Id=8183.

43. After the closure of Minority Vegetable Garden in August 2013, Chen Cun started a new and currently ongoing 2014 thread in this series on a different site. The URL is http://www.longdang.org/bbs/thread-38998-1-1.html.

44. Not currently available on the live web but archived at https://www.zotero.org/groups/252231/items/CGNUQWUN/file/view.

45. "Relie qingzhu cunzhang shuailing anmen pinxia cainong chongchu caiyuan zouxiang shijie" (Warmest Congratulations to Our Village Head for Leading Us Poor and Middle Vegetable Farmers as We Surge out of the Garden and into the World). A copy of this post is still available on Yang Xiaobin's blog: http://blog.sina.com.cn/s/blog_3f7b999e0100038w.html. The use of the term "village head" (*cunzhang*), a pun on Chen's prominent status and the character *cun* (village) of his name, dates back to his days on Banyan Tree. Nowadays it is still the common appellation used by others to address him online.

46. Archived at https://www.zotero.org/groups/252231/items/V5A2WF7B/file/view; scroll down to post numbers 3304 and 3305.

47. Chen Cun's comments originally appeared at the URL http://bbs.99read.com/dispbbs.asp?boardid=18&id=149535&page=&star=78, posts 775 and 776. The thread "Fanfeng xing biji" (Ironic Random Notes on Sex) was originally available at http://bbs.99read.com/dispbbs.asp?BoardID=18&ID=71556. Both are not available online at this writing and have not been archived.

48. Archived at https://www.zotero.org/groups/252231/items/EMT4IZRS/file/ view; scroll down to post numbers 813 and 814.

49. Ibid., post number 813.

50. On November 8, 2012, the Alexa rankings showed that Twitter was in the top 10 of most popular websites in most countries (and no. 8 globally), but in Taiwan it was ranked 73rd, whereas Weibo was ranked 35th. The Taiwanese alternative to Twitter, called Plurk, was ranked 53rd. In Hong Kong, Weibo was ranked 15th and Twitter 41st. In comparison, YouTube (global ranking 3), was ranked 4 in Taiwan and 5 in Hong Kong.

51. Sina Weibo, http://en.wikipedia.org/wiki/Sina_Weibo.

52. This becomes evident if one looks at the self-proclaimed first ever Twitter novel in English, *The French Revolution*, by Matt Stewart, which was completed as a full-length novel manuscript and then chopped into tweets more or less at random, with hardly any of the tweets containing even a single full sentence. See @thefrenchrev on Twitter as well as "Tweeting the Revolution," http://www.thefrenchrev.com. Much more akin to Wen Huajian's work is the Twitter-based fiction writing by Shawn Kupfer (@Tweet_Book), which has been ongoing since February 2009 (and thus predates Stewart's work, which began publication in July 2009). Kupfer's novels consist of self-contained tweets, posted to Twitter on a daily basis and copied in longer installments onto the author's blog site at irregular intervals. See "The Twitter Novel Project," http://twitternovel.blogspot.co.uk/p/index.html. Both Stewart and Kupfer write for a very small number of followers and rarely use their Twitter accounts for interaction with their readers like Wen Huajian, who had a much larger following.

53. The Chinese title employs a common pun by writing *weibo* with the characters 围脖, literally meaning "scarf" but widely used by Weibo users as a homonym for the word *weibo* 微博, meaning "microblog."

54. Wen Huajian, *Weibo shiqi de aiqing* (*Love in the Time of Microblog*) (Shenyang: Shenyang chubanshe, 2011). For media coverage, see, for instance, "China's First Microblog Novel Published," *Global Times*, April 13, 2011, http://www.globaltimes.cn/life/art/2011–04/644298.html.

55. Wen Huajian, *Tong, jiu kuchu sheng lai* (*Cry If It Hurts*) (Taipei: Taiwan shangwu, 2006). A PRC edition was published by Chongqing chubanshe in 2010.

56. In the printed version of the novel, copies of "Uncle's Longings" texts additionally serve as chapter epigraphs.

57. In his response to a comment on post number 368, the author admits that an image he appended to the post was found on the Internet using the Baidu search engine.

58. "Twitter: Integrated Photo-Sharing Service," http://en.wikipedia.org/wiki/Twitter#Integrated_photo-sharing_service.

59. My impression is that numbers of followers on Weibo are hugely inflated. In order to be able to read Wen Huajian's novel, I had to register a Weibo ID myself, and even though I never used it to write anything, I still gained new followers on almost a daily basis, presumably most of them automated advertising or phishing accounts.

60. The first 105 posts appear on a dedicated page on Banyan Tree, http://www.rongshuxia.com/book/volume/bookid-5057460.html. The version on Tianya is longer, containing 227 posts submitted between March 2010 and January 2011 and receiving quite a few comments from Tianya readers; http://www.tianya.cn/publicforum/content/culture/1/344563.shtml.

61. "Shou bu weibo xiaoshuo cuanhong wangluo: Chidu dadan bei pi gediao bu gao" (First-Ever Microblog Novel Takes Web by Storm: Rated as Daring but Criticized for Lack of Style), *Xinhuawang*, March 17, 2010, http://news.xin huanet.com/book/2010–03/17/content_13187889.htm.

62. Willis Wee, "China Has a Microblog Love Novel," *Tech in Asia*, April 15, 2011, http://www.techinasia.com/china-has-a-microblog-love-novel/.

63. "China's First Twitter Novel," *Wall Street Journal*, March 11, 2010, http://blogs.wsj.com/chinarealtime/2010/03/11/chinas-first-twitter-novel/.

64. "Gay Novels Went Popular in the First Microblog Novel Contest in China," http://www.bukisa.com/articles/403440_gay-novels-went-popular-in-the-first-microblog-novel-contest-in-china. (At this writing, this link no longer works and no archived version appears to be available.)

65. "Twitter Fiction: 21 Authors Try Their Hand at 140-Character Novels," *Guardian*, October 12, 2012, http://www.guardian.co.uk/books/2012/oct/12/twitter-fiction-140-character-novels.

66. The URL for the first competition is http://www.weibo.com/zt/2010weix-iaoshuo. The second and third competitions can be accessed through what is now the main Weibo page for the genre, http://weibo.com/weixiaoshuo.

67. Jin Feng, *Romancing the Internet: Producing and Consuming Chinese Web Romance* (Leiden: Brill, 2013), 53–83.

68. Since early 2012, as a result of a series of online articles by Fang Zhouzi on his website *New Spinners of Words* (see chapter 1), there has been doubt about the extent to which all of Han Han's printed and online work was written by one and the same person. Han Han has strongly denied the accusation that he used ghost writers. In February 2012 he briefly launched, and then almost immediately withdrew, a lawsuit against Fang for defamation. Han Han's reputation did suffer as a result, and he has been relatively less prolific since then, although as this chapter shows, he has been active in promoting new publish-

ing initiatives. For the analysis of specific blog posts and debates presented in this chapter, the question as to who actually wrote the texts ascribed to Han Han does not necessarily require an answer, nor was it a factor at the time the posts were published. For a good and impartial overview of the debate between Fang and Han, see Joel Martinsen, "Han Han the Novelist Versus Fang Zhouzi the Fraud-Buster," n.d., http://www.danwei.com/blog-fight-of -the-month-han-han-the-novelist-versus-fang-zhouzi-the-fraud-buster/.

69. All information about Han Han's early career is based on the discussion of his career trajectory in Marco Fumian, "The Temple and the Market: Controversial Positions in the Literary Field with Chinese Characteristics," *Modern Chinese Literature and Culture* 21, no. 2 (2009): 126–66.

70. A selection of essays from the period 2007–2011 was presented in English translation (by an anonymous translator or translators) on the website Han Han Digest at the now suspended URL http://www.hanhandigest.com. The IAWM has preserved snapshots of this site, taken mainly in 2011, at, for instance, https://web.archive.org/web/20110401115002/http://www.hanhan digest.com/?.

71. Han Han, *This Generation: Dispatches from China's Most Popular Blogger*, ed. and trans. Allan H. Barr (London: Simon and Schuster, 2012). This collection contains translations of blog essays from the period 2006–2012. The bulk of the material is translated from a Taiwanese collection that came out in 2010 and contained mainly current affairs essays from the period around the Olympics.

72. Liu Yunyun, "Handong shehui de liliang: Qianxi Han Han de bowen" (The Power to Shake Up Society: A Tentative Analysis of Han Han's Blog Writings), *Qingnian zuojia*, no. 11 (2010): 82.

73. http://web.archive.org/web/20051103050633/http://blog.sina.com .cn/u/4701280b01000080.

74. Han Han, "Wentan shi ge pi, shei dou bie zhuang bi" (The Literary Scene is Crap and People Should Stop Acting Like Cunts), http://web.archive.org/ web/20060322080202/http://blog.sina.com.cn/u/4701280b010002kb.

75. A measure of Han Han's significance as an independent blogger and the distance between his blogging activity and his literary activity can be found in this quote from Jeffrey Wasserstrom: "For us [scholars of present-day Chinese culture], it's not Han's novels that matter (I've never read one), but his online essays." Jeffrey Wasserstrom, "Make Way for Han Han," http://wordswithout borders.org/dispatches/article/make-way-for-han-han.

76. For a detailed and authoritative discussion of the Lower Body group and its literary achievements, see Maghiel van Crevel, *Chinese Poetry in Times of Mind, Mayhem and Money* (Leiden: Brill, 2008), 305–44.

77. Han Han, "Xiandai shi he shiren zenme hai cunzai" (How Come Modern Poetry and Poets Still Exist?), http://web.archive.org/web/20061203064454/http://blog.sina.com.cn/u/4701280b0100064x.

78. For a succinct discussion of the Zhao Lihua affair, see Heather Inwood, "On the Scene of Contemporary Chinese Poetry" (Ph.D. diss., SOAS, University of London, 2008), 254–59. I am grateful to Heather Inwood for sharing her knowledge of the primary sources related to the affair, as referred to in my subsequent discussion.

79. "Shi shang zui han de shi" (The Most Embarrassing Poems in History), cited from forwarded message on the Shui Mu Shequ forum, http://www.newsmth. net/bbsanc.php?path=%2Fgroups%2Frec.faq%2FJoke%2Ftestsep%2Fjoke_special%2Fsdf%2Flihua%2Flihuathepoem%2FM.1158017906.H0.

80. Han Han, "Shiren ji le, bu xie shi le" (When Poets Get Nervous, They Stop Writing Poetry), http://web.archive.org/web/20061027102459/http://blog .sina.com/u/4701280b0100066s.

81. For a detailed overview of the "popular" poetry style and its protracted opposition against the "intellectual" style, see van Crevel, *Chinese Poetry in Times of Mind, Mayhem and Money*.

82. The blog in question is still available but is no longer maintained. The URL is http://blog.sina.com.cn/u/1257069605.

83. Han Han, "Guoqing changjia, xiandai shiren ye zutuan" (During the National Day Long Holiday, Modern Poets Get Organized Too), originally posted on his blog on October 3, 2006, and not archived by the IAWM but still widely available on the live web, for instance at http://culture.163 .com/06/1005/09/2SLMVQ8600280003.html.

84. Van Crevel, *Chinese Poetry in Times of Mind, Mayhem and Money*, 319.

85. http://web.archive.org/web/20060805153022/http://blog.sina.com.cn/m/twocold.

86. Han Han, "Zhongguo zhe bang ernai zuojia, Zuoxie zhe ge ernai xiehui" (That Bunch of Chinese Mistress Writers and That Mistresses Club Called the Writers Association). This blog post has not been archived by the IAWM but has been widely copied by other bloggers, for instance at http://blog.sina.com .cn/s/blog_48f57c9c010006kz.html.

87. Han Han, "Xin zazhi de zhenggao xin, zhengren xin, gaofei biaozhun, tougao youxiang" (New Magazine: Call for Contributions, Staff Vacancy, Fee Levels, Address for Manuscript Submission), http://blog.sina.com.cn/s/blog_4701280b0100d03h.html.

88. For a discussion of this specific issue in the context of Han Han's contribution to debates about sex and pornography, see Katrien Jacobs, *People's Pornography: Sex and Surveillance on the Chinese Internet* (Bristol, U.K.: Intel-

lect Books, 2011), 90. For other images used to promote *Chorus of Solos*, see "*Duchangtuan* haibao" (Promotional Images for *Chorus of Solos*), http://blog .sina.com.cn/s/blog_493406430100gevi.html.

89. See "Han Han's Magazine Lacks Bite," http://paper-republic.org/news/ newsitems/29/.

90. Ibid.

91. Han Han, "Houhuiyouqi" (Until We Meet Again), http://blog.sina.com.cn/s/ blog_4701280b010176x6.html.

92. For a discussion of the term "studio" in the context of Chinese second-channel publishing, see Shuyu Kong, *Consuming Literature: Best Sellers and the Commercialization of Literary Production in Contemporary China* (Stanford: Stanford University Press, 2005), 5.

93. "Printing Revolution," http://europe.chinadaily.com.cn/digest/2010–12/10/ content_11684101.htm.

94. Han Han, "A Letter to Robin Li," Han Han Digest, archived by the IAWM at https://web.archive.org/web/20110401234457/http://www.hanhandigest .com/?p=369.

95. "Han Han's Anti-Piracy Union Takes Aim at Apple," http://www.wantchina times.com/news-subclass-cnt.aspx?id=20110707000041&cid=1104.

96. Han Han, "Rang dajia saoxing le" (Sorry to Disappoint Everyone), http:// blog.sina.com.cn/s/blog_4701280b0102ecxd.html.

3. THE BOTTOM LINE

1. Edward L. Davis, ed., *Encyclopedia of Contemporary Chinese Culture* (London: Routledge, 2005), 758.

2. This chronicle is no longer available on the live web but can be found incorporated into a Baike wiki article, http://www.baike.com/wiki/%E8%B5%B7%E 7%82%B9%E4%B8%AD%E6%96%87%E7%BD%91.

3. The IAWM has preserved a snapshot of the very earliest version of their website: http://web.archive.org/web/20011203090315/http://www.cmfu.net/.

4. *Xuanhuan* is considered to be generically distinct from *qihuan*, with the latter term referring to the international fantasy genre made famous by books such as *Lord of the Rings*. As explained by Shih-chen Chao, who translates *xuanhuan* as "Eastern fantasy," the core generic trait of *xuanhuan* is that it always features protagonists who are recognizably Chinese and who invariably establish superiority in the fantasy world because of their knowledge of Chinese philosophy, martial arts, and so on. See Shih-chen Chao, "Desire and Fantasy On-Line: A Sociological and Psychoanalytical Approach to the Pro-

sumption of Chinese Internet Fiction" (Ph.D. diss., University of Manchester, 2012), 114–15.

5. The IAWM has captured the front page of their site from early June 2004, on which they proudly announce this achievement: http://web.archive.org/web/20040606095624/http://www.cmfu.com/.

6. The China Webmaster ranking site has a separate ranking for fiction sites, indicating their Alexa ranking as well as several other rankings. Starting Point is invariably in the first spot. See http://top.chinaz.com/list.aspx?t=77&fn=bd. Based on the methodology used by China Webmaster, which takes into account not only page views but also links, search engine results, and so on, and which looks only at Chinese-language sites, the overall ranking of Starting Point among all Chinese-language sites is in the top thirty.

7. For a detailed discussion of the business management and editorial practices of Harlequin enterprises in different countries, see Eva Hemmungs Wirtén, *Global Infatuation: Explorations in Transnational Publishing and Texts; The Case of Harlequin Enterprises and Sweden* (Uppsala: Section for Sociology of Literature at the Department of Literature, Uppsala University, 1998). For a general study of the romance novel genre in Western languages, see George Paizis, *Love and the Novel: The Poetics and Politics of Romantic Fiction* (New York: St. Martin's Press, 1998).

8. See Michel Hockx, "Links with the Past: Mainland China's Online Literary Communities and Their Antecedents," *Journal of Contemporary China* 13, no. 38 (2004): 105–27.

9. Chao, "Desire and Fantasy On-Line," 34–49.

10. Ibid.

11. The English translation here is borrowed from Cao Xueqin, *The Story of the Stone*, trans. David Hawkes (Harmondsworth, U.K.: Penguin, 1973), 1:146. For an insightful discussion of YY fiction and its place in the Chinese literary system, see Shao Yanjun, "Chuantong wenxue shengchan jizhi de weiji he xinxing jizhi de shengcheng" (The Crisis in the Traditional Literary Production Mechanism and the Emergence of a New-Style Mechanism), *Wenyi zhengming*, no. 12 (2009): 19–21.

12. Information based on an interview with a government official in charge of the regulation of digital publishing, Beijing, April 13, 2011. The official spoke in a nonofficial capacity, allowing me to use but not attribute the information.

13. Jin Feng, *Romancing the Internet: Producing and Consuming Chinese Web Romance* (Leiden: Brill, 2013), 24–28.

14. For a very good discussion of the role of pornography in such debates in Europe, see Lynn Hunt, "Introduction: Obscenity and the Origins of Modernity,

1500–1800," in *The Invention of Pornography: Obscenity and the Origins of Modernity, 1500–1800*, ed. Lynn Hunt, 9–46 (New York: Zone Books, 1996). For specific discussion of these issues with reference to literature written by and for women, and its later exclusion from the realms of "proper" literature, see Bradford K. Mudge, *The Whore's Story: Women, Pornography, and the British Novel, 1684–1830* (Oxford: Oxford University Press, 2000). See also my discussion of transgressive poetry in the next chapter.

15. Erotic fiction and pornography also lend themselves to a wide range of other approaches, perhaps especially to an investigation into gender roles and relationships. I have no intention to deny or subvert the important questions of gender that are linked to this kind of material. However, in studying this and other genres of Internet literature, my intention is to show that the material is also of intrinsic interest for the study of literature, broadly defined. By focusing only on the social aspects of this kind of writing, one would a priori remove its literary significance and thereby reenact existing distinctions that have been generated by the literary field itself.

16. Feng, *Romancing the Internet*, 53–83.

17. Ibid., 123–25.

18. For an example of a Chinese SS/HP novel on the Jinjiang site, see http://www.jjwxc.net/onebook.php?novelid=462139. For an extensive discussion of Harry Potter imitations and fan fiction in China, see Lena Henningsen, "Harry Potter with Chinese Characteristics: Plagiarism between Orientalism and Occidentalism," *China Information* 20, no. 2 (July 2006): 275–311.

19. Feng, *Romancing the Internet*, 58.

20. Following the editors of the 2006 *Encyclopedia of Erotic Literature*, I prefer to use "erotic" rather than "pornographic" or "obscene," in order to circumvent the subjective connotations of the latter two terms. The usage of all three terms in legislation and criticism will be discussed later. See Gaëtan Brulotte and John Phillips, eds., *Encyclopedia of Erotic Literature* (New York: Routledge, 2006), x–xii.

21. In March 2013, it was announced that GAPP would be merged with the State Administration of Radio, Film and Television (SARFT) to form a new organization called General Administration of Press, Publication, Broadcast, Film, and Television (Guojia Xinwen Chuban Guangdian Zongju). At this writing (summer 2013) this decision had not yet been implemented. The new organization has a skeleton website providing links to the websites of GAPP and SARFT, which continue to function as normal.

22. The original publication can no longer be found on the GAPP website but was reproduced on various other sites, for instance at http://www.china.com.cn/policy/txt/2007–09/08/content_8840517.htm.

3. THE BOTTOM LINE   **217**

23. The very short deadline given to the lower offices to carry out these censoring measures seems a good example of the financial motives underlying many of the purported antiporn activities in the PRC, i.e., they are mainly about creating revenue for central government offices, which are allowed to fine regional offices that fail to meet the deadlines that they are set. See Gary Sigley, "Sex, Politics and the Policing of Virtue in the People's Republic of China," in *Sex and Sexuality in China*, ed. Elaine Jeffreys (London: Routledge, 2006), 53.

24. I am grateful to Ashley Esarey for telling me about these lists.

25. See http://www.legislation.gov.uk/ukpga/Eliz2/7-8/66/section/1.

26. What is also unusual about the GAPP statement, when compared with U.K. legislation (and presumably that of most Western countries), is its emphasis on banning obscenity in printed works. In the United Kingdom, current guidance published by the Crown Prosecution Service indicates that the harmful impact of the printed word is considered to be less than that of film or photographs. Indeed it is rare these days in the United Kingdom for obscenity charges to be brought against printed publications. See http://www.cps.gov .uk/legal/l_to_o/obscene_publications/.

27. English translation taken from the English-language database of Chinese laws and regulations provided by Lawinfochina at Peking University (http:// www.lawinfochina.com). Other (not necessarily better) English translations exist. The Chinese original can be found online in many places, for instance at http://www.china.com.cn/policy/txt/2012-01/14/content_24405327.htm. The following discussions of later interpretations of the law are also based on material available through the Lawinfochina database.

28. See http://www.law.cornell.edu/supct/html/historics/USSC_CR_0413_0015 _ZS.html.

29. Fang Qiang and Hai Yun, "'Yinhui wupin' bianxi" (The Differentiation of "Obscene Objects"), *Zhongguo xing kexue* 14, no. 9 (2005): 46.

30. http://www.law.cornell.edu/supct/html/historics/USSC_CR_0413_ 0015_ZS.html.

31. Zhang Rui and Yang Zhi, "Jiankang wenxue yu seqing wenxue de qubie" (The Distinction Between Healthy Literature and Pornographic Literature), *Beijing jiaoyu xueyuan xuebao* 20, no. 1 (2006): 34–37.

32. Ibid., 36.

33. This might seem implausible to those familiar with the censoring practices that are often encountered on platforms such as Weibo, where the use of certain keywords often leads to the immediate deletion of material. However, the point here is that such censorship is done by the Sina Weibo editors themselves, as a crude yet effective way of staying out of trouble with the authorities. The key role of editors in the PRC censorship system is discussed later in this chapter.

34. See Yi Chen, "Publishing in China in the Post-Mao Era: The Case of *Lady Chatterley's Lover*," *Asian Survey* 32, no. 6 (June 1, 1992): 568–82.

35. A Google search for the number one title on the list, "Jianghu yinniang" (Wandering Licentious Lady), yields plenty of links to sites claiming to host the full text of the work, but many of the links are dead or lead to sites that confront the user with a plethora of ads and pop-up windows among which it is virtually impossible to find the text (assuming it is actually there). Some sites claim to provide full-text downloads for members in possession of a password, without guarantees that the file one would be downloading is genuine and indeed safe. On the whole it is safe to say that, even if this text, which features graphic descriptions of incest between mother and son, may still be available on Chinese servers, its dissemination has been successfully minimized and restricted to the margins of the Chinese Internet, accessible only to those with access to password-protected communities or those who are unafraid to expose their computers to dubious downloading sites. However, the text is easily and freely available on websites hosted in Hong Kong.

36. http://bbs.v15i.com/viewthread.php?tid=103917&extra=&ordertype= 1&page=1.

37. The page is still available on the live web, although the accompanying text no longer appears; http://tupian.baike.com/a0_52_24_0130000025867812537 5242112031_jpg.html.

38. http://www.u148.net/article/421.html.

39. The site owners claimed to have a thousand authors under contract when I met them but added that most authors do not stay around for long. Contracts can be offered either for the serialization of a specific work or for contributions made over a specific period of time.

40. See http://www.luoqiu.com/html/36/36092/3893209.html. Beware of large numbers of pop-up windows opening when following this link.

41. For an in-depth and ongoing study of online political discourse, see Xiao Qiang, "The Grass-Mud Horse Lexicon: Translating the Resistance Discourse of Chinese Netizens," n.d., http://chinadigitaltimes.net/space/The_Grass -Mud_Horse_Lexicon.

42. This novel, serialization of which was ongoing when I visited the site in 2011, is now no longer available on Flying Gourd.

43. See, for instance, Guobin Yang's analysis of the "playful style of digital contention," Guobin Yang, *The Power of the Internet in China: Citizen Activism Online* (New York: Columbia University Press, 2009), 89–91.

44. http://b.faloo.com/p/185150/18.html.

45. http://bbs.faloo.com/t/1612604.html.

46. http://b.faloo.com/p/185150/263.html.

47. I should add that the Flying Gourd editors, during my interview with them in Beijing on April 14, 2011, did express an interest in artistic value and strenuously denied any suggestion that their website was merely a commercial operation.

48. For instance, in September 2011, the ballet adaptation of the classic erotic novel *Jin Ping Mei* voluntarily imposed an "eighteen and over" age restriction on its performances in mainland China. See http://www.ministryoftofu .com/2011/09/video-erotic-novel-adapted-for-ballet-takes-center-stage-in -china-admitting-adults-only/.

49. For a comprehensive discussion and bibliography of unofficial literary journals, especially poetry journals, see Maghiel van Crevel, "Unofficial Poetry Journals from the People's Republic of China: A Research Note and an Annotated Bibliography" (MCLC Resource Center, 2007), http://mclc.osu.edu/rc/ pubs/vancrevel2.html.

50. My relatively late discovery of the Black and Blue site was prompted by reading an excellent overview article about Chinese online literature by Adam J. Schokora, first published online in April 2009 and archived by the IAWM: https://web.archive.org/web/20111227162505/http://56minus1 .com/2009/04/chinese-internet-literature/. The Black and Blue site has been regularly archived by the IAWM, with snapshots dating back to 2002.

51. http://www.heilan.com/about.htm. Unless otherwise mentioned, information about the history of the group and the site presented in the following is all taken from this source.

52. Van Crevel, "Unofficial Poetry Journals." Van Crevel notes that *Black and Blue* is unusual among unofficial journals of the period in that its editors are not also its main contributors.

53. http://web.archive.org/web/20030205085209/http://www.heilan.com/ main.htm.

54. For a discussion of the forms and functions of abusive criticism in modern Chinese literature, see Michel Hockx, *Questions of Style: Literary Societies and Literary Journals in Modern China, 1911–1937* (Leiden: Brill, 2003), 191–201.

55. When I was writing this chapter in late September 2013, the Duokan site was in the process of migrating its account to the online shopping portal http:// www.xiaomi.com.

56. Wang Yang, "Wangluo he wenxue bantu shang de Heilan" (Heilan as a Web Domain and a Literary Domain), *Shanhua*, no. 8 (2007): 140.

57. http://www.heilan.com/main.htm.

58. Tian Er, "Bie ba 'xianfeng' dangcheng zhexiubu" (Don't Turn the "Avant-Garde" into a Fig Leaf), *Shanxi wenxue*, no. 10 (2007): 82.

59. Lexiaozhu, "Lin Xiaohe ruce" (Lin Xiaohe Visits the Toilet), *Heilan* 127 (July 2013), screen 54/280.

60. *Heilan* 127 (July 2013), screens 112–15.

61. Ibid., screens 132–35.

62. Ibid., screens 229–30.

63. Yu Hua's novel was widely criticized both online and offline. A short post by Han Han on Weibo, containing a screenshot of a few notes about novel writing recorded on his iPhone Notes application, was also widely interpreted as criticism of Yu Hua. However, whereas Han Han's critique was about the choice of subject matter, the Black and Blue group typically commented on Yu Hua's use of language. For Han Han's post, see http://www.weibo.com/1191258123/zBXNfFpoM?mod=weibotime.

64. Ibid., note to screen 250.

65. See Michel Hockx, "Born Poet and Born Lover: Wang Jingzhi's Love Poetry within the May Fourth Context," *Modern Chinese Literature* 9, no. 2 (October 1, 1996): 272.

66. On one of the Black and Blue forums I even encountered on one occasion the character *bi* 屄 (cunt), which is very rarely seen in print, routinely changed into a homophone character (逼) by editors and definitely not used in any of the erotic stories on the Flying Gourd site (nor in Han Han's blog posts using the term, as mentioned in chapter 2). Interestingly, the character was not censored, but comments on the story by other contributors to the forum expressed the opinion that its use had been somewhat gratuitous, thereby harming the story's literary achievement. For less clear-cut examples of what is and is not obscene or "serious," see chapter 4.

4. ONLINE POETRY IN AND OUT OF CHINA

1. See Christopher Bush, *Ideographic Modernism: China, Writing, Media* (Oxford: Oxford University Press, 2010).

2. Following the pioneering efforts of Shu-mei Shih, the corpus of world literature written in some form of Chinese is generally referred to as sinophone, even though the nonphonetic nature of Chinese writing would make the term "sinographic" preferable. The difficulty here is that the term "sinography" is also used to refer to writings about China, rather than writings in Chinese. See Shu-mei Shih, *Visuality and Identity: Sinophone Articulations across the Pacific* (Berkeley: University of California Press, 2007); Shu-mei Shih, Chien-hsin Tsai, and Brian Bernards, eds., *Sinophone Studies: A Critical Reader* (New York: Columbia University Press, 2013); Eric Hayot, Haun Saussy, and

Steven G. Yao, eds., *Sinographies: Writing China* (Minneapolis: University of Minnesota Press, 2008).

3. Maghiel van Crevel, *Chinese Poetry in Times of Mind, Mayhem and Money* (Leiden: Brill, 2008), 8–9.

4. Christen Cornell, "'Once Were Cultural Heroes' or 'A Kind of Geek Art'? Interview with Hu Xudong about Contemporary Chinese Poetry," *Artspace China*, July 15, 2011, http://blogs.usyd.edu.au/artspacechina/2011/07/once_were_cultural_heroes_or_a.html.

5. Ibid.

6. See Michel Hockx, *Questions of Style: Literary Societies and Literary Journals in Modern China, 1911–1937* (Leiden: Brill, 2003), 17–26.

7. See Michel Hockx, "To Tong or Not to Tong: The Problem of Communication in Modern Chinese Poetics," *Monumenta Serica* 53 (January 1, 2005): 261–72. I borrow the term "involutionary" (as opposed to "revolutionary") from David Der-wei Wang. See especially his explication of the term "involution" in Kang-i Sun Chang and Stephen Owen, eds., *The Cambridge History of Chinese Literature* (Cambridge: Cambridge University Press, 2010), 2:457.

8. There were Chinese poetry sites with their own domain names in existence prior to 2000, but they were not based in the PRC. See Mei Hong et al., eds., *Wangluo wenxue* (*Internet Literature*) (Chengdu: Xinan jiaotong daxue chubanshe, 2010), 39–40.

9. "Forum Rules and Etiquette," http://www.thepoetryforum.co.uk/view.php?pg=info_forumrules.

10. The site itself, in its information for potential advertisers (http://www.everypoet.com/mediakit.htm), mentions that over 80 percent of its members are based in the United States. The Alexa statistics for the site confirm this, indicating that 95 percent of visitors to the main forums page are from the United States.

11. Howard Miller, "New Posters' Orientation—Please Read Before Posting," http://www.everypoet.org/pffa/showthread.php?44995-New-posters-orientation-please-read-before-posting. Emphasis added.

12. "Shaìma jinzuo shisan shou, dajia piping!" http://bbs.poemlife.com/thread-616636-1-1.html.

13. Laier, ed., *Shi shenghuo nianxuan: 2006 nian juan* (*Poemlife Annual Selection: 2006*) (Guangzhou: Huacheng chubanshe, 2007).

14. The table of contents of the 2007 annual selection was widely circulated on the Internet, and I have found one website carrying a photograph of the printed version. In contrast to the 2006 selection, however, the 2007 selection does not appear in any of the major online Chinese library catalogues, nor

in WorldCat. This suggests that it was published through unofficial channels. See "*Shi shenghuo nianxuan* 2007 nian juan chuban," http://hi.baidu.com/liyuning/blog/item/32d28154acbc23183a2935d3.html.

15. Sang Ke, "*2000 nian wangluo shixuan* xu," http://80hou.poemlife.com/index.php?mod=libshow&id=302. For a general discussion of the significance of annual selections and anthologies on the current Chinese poetry scene, see Heather Inwood, "On the Scene of Contemporary Chinese Poetry" (Ph.D. diss., SOAS, University of London, 2008), 129–99.

16. For an in-depth study of classical poetry in modern times, including the genre's renewed popularity since the arrival of the Internet, see Xiaofei Tian, "Muffled Dialect Spoken by Green Fruit: An Alternative History of Modern Chinese Poetry," *Modern Chinese Literature and Culture* 21, no. 1 (2009): 1–45.

17. The Chongqing-based site Jiexian (Limitpoem, http://www.limitpoem.com) claims to have launched in November 1999, although again this claim is not substantiated by its domain registration record, which gives November 20, 2000, as its date of first registration. Chinapoet has always mentioned on its front page that it was founded in December 1999. Inside the site there is a brief overview that gives December 29, 1999, as the exact founding date; http://www.chinapoet.net/forum.php?mod=forumdisplay&fid=33. For a more de-tailed overview of the early history of Chinese online poetry forums, including those active before 2000 without a dedicated domain name or with "virtual" domain names (i.e., domain names pointing to subdomains on other sites), see Sang Ke, "Hulianwang shidai de Zhongguo shige" (Chinese Poetry in the Internet Age), *Shi tansuo* 1 (2001): 5–9.

18. When I visited the site in May 2004, over 15,000 members were claimed to be subscribed to the forums. When I visited again on September 20, 2004, mem-bership was claimed to be over 19,000. At this writing (February 2013) China-poet boasts 43,720 subscribers. During a visit in 2005, I noticed that the site had temporarily stopped accepting new subscriptions. Although no reason for this was given, the appearance of a two-line slogan under the announcement ("Let us jointly establish a healthy, civilized, law-abiding poetry community. Actively suppress and eliminate bad information and lend your strength to the cleaning up of the web environment.") suggested that this was most likely an act of self-regulation following state intervention, similar to what we have seen in the case of the Flying Gourd site in chapter 3.

19. See Michel Hockx, "Virtual Chinese Literature: A Comparative Case Study of Online Poetry Communities," *China Quarterly* 183 (2005): 670–91.

20. I borrow my usage of this term from C. J. van Rees's model for the description of literary communities. See, for instance, Kees van Rees and Jeroen Vermunt,

"Event History Analysis of Authors' Reputation: Effects of Critics' Attention on Debutants' Careers," *Poetics* 23, no. 5 (April 1996): 317–33.

21. Howard S. Becker, *Art Worlds* (Berkeley: University of California Press, 1982).

22. Howard Becker, "A New Art Form: Hypertext Fiction," http://home.earthlink.net/~hsbecker/articles/lisbon.html.

23. http://web.archive.org/web/20050113054449/http://www.hd315.gov.cn/beian/view.asp?bianhao=021102001091200370.

24. It is likely that, already in 2004, the Chinese site also screened submissions automatically with the help of filters that flag posts containing certain terms that are deemed unacceptable. In 2004, Chinese Internet watchers were beginning to draw attention to such filtering mechanisms. See, for instance, Xiao Qiang, "The Words You Never See in Chinese Cyberspace," originally published online in *China Digital News*, August 30, 2004. A copy of the text can still be found on the live web at http://www.hrw.org/reports/2006/china0806/9.htm.

25. The IAWM has preserved much of this material. The earliest online edition of the modern poetry webzine dates back to 2003. See http://web.archive.org/web/20041017022201/http://www.chinapoet.net/zswk/zswk.htm. The September 2004 issue of the classical poetry webzine can be found at http://web.archive.org/web/20050204214755/http://www.chinapoet.net/zazhi/200409gt/1.htm.

26. This rule appeared in a pop-up window when accessing the forums. It also appears when accessing the pages archived by the IAWM.

27. The discussion in question has not been preserved online, but a screenshot of the exchange appears as an illustration in Hockx, "Virtual Chinese Literature," 687.

28. Still available on the live web at http://www.chinapoet.net/forum.php?mod=viewthread&tid=118472&extra=page%3D1.

29. An image of the cover of the 2010 anthology found on a blog site mentions Zhongguo Guoji Chubanshe as publisher. See *"2010 Zhongguo shiren luntan nianxuan* fengmian, mulu" (Cover and Table of Contents of *Chinapoet Forum 2010 Annual Selection*), http://blog.sina.com.cn/s/blog_517210540100qgvo.html.

30. Zhongguo Shige Luntan, http://bbs.yzs.com/forum.php.

31. Tian, "Muffled Dialect Spoken by Green Fruit," 37.

32. Ibid.

33. Hockx, "Virtual Chinese Literature," 689.

34. For a succinct English-language overview of the early history of the journal, see Maghiel van Crevel, *Language Shattered: Contemporary Chinese Poetry and Duoduo* (Leiden: CNWS, 1996), 63–69.

35. The exilic nature of post-1989 writings by Chinese authors residing overseas is discussed at length in Oliver Krämer, "No Past to Long For? A Sociology of Chinese Writers in Exile," in *The Literary Field of Twentieth-Century China*, ed. Michel Hockx, 161–77 (Richmond, U.K.: Curzon Press, 1999).

36. Quoted from the IAWM February 17, 2004, snapshot of the website, http://web.archive.org/web/20040217104253/http://jintian.net/jthome.html.

37. Statistics here and following are taken from the site's statistics page: "Luntan tongji" (Forum Statistics), http://jintian.net/bb/stats.php. Based on visits to the site in 2011.

38. One should bear in mind here that *Jintian* is much more than just a poetry journal and also includes other genres. The Alexa rankings might be slightly skewed because they consider Hong Kong to be part of the .cn domain, i.e., it is not possible to determine if the high ranking of *Jintian* in China is perhaps due to a relatively high popularity in Hong Kong, where Bei Dao is now based.

39. James Farrer, *Opening Up: Youth Sex Culture and Market Reform in Shanghai* (Chicago: University of Chicago Press, 2002), 148.

40. Geremie Barmé, *In the Red: On Contemporary Chinese Culture* (New York: Columbia University Press, 1999), 181–87.

41. The opposition between "earthly" and "elevated" in contemporary Chinese poetry and poetics and the various clashes between the two styles, especially in the late 1990s, are analyzed in several chapters of van Crevel, *Chinese Poetry in Times of Mind, Mayhem and Money*.

42. The IAWM has many archived copies of the site, the last snapshot dating from December 2010, http://web.archive.org/web/20101209020227/http://www.wenxue2000.com/mk/xbs001.htm.

43. Van Crevel, *Chinese Poetry in Times of Mind, Mayhem and Money*, 307.

44. Ibid., 309.

45. Ibid.

46. A search of the Chinese Academic Journals database on March 31, 2013, yielded sixty-two articles mentioning Yin's poem, the earliest dating back to 2002.

47. The interview took place at the Beijing offices of the General Administration of Press and Publication on April 13, 2011.

48. "Guanyu wo he wo de shige, yiji zuijin de yidian xinqing zhaji" (Notes About Me, My Poetry, and My Recent Mood), http://www.tianya.cn/techforum/content/187/555040.shtml.

49. Datui, "Shouji yijing fang bi li le." The online collection I used is no longer available on the live web, nor on the IAWM, but has been archived at https://www.zotero.org/groups/252231/items/EJB9DZZ3/file/view.

50. "Biyun Beijing," ibid.

51. "Dongfang hong," ibid.

52. "Han Han: SB daiyanren," http://www.douban.com/group/topic/11204002/. The acronym "SB" is commonly used online to represent the obscene expression *shabi* (stupid cunt). Apart from the title, the rest of the poem writes this term in characters as 傻逼, where *bi* 逼 is the commonly used homophone for *bi* 屄, which rarely appears in print or on-screen anywhere.

53. "Wei chengnianren bu yi: Nü xianfeng shiren Datui zixuan 10 shou jingdian," http://bbs.headphoneclub.com/thread-139319-1-1.html.

54. "Han Han: SB daiyanren."

55. Cayley graduated from the Chinese program at the University of Durham in the United Kingdom and was for many years active as an independent scholar, writer, translator (of Chinese poetry), and publisher based in London. Since 2007 he has been a professor in the Literary Arts at Brown University. His status as one of the foundational figures of both the practice and the theory of electronic literature has been widely acknowledged. For a succinct introduction to his work in the area of "textual morphing," see N. Katherine Hayles, *Electronic Literature: New Horizons for the Literary* (Notre Dame: University of Notre Dame Press, 2008), 145–47. Cayley's website, with links to downloadable versions of much of his work, can be found at http://programmatology.shadoof.net.

56. Here and elsewhere my understanding of the aesthetic experience of reading this kind of literature is informed in part by Cosima Bruno's work on the translatability of Chinese concrete poetry. See Cosima Bruno, "Words by the Look: Issues in Translating Chinese Visual Poetry," in *China and Its Others: Knowledge Transfer and Representations of China and the West*, ed. James St. André, 245–76 (Amsterdam: Rodopi, 2012).

57. The morphs can still be found online (http://www.shadoof.net/in/digitalwen/dwframes.html), although they no longer work in all browsers.

58. John Cayley, "Digital Wen: On the Digitization of Letter- and Character-Based Systems of Inscription," in *Reading East Asian Writing: The Limits of Literary Theory*, ed. Michel Hockx and Ivo Smits, 277–94 (London: Routledge-Curzon, 2003).

59. See http://www.eliterature.org/Awards2001/poetry-CayleyJohn.php.

60. http://collection.eliterature.org/1/works/cayley__windsound.html.

61. Xu Bing's "Square Word Calligraphy" is a writing system presenting English words as if they were Chinese characters. See, for instance, http://www.xubing.com/index.php/site/texts/xu_bings_square_work_calligraphy/.

62. http://www.vispo.com/animisms/enigman/index.htm.

63. The Chinese translation is linked from the front page of the English version. To access the Chinese version directly, go to http://vispo.com/animisms/

enigman/chinese/enigmanintro.htm. Note that the Chinese version works on only PCs, not on Macs.

64. I am grateful to Andrea Bachner for pointing out this possibility and its significance to my argument in this section.

65. http://vispo.com/arteroids/indexenglish.htm.

66. Jonathan Stalling, *Yingelishi: Sinophonic English Poetry and Poetics* (Denver: Counterpath Press, 2011).

67. http://jonathanstalling.com/yingelishi.html.

68. See page 77 in the printed edition, or fast-forward to 12:22 in the online recording.

69. Stalling, *Yingelishi*, 9.

70. Printed edition, page 62; online version, 08:25.

71. It should be pointed out that, outside the PRC, formal experimentalism by Chinese-language online poets does exist, especially in Taiwan. The Taiwanese work has also drawn attention from PRC scholars. See, for instance, Chen Zhongyi, "'Sheng, xiang, dong' quanfangwei zuhe: Taiwan xinxing de chaowenben wangluo shige" (The Avant-Garde Combination of "Sound, Image, and Motion": Taiwan's New-Style Avant-Garde Internet Poetry), *Jianghan daxue xuebao (renwen kexue ban)* 27, no. 4 (2008): 11–16. In terms of actual practice, however, experiments with the creative use of Chinese characters taking place in the PRC appear generally to be grouped under the rubric of "art" rather than "poetry." The most notable example of this tendency is the work of Xu Bing, which although profoundly occupied with writing and text, is not normally considered to be a form of literature.

72. See Wang Guo'an, "Shuwei de Miusi—shilun *Miao miao miao*" (The Digital Muse: An Overview of *Wonderfully Absurd Temple*), *Renwen yu shehui* 1, no. 10 (2007): 101–30.

73. The character 謬 in the meaning "absurd" is more commonly read *miu* and more commonly written 謬.

74. The domain http://www.sinologic.com has been unreachable since 2008. Snapshots remain available on the IAWM. I downloaded copies of the domain files prior to its disappearance. I am grateful to Dajuin Yao for granting me permission to keep those files as an archive of the site and to cite from them in my research. Yao assured me in correspondence that the disappearance of the domain was not intentional and that he hopes it will be revived in future. When referencing specific works in the following, links given are to the works as they appear in the last version available on the IAWM.

75. http://web.archive.org/web/20080514034832/http://www.sinologic.com/webart/jueju/jueju.html.

76. It is worth mentioning that Yao's critique in this case, at least according to my interpretation, is of the *modern* way of printing classical Chinese poetry on the page, i.e., in separate lines of equal length. Traditionally, classical Chinese poetry was printed in consecutive lines without line breaks, similar to prose.

77. http://web.archive.org/web/20080509193228/http://www.sinologic.com/ concrete/works/quatrain.html. (Only partially archived. The interactive elements do not work anymore.)

78. http://web.archive.org/web/20080514070058/http://www.sinologic.com/ concrete/works/virtualpoem1.html. (Only partially archived. The image with the Chinese text of the poem does not appear.)

79. http://www.post-concrete.com/vinyl/?m=200802.

80. http://web.archive.org/web/20080514065941/http://www.sinologic.com/ concrete/works/autoexoticism1.html. (Only partially archived. The images do not appear.)

81. "Gongneng tese," *Verticalis zhixing shuxieji,* http://www.post-concrete.com/ verticalis/?page_id=11.

82. http://www.post-concrete.com/blog/.

83. Cited from http://www.chatfestival2010.com/ideorhythm.html. At this writing, this link has become unavailable and appears not to have been archived.

CONCLUSION

1. *Statistical Report on Internet Development in China* (Beijing: China Internet Network Information Center, January 2013), 50, http://www1.cnnic.cn/IDR/ ReportDownloads/201302/P020130312536825920279.pdf.

2. Mei Hong et al., eds., *Wangluo wenxue* (*Internet Literature*) (Chengdu: Xinan jiaotong daxue chubanshe, 2010), 68–69.

3. http://www.globaltimes.cn/opinion/voice/2010–10/585218.html.

BIBLIOGRAPHY

Aarseth, Espen J. *Cybertext: Perspectives on Ergodic Literature*. Baltimore: Johns Hopkins University Press, 1997.

Barmé, Geremie. *In the Red: On Contemporary Chinese Culture*. New York: Columbia University Press, 1999.

Barmé, Geremie R., and Gloria Davies. "Have We Been Noticed Yet? Intellectual Contestation and the Chinese Web." In *Chinese Intellectuals between State and Market*, edited by Edward X. Gu and Merle Goldman, 75–108. London: RoutledgeCurzon, 2004.

Barmé, Geremie, and Sang Ye. "The Great Firewall of China." *Wired* 5, no. 6 (1997). http://www.wired.com/wired/archive/5.06/china_pr.html.

Becker, Howard S. *Art Worlds*. Berkeley: University of California Press, 1982.

——. "A New Art Form: Hypertext Fiction," n.d. http://home.earthlink.net/~hsbecker/articles/lisbon.html.

Berg, Daria. "Consuming Secrets: China's New Print Culture at the Turn of the Twenty-First Century." In *From Woodblocks to the Internet: Chinese Publishing and Print Culture in Transition, circa 1800 to 2008*, edited by Cynthia Brokaw and Christopher A. Reed, 315–32. Leiden: Brill, 2010.

——. "A New Spectacle in China's Mediasphere: A Cultural Reading of a Web-Based Reality Show from Shanghai." *China Quarterly* 205 (2011): 133–51.

Berry, Chris. *Postsocialist Cinema in Post-Mao China: The Cultural Revolution After the Cultural Revolution*. New York: Routledge, 2004.

Brandtstädter, Susanne. "Transitional Spaces: Postsocialism as a Cultural Process." *Critique of Anthropology* 27, no. 2 (June 1, 2007): 131–45.

Brulotte, Gaetan, and John Phillips, eds. *Encyclopedia of Erotic Literature*. New York: Routledge, 2006.

Bruno, Cosima. "Words by the Look: Issues in Translating Chinese Visual Poetry." In *China and Its Others: Knowledge Transfer and Representations of China and the West*, edited by James St. André, 245–76. Amsterdam: Rodopi, 2012.

Bush, Christopher. *Ideographic Modernism: China, Writing, Media*. Oxford: Oxford University Press, 2010.

Cai Zhiheng. *Di-yi ci de qinmi jiechu* (*First Intimate Contact*). Beijing: Zhishi chubanshe, 1999.

Cao Xueqin. *The Story of the Stone*. Translated by David Hawkes. Vol. 1. Harmondsworth, U.K.: Penguin, 1973.

Cayley, John. "Digital Wen: On the Digitization of Letter- and Character-Based Systems of Inscription." In *Reading East Asian Writing: The Limits of Literary Theory*, edited by Michel Hockx and Ivo Smits, 277–94. London: RoutledgeCurzon, 2003.

Chang, Kang-i Sun, and Stephen Owen, eds. *The Cambridge History of Chinese Literature*. Cambridge: Cambridge University Press, 2010.

Chao, Shih-chen. "Desire and Fantasy On-Line: A Sociological and Psychoanalytical Approach to the Prosumption of Chinese Internet Fiction." Ph.D. diss., University of Manchester, 2012.

Chen Cun. *Bainian liushou* (*Custodian of a Century*). Beijing: Qunzhong chubanshe, 1995.

——. "Liang dai ren" (Two Generations). *Shanghai wenxue*, no. 9 (1979): 17–24.

——. *Wuding shang de jiaobu* (*Footsteps on the Roof*). Wuhan: Changjiang wenyi chubanshe, 1992.

Chen Sihe. "Lun 1997 nian xiaoshuo wenti de shiyan" (The 1997 Experiments with the Form of Fiction). *Wenxue bao*, July 9, 1998.

——. *Zhongguo dangdai wenxueshi jiaocheng* (*A Course in Contemporary Chinese Literary History*). Shanghai: Fudan daxue chubanshe, 1999.

Chen, Yi. "Publishing in China in the Post-Mao Era: The Case of *Lady Chatterley's Lover*." *Asian Survey* 32, no. 6 (June 1, 1992): 568–82.

Chen Zhongyi. "'Sheng, xiang, dong' quanfangwei zuhe: Taiwan xinxing de chaowenben wangluo shige" (The Avant-Garde Combination of "Sound, Image, and Motion": Taiwan's New-Style Avant-Garde Internet Poetry). *Jianghan daxue xuebao* (*renwen kexue ban*) 27, no. 4 (2008): 11–16.

Clark, Paul. *The Chinese Cultural Revolution: A History*. New York: Cambridge University Press, 2008.

Cornell, Christen. "'Once Were Cultural Heroes' or 'A Kind of Geek Art'? Interview with Hu Xudong about Contemporary Chinese Poetry." *Artspace China*, July 15, 2011. http://blogs.usyd.edu.au/artspacechina/2011/07/once_were_cultural_heroes_or_a.html.

Daruvala, Susan. *Zhou Zuoren and an Alternative Chinese Response to Modernity*. Cambridge, Mass.: Harvard University Press, 2000.

Davis, Edward L., ed. *Encyclopedia of Contemporary Chinese Culture*. London: Routledge, 2005.

Dirlik, Arif. "Postsocialism? Reflections on 'Socialism with Chinese Characteristics.'" In *Marxism and the Chinese Experience*, edited by Arif Dirlik and Maurice Meisner, 362–84. Armonk, N.Y.: M.E. Sharpe, 1989.

Fang Qiang and Hai Yun. "'Yinhui wupin' bianxi" (The Differentiation of "Obscene Objects"). *Zhongguo xing kexue* 14, no. 9 (2005): 45–46.

Farrer, James. "China's Women Sex Bloggers and Dialogic Sexual Politics on the Chinese Internet." *China Aktuell: Journal of Current Chinese Affairs*, no. 4 (2007): 1–36.

——. *Opening Up: Youth Sex Culture and Market Reform in Shanghai*. Chicago: University of Chicago Press, 2002.

Feng, Jin. *Romancing the Internet: Producing and Consuming Chinese Web Romance*. Leiden: Brill, 2013.

Fraser, Nancy. *Justice Interruptus: Critical Reflections on the "Postsocialist" Condition*. New York: Routledge, 1997.

Fumian, Marco. "The Temple and the Market: Controversial Positions in the Literary Field with Chinese Characteristics." *Modern Chinese Literature and Culture* 21, no. 2 (2009): 126–66.

Gittings, John. "Last Testament," n.d. http://www.guardian.co.uk/technology/2000/dec/19/healthsection.lifeandhealth.

Goodman, David. *Beijing Street Voices: The Poetry and Politics of China's Democracy Movement*. London: Boyars, 1981.

Han Han. "A Letter to Robin Li." *Han Han Digest*, n.d. http://www.hanhandigest.com/?p=369.

——. *This Generation: Dispatches from China's Most Popular Blogger*. Edited and translated by Allan H. Barr. London: Simon and Schuster, 2012.

"Han Han's Anti-Piracy Union Takes Aim at Apple," n.d. http://www.wantchinatimes.com/news-subclass-cnt.aspx?id=20110707000041&cid=1104.

"Han Han's Magazine Lacks Bite." http://paper-republic.org/news/newsitems/29/.

Hayles, N. Katherine. *Electronic Literature: New Horizons for the Literary*. Notre Dame: University of Notre Dame Press, 2008.

Hayot, Eric, Haun Saussy, and Steven G. Yao, eds. *Sinographies: Writing China.* Minneapolis: University of Minnesota Press, 2008.

He Maixiao [Michel Hockx]. "Wenxue shi duandai yu zhishi shengchan: Lun 'wu si' wenxue" (The Periodization of Literary History and the Production of Knowledge: On "May Fourth" Literature). *Wenhua yu shixue* 6 (2008): 109–20.

Hemmungs Wirtén, Eva. *Global Infatuation: Explorations in Transnational Publishing and Texts; The Case of Harlequin Enterprises and Sweden.* Uppsala: Section for Sociology of Literature at the Department of Literature, Uppsala University, 1998.

Henningsen, Lena. "Harry Potter with Chinese Characteristics: Plagiarism between Orientalism and Occidentalism." *China Information* 20, no. 2 (July 2006): 275–311.

Herold, David Kurt. "Through the Looking Glass: Twenty Years of Research into the Chinese Internet," 2013. http://repository.lib.polyu.edu.hk/jspui/bit stream/10397/5789/1/Herold_Through_Looking_Glass.pdf.

Herold, David Kurt, and Peter Marolt, eds. *Online Society in China: Creating, Celebrating, and Instrumentalising the Online Carnival.* Abingdon, U.K.: Routledge, 2011.

Hewitt, Duncan. "Cancer Diary Man Dies." *BBC*, December 11, 2000. http://news .bbc.co.uk/1/hi/world/asia-pacific/1066203.stm.

Hockx, Michel. "Born Poet and Born Lover: Wang Jingzhi's Love Poetry within the May Fourth Context." *Modern Chinese Literature* 9, no. 2 (October 1, 1996): 261–96.

——. "Links with the Past: Mainland China's Online Literary Communities and Their Antecedents." *Journal of Contemporary China* 13, no. 38 (2004): 105–27.

——. "The Literary Field and the Field of Power: The Case of Modern China." *Paragraph* 35, no. 1 (March 2012): 49–65.

——, ed. *The Literary Field of Twentieth-Century China.* Honolulu: University of Hawai`i Press, 1999.

——. *Questions of Style: Literary Societies and Literary Journals in Modern China, 1911–1937.* Leiden: Brill, 2003.

——. "To Tong or Not to Tong: The Problem of Communication in Modern Chinese Poetics." *Monumenta Serica* 53 (January 1, 2005): 261–72.

——. "Virtual Chinese Literature: A Comparative Case Study of Online Poetry Communities." *China Quarterly* 183 (2005): 670–91.

Hong Zicheng. *A History of Contemporary Chinese Literature.* Translated by Michael M. Day. Leiden: Brill, 2007.

"Hua Xia Wen Zhai—The World First Chinese E-Magazine," n.d. http://www.cnd .org/HXWZ/about-cm.html.

Hunt, Lynn. "Introduction: Obscenity and the Origins of Modernity, 1500–1800." In *The Invention of Pornography: Obscenity and the Origins of Modernity, 1500–1800*, edited by Lynn Hunt, 9–46. New York: Zone Books, 1996.

Idema, Wilt, and Lloyd Haft. *A Guide to Chinese Literature*. Ann Arbor: Center for Chinese Studies, University of Michigan, 1997.

Inwood, Heather. "Multimedia Quake Poetry: Convergence Culture After the Sichuan Earthquake." *China Quarterly* 208 (2011): 932–50.

——. "On the Scene of Contemporary Chinese Poetry." Ph.D. diss., SOAS, University of London, 2008.

Jacobs, Katrien. *People's Pornography: Sex and Surveillance on the Chinese Internet*. Bristol, U.K.: Intellect Books, 2011.

Jenner, W. J. F. "1979: A New Start for Literature in China?" *China Quarterly* 86 (1981): 274–303.

King, Gary, Jennifer Pan, and Margaret E. Roberts. "A Randomized Experimental Study of Censorship in China." Paper prepared for the annual meetings of the American Political Science Association, August 31, 2013, Chicago. Available for download from http://papers.ssrn.com/sol3/papers.cfm ?abstract_id=2299509.

Kipnis, Andrew. *China and Postsocialist Anthropology: Theorizing Power and Society After Communism*. Norwalk, Conn.: Eastbridge, 2008.

Kong, Shuyu. *Consuming Literature: Best Sellers and the Commercialization of Literary Production in Contemporary China*. Stanford: Stanford University Press, 2005.

Krämer, Oliver. "No Past to Long For? A Sociology of Chinese Writers in Exile." In *The Literary Field of Twentieth-Century China*, edited by Michel Hockx, 161–77. Richmond, U.K.: CurzonPress, 1999.

Laier, ed. *Shi shenghuo nianxuan: 2006 nian juan* (*Poemlife Annual Selection: 2006*). Guangzhou: Huacheng chubanshe, 2007.

Lei Shiwen. "Xiandai baozhi wenyi fukan de yuanshengtai wenxue tujing" (The Landscape of Primitive-State Literature in Literary Supplements to Modern Newspapers). *Zhongguo xiandai wenxue yanjiu congkan*, no. 1 (2003): 156–66.

Li Jiaming. *Zui hou de xuanzhan: "Zhongguo zui shenmi de aizi bingren Li Jiaming wangluo shouji"* (*The Last Declaration of War: "Online Notes by Li Jiaming, China's Most Mysterious AIDS Patient"*). Tianjin: Tianjin renmin chubanshe, 2002.

Link, Perry. *An Anatomy of Chinese: Rhythm, Metaphor, Politics*. Cambridge, Mass.: Harvard University Press, 2013.

——. *The Uses of Literature: Life in the Socialist Chinese Literary System.* Princeton: Princeton University Press, 2000.

Liu, Lydia H. "Beijing Sojourners in New York: Postsocialism and the Question of Ideology in Global Media Culture." *positions: east asia cultures critique* 7, no. 3 (1999): 763–98.

Liu Yunyun. "Handong shehui de liliang: Qianxi Han Han de bowen" (The Power to Shake Up Society: A Tentative Analysis of Han Han's Blog Writings). *Qingnian zuojia*, no. 11 (2010): 81–82.

Liu Zengren. *Zhongguo xiandai wenxue qikan shilun* (*An Overview of Modern Chinese Literary Journals*). Beijing: Xinhua chubanshe, 2005.

Lu, Sheldon H. "Postscript: Answering the Question, What Is Chinese Postsocialism?" In *Chinese Modernity and Global Biopolitics: Studies in Literature and Visual Culture*, 204–10. Honolulu: University of Hawai`i Press, 2007.

Lu Youqing. *Huan cheng* (*Happy City*). Shanghai: Shanghai wenhua chubanshe, 2001.

——. *Shengming de liuyan: "Siwang riji" quanxuan ben* (*Words Leftover from a Life: The Full Text of "Death Diary"*). Beijing: Huayi chubanshe, 2000.

——. *Weiwei kafeiwu* (*VV Coffee Shop*). Shanghai: Shanghai wenhua chubanshe, 2001.

Ma Yuan. "Fabrication." In *The Lost Boat: Avant-Garde Fiction from China*, edited by Henry Y. H. Zhao, translated by J. Q. Sun, 101–44. London: Wellsweep, 1993.

MacKinnon, Rebecca. *Consent of the Networked: The World-Wide Struggle for Internet Freedom.* New York: Basic Books, 2012.

Mao Keqiang and Yuan Ping. "Dangdai xiaoshuo xushu xintan" (A New Inquiry into Narration in Contemporary Fiction). *Dangdai wentan*, no. 5 (1997): 10–14.

Martinsen, Joel. "Han Han the Novelist Versus Fang Zhouzi the Fraud-Buster," n.d. http://www.danwei.com/blog-fight-of-the-month-han-han-the-novelist-versus-fang-zhouzi-the-fraud-buster/.

Mattix, Micah. "Periodization and Difference." *New Literary History* 35, no. 4 (2004): 685–97.

McGrath, Jason. *Postsocialist Modernity: Chinese Cinema, Literature, and Criticism in the Market Age.* Stanford: Stanford University Press, 2008.

Mei Hong et al., eds. *Wangluo wenxue* (*Internet Literature*). Chengdu: Xinan jiaotong daxue chubanshe, 2010.

Mitra, Ananda, and Elisia Cohen. "Analyzing the Web: Directions and Challenges." In *Doing Internet Research: Critical Issues and Methods for Examining the Net*, edited by Steve Jones, 179–203. Thousand Oaks, Calif.: Sage, 1999.

Mudge, Bradford K. *The Whore's Story: Women, Pornography, and the British Novel, 1684–1830*. Oxford: Oxford University Press, 2000.

Ouyang Youquan. *Wangluo wenxue benti lun* (*An Ontology of Internet Literature*). Beijing: Zhongguo wenlian chubanshe, 2004.

——, ed. *Wangluo wenxue fazhan shi—Hanyu wangluo wenxue diaocha jishi* (*A History of the Development of Internet Literature: Research Notes on Chinese-Language Internet Literature*). Beijing: Zhongguo guangbo dianshi chubanshe, 2008.

Paizis, George. *Love and the Novel: The Poetics and Politics of Romantic Fiction*. New York: St. Martin's Press, 1998.

Pickowicz, Paul G. "Huang Jianxin and the Notion of Postsocialism." In *New Chinese Cinemas: Forms, Identities, Politics*, edited by Nick Browne, Paul G. Pickowicz, Vivian Sobchack, and Esther Yau, 57–87. Cambridge: Cambridge University Press, 1994.

"Printing Revolution," n.d. http://europe.chinadaily.com.cn/digest/2010-12/10/content_11684101.htm.

Qiu, Jack Linchuan, and Wei Bu. "China ICT Studies: A Review of the Field, 1989–2012." *China Review* 13, no. 2 (2013): 123–52.

Reed, Christopher A. "From Woodblocks to the Internet: Chinese Printing, Publishing, and Literary Fields in Transition, circa 1800 to 2008." In *From Woodblocks to the Internet: Chinese Publishing and Print Culture in Transition, circa 1800 to 2008*, 1–35. Leiden: Brill, 2010.

Sang Ke. "Hulianwang shidai de Zhongguo shige" (Chinese Poetry in the Internet Age). *Shi tansuo* 1 (2001): 5–19.

Shao Yanjun. "Chuantong wenxue shengchan jizhi de weiji he xinxing jizhi de shengcheng" (The Crisis in the Traditional Literary Production Mechanism and the Emergence of a New-Style Mechanism). *Wenyi zhengming*, no. 12 (2009): 12–22.

——. *Qingxie de wenxuechang: Dangdai wenxue shengchan jizhi de shichanghua zhuanxing* (*The Inclined Literary Field: The Commercial Transformation of the Contemporary Literary Production Mechanism*). Nanjing: Jiangsu renmin chubanshe, 2003.

Shih, Shu-mei. *Visuality and Identity: Sinophone Articulations across the Pacific*. Berkeley: University of California Press, 2007.

Shih, Shu-mei, Chien-hsin Tsai, and Brian Bernards, eds. *Sinophone Studies: A Critical Reader*. New York: Columbia University Press, 2013.

Sigley, Gary. "Sex, Politics and the Policing of Virtue in the People's Republic of China." In *Sex and Sexuality in China*, edited by Elaine Jeffreys, 43–61. London: Routledge, 2006.

Stalling, Jonathan. *Yingelishi: Sinophonic English Poetry and Poetics*. Denver: Counterpath Press, 2011.

Statistical Report on Internet Development in China. Beijing: China Internet Network Information Center, January 2013. http://www1.cnnic.cn/IDR/Report Downloads/201302/P020130312536825920279.pdf.

Tian Er. "Bie ba 'xianfeng' dangcheng zhexiubu" (Don't Turn the "Avant-Garde" into a Fig Leaf). *Shanxi wenxue*, no. 10 (2007): 82–83.

Tian, Xiaofei. "Muffled Dialect Spoken by Green Fruit: An Alternative History of Modern Chinese Poetry." *Modern Chinese Literature and Culture* 21, no. 1 (2009): 1–45.

Tsu, Jing. *Sound and Script in Chinese Diaspora*. Cambridge, Mass.: Harvard University Press, 2010.

Tsui, Lokman. "An Inadequate Metaphor: The Great Firewall and Chinese Internet Censorship." *Global Dialogue* 9, no. 102 (2007). http://www.world dialogue.org/content.php?id=400.

van Crevel, Maghiel. *Chinese Poetry in Times of Mind, Mayhem and Money*. Leiden: Brill, 2008.

——. *Language Shattered: Contemporary Chinese Poetry and Duoduo*. Leiden: CNWS, 1996.

——. "Unofficial Poetry Journals from the People's Republic of China: A Research Note and an Annotated Bibliography." MCLC Resource Center, 2007. http://mclc.osu.edu/rc/pubs/vancrevel2.html.

van Rees, Kees, and Jeroen Vermunt. "Event History Analysis of Authors' Reputation: Effects of Critics' Attention on Debutants' Careers." *Poetics* 23, no. 5 (April 1996): 317–33.

Visser, Robin. *Cities Surround the Countryside: Urban Aesthetics in Post-Socialist China*. Durham, N.C.: Duke University Press, 2010.

Wang Guo'an. "Shuwei de Miusi—shilun *Miao miao miao*" (The Digital Muse: An Overview of *Wonderfully Absurd Temple*). *Renwen yu shehui* 1, no. 10 (2007): 101–30.

Wang, Jing. *China's Avant-Garde Fiction: An Anthology*. Durham, N.C.: Duke University Press, 1998.

Wang Yang. "Wangluo he wenxue bantu shang de Heilan" (Heilan as a Web Domain and a Literary Domain). *Shanhua*, no. 8 (2007): 136–41.

Wasserstrom, Jeffrey. "Make Way for Han Han," n.d. http://wordswithoutborders. org/dispatches/article/make-way-for-han-han.

Wen Huajian. *Tong, jiu kuchu sheng lai* (*Cry If It Hurts*). Taipei: Taiwan shangwu, 2006.

——. *Weibo shiqi de aiqing* (*Love in the Age of the Microblog*). Shenyang: Shenyang chubanshe, 2011.

Xiao Qiang. "The Grass-Mud Horse Lexicon: Translating the Resistance Discourse of Chinese Netizens," n.d. http://chinadigitaltimes.net/space/The_Grass-Mud_Horse_Lexicon.

Xin Guangwei. *Publishing in China*. Translated by Li Hong, Zhao Wei, Peter F. Bloxham, and Tang Hongzhao. 2nd ed. Singapore: Cengage Learning Asia, 2010.

Xu Fang. "Xing'ershang zhuti: Xianfeng wenxue de yizhong zongjie he ling yizhong zhongjie" (The Metaphysical Subject: A Conclusion and an Ending for Avant-Garde Literature). *Wenxue pinglun*, no. 4 (1995): 86–96.

Yang, Guobin. "Chinese Internet Literature and the Changing Field of Print Culture." In *From Woodblocks to the Internet: Chinese Publishing and Print Culture in Transition, circa 1800 to 2008*, edited by Cynthia Brokaw and Christopher A. Reed, 333–52. Leiden: Brill, 2010.

——. *The Power of the Internet in China: Citizen Activism Online*. New York: Columbia University Press, 2009.

Yu, Haiqing. *Media and Cultural Transformation in China*. London: Routledge, 2009.

Zhang Rui and Yang Zhi. "Jiankang wenxue yu seqing wenxue de qubie" (The Distinction Between Healthy Literature and Pornographic Literature). *Beijing jiaoyu xueyuan xuebao* 20, no. 1 (2006): 34–37.

Zhang, Xudong. *Chinese Modernism in the Era of Reforms: Cultural Fever, Avant-Garde Fiction, and the New Chinese Cinema*. Durham, N.C.: Duke University Press, 1997.

——. *Postsocialism and Cultural Politics: China in the Last Decade of the Twentieth Century*. Durham, N.C.: Duke University Press, 2008.

Zhu, Aijun. *Feminism and Global Chineseness: The Cultural Production of Controversial Women Authors*. Youngstown, N.Y.: Cambria Press, 2007.

▶ **Bold** denotes photos

yinhui seqing xiaoshuo (obscene and pornographic fiction), 163

Yin Lichuan, 161, 162, 164, 167

Yi Sha, 99

yishu zongjian (chief artistic officer) (CAO), 36, 37

yiyin (lust of the mind), 111, 138

you dianr qingse (somewhat erotic), 125

you qu, 76

yousheng wenzhang (texts with sound), 38

YouTube, 9, 84

Yu, Haiqing, 56

yuanshengtai wenxue (literature in its primary state), 29

Yu Hua, 61, 66, 139, 206n8

Yu Jian, 161

Yünü tianwang zai dushi (*The King of Copulation in the City*), 128

Yu Qiuyu, 70

Yusi, 30

YY xiaoshuo (YY fiction), 111, 126

zawen (critical essay) genre, 94

Zhang, Xudong, 13–14, 17, 25

Zhang Rui, 119

Zhang Yuan, 16

Zhao Lihua, 97, 98, 99, 147

"Zhendang de manzu" (Satisfaction of Oscillation) (Yao), 182

zhiyin (soul mate), reader as, 39, 49

Zhongguo Quanguo Wenxue Yishu Jie Lianhehui (All-China Federation of Literary and Artistic Circles) (Wenlian), 25

Zhongguo Shige Luntan (Chinese Poetry Forum), 156

Zhongguo Shige Xuehui (Chinese Poetry Study Society), 156

Zhongguo Shiren (Chinapoet) (website), 148–56, **149**

Zhongguo Zuojia Xiehui (Chinese Writers Association) (Zuoxie), 25. *See also* Writers Association

Zhong shi wangkan (*Chinapoet Webzine*), 155

Zhou Zuoren, 30, 71

zhuti (thread titles), 33

Zhu Weilian (William Zhu), 35, 36, 46, 47, 68

"Zhuyuan Rongshu Xia" (Wishing Banyan Tree Well) (Chen Cun), 68

ziti yihua (auto-exoticism, self-estrangement), 182

Zotero, 18

"Zui hou de xuanzhan" (The Last Declaration of War) (Li Jiaming), 55, **55**, 57

zuojia (authors), 5

Zuojia Weiquan Lianmeng (Writers Legal Protection Union), 105

zuopinku (site archive), 43